The Homesick Phone Book

THE HOMESICK PHONE BOOK

Addressing Rhetorics in the Age of Perpetual Conflict

CYNTHIA HAYNES

Southern Illinois University Press • *Carbondale*

Southern Illinois University Press
www.siupress.com

Figure 2.1, of a Hollerith tabulating machine from IBM (USHMM # 9048–1), reprinted with permission from the United States Holocaust Memorial Museum; the views or opinions expressed in this book, and the context in which the images are used, do not necessarily reflect the views or policy of, nor imply approval or endorsement by, the United States Holocaust Memorial Museum. Poem fragment by Friedrich Hölderlin, from *Hymns and Fragments*, trans. Richard Sieburth (Princeton: Princeton University Press, 1984), 32, reprinted in chapter 3 with permission of Princeton University Press conveyed through Copyright Clearance Center, Inc. Poem "improvised verses," by Rainer Maria Rilke (16 l.), from *Poetry, Language, Thought,* by Martin Heidegger, trans. and introd. Albert Hofstadter, copyright © 1971 by Martin Heidegger, reprinted in chapter 4 by permission of HarperCollins Publishers. Poem, "Needing the Sea," by Desmond Egan, reprinted in chapter 4 with permission of the poet.

19 18 17 16 4 3 2 1

Cover illustrations: *Top*, artwork, by Beatrice Turquand d'Auzay, from page 173 of *Notre Combat*, altered book project of *Mein Kampf* by Linda Ellia (courtesy of Linda Ellia); *background*, cover of Berlin phone book, 1941 (lightened and cropped; author's collection).

Library of Congress Cataloging-in-Publication Data

Names: Haynes, Cynthia (Cynthia A.) author.
Title: The homesick phone book : addressing rhetorics in the age of perpetual conflict / Cynthia Haynes.
Description: Carbondale : Southern Illinois University Press, 2016. | Includes bibliographical references and index.
Identifiers: LCCN 2016006856 | ISBN 9780809335084 (pbk. : alk. paper) | ISBN 9780809335091 (e-book)
Subjects: LCSH: Rhetoric—Social aspects—History—20th century. | Rhetoric—Social aspects—History—21st century. | Academic writing—Social aspects.
Classification: LCC P301.5.S63 .H39 2016 | DDC 814/.6—dc23 LC record available at https://lccn.loc.gov/2016006856

Printed on recycled paper. ♲

To my father, Morris A. Haynes

Contents

Illustrations

Acknowledgments

I am grateful to Clemson University for a sabbatical, summer research grant, and project completion grant, all of which made it possible to complete the research and writing of this book. I owe my thanks, also, to the staffs of the Landesarchiv Berlin, the Bundesarchiv Berlin, the Topography of Terror Museum Library (Berlin), the United States Holocaust Memorial Museum Library, and the Library of Congress Manuscript Division.

Karl Kageff has been a patient and supportive editor who believed in this project from the start, and I am extremely grateful for the care with which he guided the book toward publication. I owe a great deal to the reviewers of the manuscript for their recommendations and comments. Their encouragement made the process of completing the book a joy. Among my colleagues, friends, and graduate students, I am particularly grateful to Sid Dobrin, Raúl Sánchez, Gregory Ulmer, Stuart Moulthrop, Sarah Arroyo, Diane Davis, Michelle Ballif, Jenny Bay, Lisa Coleman, Rebecca Sabounchi, Thomas Rickert, Byron Hawk, Lorien Goodman, Jenny Rice, Jeff Rice, Anne Wysocki, Bonnie Kyburz, Geoffrey Sirc, Lynn Worsham, Bradley Dilger, Espen Aarseth, Markku Eskelinen, Matt Levy, Steve Katz, Brian McGrath, Walt Hunter, Lee Morrissey, Barbara Weaver, Aga Skrodzka, Elisa Sparks, Jimmy Butts, Josh Hilst, Nicole McFarlane, Jason Helms, Justin Hodgson, Trish Fancher, Sharon Henry, Sergio Figueiredo, Anthony Collamati, Sean Callot, Data Tolentino-Canlas, Hayley Zertuche, Walter Iriarte, Toni Vitanza, and Jonathan Lashley. These and countless others have contributed to the development of my thinking through seminars and academic conferences over the years, many of whom listened to early drafts of chapters presented as research talks and whose kind comments and support have meant more than they will ever know.

A very special thank you goes to Victor J. Vitanza, who has been my mentor and friend for over thirty years. His enduring support of me and my work has been invaluable and unconditional. Luanne T. Frank deserves an equal portion of my gratitude for always allowing me to be who I am and for showing up (in every sense of those words) through her devotion to thought and writing. I would also like to thank Esther Dorothy Buschke Federman, granddaughter of Abraham and Erna Buschke. Esther's memories of her grandparents brought them to life, and she reminds me how precious life and family are. This book is dedicated to my late father, Morris A. Haynes, but I would also like to thank my amazing mother, Norma Hickson, whose love and abiding friendship knows no limits. Both of my parents gave me a thirst for knowledge and the education necessary to pursue it, and were models of love and commitment to family, family history, and the art of telling stories. I am especially grateful to other family members, Jackie Parker, Sherry Haynes McReynolds, Shirley Haynes, Johnny Hickson, Bente Holmevik, and my chosen family/friends, Steve and Barbara Black. Finally, I am certain that without the support, love, and encouragement from my husband, Jan Rune Holmevik, this book would not have been possible. My gratitude to him will take a lifetime to convey.

The Homesick Phone Book

Introduction

The trouble with phone books is that they're heavy, not to mention fairly useless in the twenty-first century. Nowadays people use them as seats, doorstops, weapons, art (fig. 0.1). There are plenty of clichés about phone books, even famous scenes in films. But after four years of reading this phone book, a gift from my father, Morris A. Haynes, before he died in 2012, I now understand that phone books are not heavy *enough*. They should weigh as much as a mountain. They should sink like ships. They should *not* sit on tables so innocently, so type-lightly pressing the *S*'s in Straße and SS, such that my sibilant syllables want to stutter, not hiss, in the abject proximity of the hard, heartless consonants that storm each page. I want to slow them down, these *SS's*, to sound them out, to drop anchor in deep waters, to stop their incessant slithering.

Fig. 0.1. Peter Rösel, "Untitled" (two telephone benches, installation view, Loock Galerie, 2011, 95 × 75 × 45 cm). *Courtesy the artist and Loock Galerie, Berlin.*

Whereas phone books are tied to land/lines, cell phones are tied to no physical place. And yet, in *this* phone book it is not difficult to see the switchboard that dials into future circuitry as ideal for teenage texting as it is for stealth prepaid unlisted terrorism, at home, yet on the move, at some farm on the outskirts of Karachi, Pakistan. Some compound in Abbottabad. Some skiff full of armed pirates off the coast of Somalia. Some car. Some plane. Some radio frequency. In this switchboard I find not only Berlin of 1941, but also the architecture and pathology of a kind of home/sickness that links this early printbound search engine to the uptown address of cloud-based jets. Violence and vitality (even children lived there) not only shared a Berlin bunker at Hitler's Reich Chancellery, his headquarters at Voßstraße 6 (fig. 0.2); they shared the same rhetorical address as Ground Zero, both of which render an inferno that leads Derrida to remind us: "cinders there are [*il y a là cendre*]" (*Cinders* 21). Derrida chooses to inflect the definite article "la" with the *grave* accent "là" in order to mark the "mention or memory of the place," which the simple "la" "risks effacing" (21). Incineration has never been and never will be a way to clean up the bloodlines of congenital conflict, though it may temporarily relocate its genocidal headquarters.

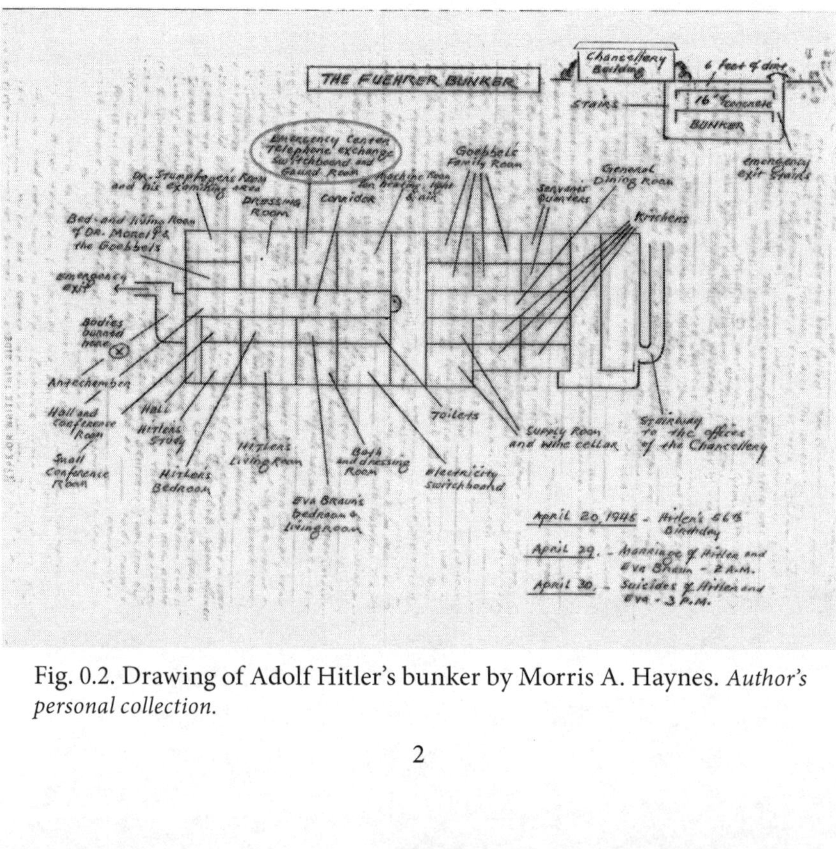

Fig. 0.2. Drawing of Adolf Hitler's bunker by Morris A. Haynes. *Author's personal collection.*

Homesickness (as discussed here) is not about missing home, it is about the sickness called *Homeland Security* and our rhetorical task of addressing it in an age of perpetual conflict. Rhetoric is not newly or even uniquely able to address conflict; therefore, I situate rhetoric's address not just next door to evil, or across the theoretical fence, but I install rhetoric *at the same address*, with the same phone number, connected to the same switchboard, and utilized and understood by the same operators.

In some respects, this phone book has been on a seventy-five-year journey and wants to go home. In fact, by addressing rhetoric in the age of perpetual conflict, this book becomes ever more infected with acute homesickness. The rhetorical task is to find rhetoric's home address, not to cure it so much as to allow it to speak of the unspeakable, to examine its relation to autoimmunity, and to unbuild the politics of Homeland Security. *Calling* to mind one of the most groundbreaking works to hit our rhetorical streets in 1989, Avital Ronell's *The Telephone Book: Technology, Schizophrenia, Electric Speech*, this book aims to dial up the address of rhetoric as opposed to Ronell's focus on the "call." The affiliation with Ronell's text is rather like a shared party line, which I can still recall at my grandparents' ranch in West Texas when I was growing up. You shared the line in both directions, incoming/outgoing, but never simultaneously. We are always in the mode of asynchronous usability of a history, or of ghostly transmissions. There is only one medium capable of getting through to the other side. It is the historico-rhetorical line to which my book pays its debt recorded in a specific ledger of missing souls—the Berlin 1941 phone book.

Chapter 1 specifically addresses the "Party Lines" of Berlin 1941. This opening chapter targets multiple addresses of rhetorical architects of the Holocaust and locates Holocaust victims along the same spectacular boulevards and parade grounds. The 1941 phone book provides the rhetorical switchboard as well as the telephonic railway switching mechanism that deports victims to their certain deaths. The remaining chapters of the book function as listings in another phone book, one that I have written to counteract the seemingly banal nature of phone books in general. But phone books are not innocuous directories, a claim that necessitates I take issue with George Kennedy's classical example of the low level of rhetoric in the white pages of a phonebook (versus the high level of rhetoric contained in the yellow pages) (Kennedy 4). In her book *Contesting Cultural Rhetorics: Public Discourse and Education, 1890–1900*, Margaret Marshall argues that Kennedy's distinction "reduces 'rhetoric' to 'persuasion'" (5).

> You would be right in claiming that the white pages of a telephone book are minimally rhetorical if by that term you mean "persuasive"; the white pages do not attempt to influence belief or action in overt ways. But these same pages are *very* rhetorical if by that term you mean that they have a purpose, and that they use conventions of print and culture to satisfy that purpose. Phone books are also rhetorical in the way they function in society; they reflect beliefs and debates about beliefs, they conform to conventions, they reinforce cultural values, and they contribute to particular practices and ways of organizing our lives. . . . In addition to this more or less practical context of usage, there are more elaborate, hidden assumptions within a phone book: a complicated technology that is only partially understood by its users; a society that is organized around, and operates with, an expectation that people have phones and use them from their homes and businesses; and a society that spends a great deal of time, money, and effort to produce texts to help people utilize phones. These assumptions constitute the more fully complex "rhetorical" system to be found in the telephone white pages, a text we would usually dismiss as not rhetorical. (5–7)

With Marshall's rebuttal to Kennedy in mind, it is necessary to think beyond classical rhetoric and rhetorics of persuasion, such as advertisements or even propaganda. Such rhetorical machinery exists, naturally, but is not of primary concern in this book. It is necessary to look closer, dig deeper, to construct one's *ontological ancestry* (if not ancestry's ontology).

Martin Davidson, a writer/producer at the BBC, was prompted to undertake such a project after his maternal grandfather passed away in 1992 at the age of 85. The resulting book, *The Perfect Nazi: Uncovering My Grandfather's Secret Past*, enabled me to understand something I was seeing as I read the 1941 Berlin phone book—namely, that names and addresses are enmeshed in a rhetorical relation with violence, the nature of which my project could reveal, both during 1941 in Berlin and beyond.

Davidson had always known that his mother's German family had ties to the military, but she was tight-lipped about her father, Bruno Langbehn, a dentist like his mother, Ida Pahnke-Lietzner, but a dentist who wore a uniform. After he died, Martin was speaking with his mother by phone one day, and it happened. Martin blurted out the questions,

> "What kind of soldier takes his family with him to foreign postings? Why were you with him in Prague at all?" She didn't answer. "Come on," [he

> said] "it doesn't make any sense . . . What was he *doing* there?" She paused, and I carried on: "He wasn't in the army, was he?" . . . "No, you're right, he wasn't, he was in the SS." For all my dispassionate bluster, nothing had prepared me for the echoing hiss of two tiny letters, whispered over the telephone line. (25–26)

Davidson would learn over the next few years of investigation that his grandfather had joined the SS and the family had enjoyed the perks of an enviable lifestyle in Berlin. According to Davidson,

> I got a sense of this charmed life from an unlikely source. My cousin had been given a document, which he had passed on to me; it was a page from the 1942 Berlin telephone directory that offered a fascinating snapshot of everyday life at the heart of the Reich during these early states of the war. There, sure enough, was Bruno. (239)

"Langbehn, Bruno, Landesdienststellenleit, Chlb 1, Berliner Str 86.87 34 25 00" (fig. 0.3). Davidson was struck by the "sheer ordinariness" of the page; it was "pristine, modern, and untouched by war . . . a crisp list of names, addresses, and telephone numbers [that] depicts a city completely at odds with the later burned-out husk destroyed by three years of bombing and Russian artillery shells" (239). On that very page, Davidson noticed another entry for "Landsberger, Kurt Israel, Dr. Med." While the name "Landsberger was ethnically vague," he knew that Israel was not. Because of the Nuremberg Laws, after January 1939 Landsberger would have been forced to take the middle name Israel, along with Jewish women, who would have had to take the middle name Sarah, "precisely to remove the camouflage of [their]

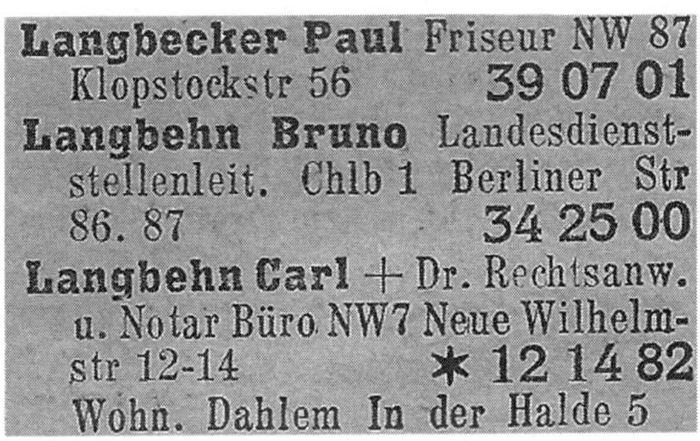

Langbecker Paul Friseur NW 87 Klopstockstr 56 **39 07 01**
Langbehn Bruno Landesdienststellenleit. Chlb 1 Berliner Str 86. 87 **34 25 00**
Langbehn Carl + Dr. Rechtsanw. u. Notar Büro NW7 Neue Wilhelmstr 12-14 **✱ 12 14 82** Wohn. Dahlem In der Halde 5

Fig. 0.3. 1941 Berlin phone book entry for Bruno Langbehn. *Photo by author.*

generic surname" (240). As Marion Kaplan explains, "These names were also inserted in telephone books, announcing a person's racial status to anyone who cared to look" (146). Davidson's grandfather had been promoted to *Landesdienststellenleiter* in charge of Berlin's dentists, which required him to "list and keep tabs on any Jew still practicing in Berlin" (Davidson 241). In 1942 the Nazi press began to question why these Jews were still living in Berlin at all. "The lists of names and addresses compiled by Bruno's office were handed over to the Gestapo, and the roundups began" (241).

This account highlights a rhetorical mystery I had encountered early in my reading of the 1941 phone book, namely, the fact that the *only* entries for Jewish people in the phone book seemed to be doctors and dentists. But it does not solve the question of how they actually lived. Each phone book entry for Jews lists only an address and phone number, along with their medical profession, such as medical doctor, doctor chemist, dentist, eye-ear-nose-and-throat doctor, pediatrician, and so forth. But looking them up in the Holocaust victim database yielded the more ominous results, such as with Dr. Abraham Buschke, a renowned dermatologist, who was transported to Theresienstadt in 1942, where he died a few months later (fig. 0.4). One after the other, as I looked up these doctors and dentists, the entries belied a prelude to deportation and slaughter. Sent to Auschwitz, fate unknown. Davidson, however, uncovered a fascinating piece of information while researching his grandfather's past. He came across a PhD thesis from the late 1990s, by Michael Kohn, in which Kohn had "set out to discover the identity of every single one of Berlin's Jewish dentists: their ages, addresses, and bleakest of all, their fate at the hands of the Nazis" (241). As Davidson scanned the list, one entry "leaped off the page: Hartmann Levy; born in Posen, in Poland, in 1882, who 'committed suicide [*Freitod*] October 1942'" (242). Davidson did not recognize the name, but the address was intimately familiar: Reichstraße 5. His great-grandmother, Ida, had lived at this address during the war and practiced her dentistry there. Davidson figured out what had happened. "After Levy's suicide, Bruno [Davidson's grandfather], in his capacity as head of Berlin's *Dentisten*, was in a prime position to spot that there were recently vacated dental offices in Charlottenburg [district]" (242). So, Bruno expropriated Levy's property on his mother's behalf knowing full well the fate that Levy had in store for him had he not committed suicide. "Berlin's Jews were being rounded up and put on trains bound first for Terezin (Theresianstadt), a large holding camp in Czechoslovakia, and thereafter sent to other camps, including Auschwitz" (243). Davidson writes that "by the time Hartmann Levy killed himself, indeed, even while Dr. Landsberger's phone entry was being printed, a threshold had been crossed" (242). The "Holocaust was at last in full swing" (242).

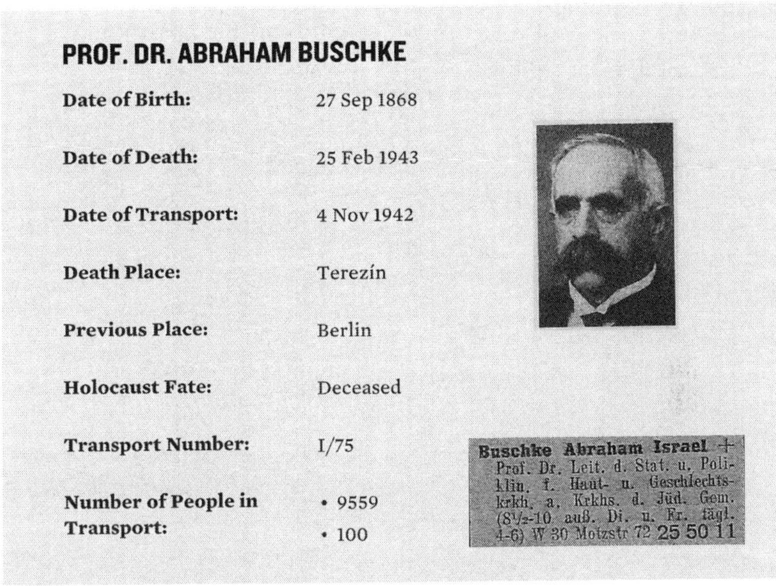

Fig. 0.4. Abraham Buschke's information from the Holocaust victims' database (U.S. Holocaust Memorial Museum) juxtaposed with the listing of his address in the 1941 Berlin phone book. *Photo of phone book listing by author.*

And this phone book was, indeed, getting heavier, and the thresholds became more and more crowded. It began to speak to me, to whisper questions that seemed to be rendering a topographic *quaquaversal* map; they pointed in all directions at once. How had my father acquired this phone book? And why? Did he ever look through it? Who had underlined in pencil certain phone numbers? Or put an *X* next to a certain train station address? Who dropped a tiny silver eyeglass screw between two pages? How should I unfold the multiple layers of complicity in the pulp of its pages? After Abraham Buschke and his wife were deported to Theresienstadt, who had moved into their apartment at Motzstraße 72, and who had sanctioned and orchestrated that move? The who, what, how, and why questions then sent me back to my own research begun in 2001 after 9/11 (see chapter 4 on "Writing Offshore"). I realized that this phone book would never tell me why because I knew that rhetoric's address is both on and offshore.

The *Homesick Phone Book* contains a series of chapters that form points on a topographical/rhetorical map of addresses. The address is a street and number, the place of *living/dwelling.* If dwelling is situated at an address, where the presence of human Being is stretched, where there are not multiple inhabitants, but multiple ghosts occupying the same address and these ghosts are Jew/German, then they must occupy, that is, live in death together in the space where they received letters, where they took off their jackboots or work boots, where they broke bread, birthed babies, made love, where they entered the sign of address and were poised briefly on the threshold of a fading postmark. But all are deported from the *address.* Only the address survives.

What *The Homesick Phone Book* reveals, chapter by chapter, address by address, is that there is no Home/land Security. In this book, one chapter acts as a hub for the book's collective argument(s). In other words, all chapters lead to the argument in chapter 4, "Writing Offshore" (that we must unbuild the "ground" as reason), which leads every other chapter's argument *offshore,* where sovereignty and topographical terror are less able to wipe out whole peoples through calculation (IBM), gassing (mobile vans), declarations of assets (paper), deportations, concentration camps, containment, then slaughter. Yet, as chapter 4 asserts, rhetoric stands in for the "refugee" ("we are all boat people") both on and offshore. For these reasons, the hub acts not as the largest chapter around which smaller pieces circulate, but as the main conductor for a network of complementary arguments that are of diverse length (which has no bearing on the manner in which they conduct the reader along the paths in the network, namely, quaquaversally, in all directions at once).

Guided in my search by my father's gift, and by Walter Benjamin's archives and thought, this book is both visually and conceptually structured like a map. In Benjamin's essay, "A Berlin Chronicle," he explains:

> I have long, indeed for years, played with the idea of setting out the sphere of life—bios—graphically on a map. . . . He who has once begun to open the fan of memory never comes to the end of its segments; no image satisfies him, for he has seen that it can be unfolded, and only in its folds does the truth reside; that image, that taste, that touch for whose sake all this has been unfurled and dissected; and now remembrance advances from small to smallest details, from the smallest to the infinitesimal, while that which it encounters in these microcosms grows ever mightier. (5–6)

Within the Berlin 1941 telephone book one can read the injustices of such "mightier" microcosms. All chapters in my book, therefore, are unfoldings in a topographical dream. As Benjamin put it: "Just as a certain kind of significant dream survives awakening in the form of words when all the rest of the dream content has vanished, here isolated words have remained in place as marks of catastrophic encounters" (14). The chapters before and after "Writing Offshore" are what remain "in place as marks of catastrophic encounters."

Chapters 2 ("Casuistic Code") and 3 ("Mechanical Faith") continue the work of chapter 1 ("Party Lines") in order to examine the rhetorical address of the Holocaust through technology and ruins. Chapter 5 ("Glitch Rhetoric") and chapter 6 ("Torture and Absolution") move us to a post-9/11 world, to addresses of torture and distress: one in the Middle East, and one not situated on land or water, but rather in nonsovereign airspace. We all know the torture that happened inside four commercial airliners on 9/11. But not so many of us know what happened to Daniel Pearl inside a ramshackle farm in Pakistan, or to unknown detainees in a certain Gulfstream V aircraft, # N379P. It is probably safe to say that everyone is interested in saving lives. But it is *not* safe to say that in order to save lives some of us may feel torture is necessary. As Greg Ulmer explained in talking to Clemson University doctoral students about his own conceptual struggles with deconstruction during the course of his long career, he decided to put this question to Derrida: "OK, Derrida. What if you're right?" In the context of my own research, here is one of Derrida's answers from his book *Without Alibi*: "It is necessary to save, it is necessary to assure the salvation. . . . [and] this salutary, sanitary, or immunitary concern triggers simultaneously a gesture of war: the militant would like to cure or save by routing, precisely, a resistance" (243). If Derrida is right, there is an "indissociable tie between cruelty and state sovereignty, state violence, the state that, far from combating violence, monopolizes it" (*Without Alibi* 268).

Other monopolies exist in which the ability to critique such "indissociable ties" become strained and untested in the waters of posttextual genres. Thus, it has been necessary to integrate research using technologies comprised of networks, computer games, historical databases, and typographical artifacts such as the 1941 Berlin phone book. Physical evidence of homes, offices, schools, synagogues (in ruins), the Reich Chancellory telephone number imprinted with the same mechanization as the phone numbers of Jüdische retirement homes, culture ministries, and hospitals.

These processes and technologies, as well as postconflict and posthuman theories, are examined in chapters 7 through 11, wherein the switchboard connects us with contemporary addresses of violence, from "Postconflict Pedagogy" to "Marine Media" to "Accidental Metaphysics" and to the final chapters on "Armageddon Army" and "Endgame Rhetoric," both of which muddy the waters of serious games and the practice of theorycrafting the ultimate endgame: death. The 1941 Berlin phone book is a study in Nazi efficiency, and yet we find no phone numbers to Hitler's bunker or the camps and crematoria, the real machinery of ruins (fig. 0.5). Walter Benjamin wrote that "Allegories are, in the realm of thoughts, what ruins are in the realm of things" (*Origin* 178), and so I offer this phone book as allegory—"letting the Other speak (*allos + agoreuei*) is the very definition of allegory" (Sirc 193). It speaks, but it does not, nor never will, tell us why. Only that it is *home/sick*. We will never know the *why* when it comes to conflict and unspeakable violence. But I do know where they live: right through the front door and inside the rhetorical address of humanity, in our basements, yes, but also our living rooms, even in our gardens—especially in our gardens. For they are where we plant the seeds of every new species of alibi, where we cultivate the roots of complacency and complicity, and harvest the next crop of tacit torture. The silos in which we store every history, crime, and good intention should be emptied of their rotting grains of truth.

NSDAP.
A 1. Reichsleitung
2. Gauleitung Berlin
3. Gauleitung Mark Brandenb.
4. Leitung der Auslands-Organisation
B 1. SA.
2. ϟϟ
3. NSKK.
4. Hitler-Jugend
5. NS.-Deutscher Studentenbund
6. NS.-Frauenschaft
C 1. NS.-Rechtswahrerbund
2. NS.-Lehrerbund
3. NS.-Volkswohlfahrt
4. NSKOV.
5. NSD.-Beamtenbund
6. Die Deutsche Arbeitsfront

A 1. Reichsleitung (Sitz München, Braunes Haus)
Kanzlei des Führers der NSDAP.
W 8 Voßstr 4
Ortsdienst ✱ 12 00 54
Ferndienst ✱ 12 66 21

Fig. 0.5. 1941 Berlin phone book entry for Hitler's office. *Photo by author.*

I would like to think that my father trained me to think rhetorically. When I was about ten years old and he was studying German for his master's degree in history, I would help him while he was shaving every morning. I would quiz him with vocabulary cards (fig. 0.6) by reading a German word, and he would define it, pronounce it, and so forth. Just language going back and forth, another game for us to play.

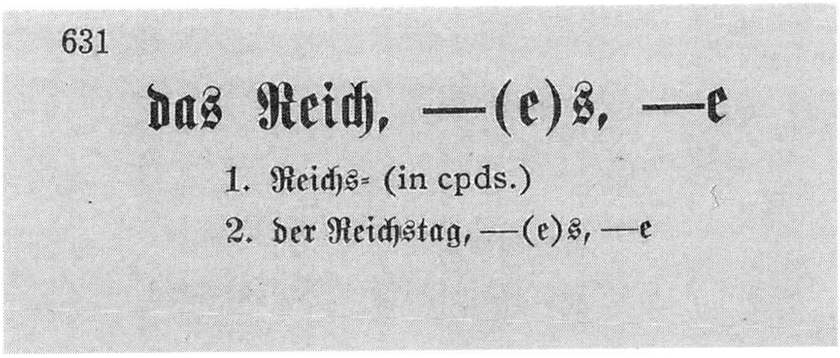

Fig. 0.6. German vocabulary card from author's personal collection. *Photo by author.*

Imagine the feeling of finding out that Heinrich Himmler's personal secretary, Rudolf Brandt, also read things to Himmler while he was shaving. According to Walter Schellenberg,

> As soon as Himmler had risen in the morning and washed, Brandt would go to him loaded with papers and files, and while Himmler shaved he would read him the most important items of the morning's mail. This was done with the greatest seriousness. If there was bad news, Brandt would preface it by saying, "Pardon, Herr Reichsführer," and thus forewarned, Himmler would temporarily suspend his shaving operations—a precautionary measure to prevent cutting himself. (302)

Twin scenarios of shaving reveal the secret address of rhetoric. There is but one address and one threshold to cross. Secretly, while my father was away, I would pull up a stool into his closet so I could reach the top shelf where he stored the books he did not want me to see, images I still remember to this day, of the Holocaust. And the phone book that lay on that shelf was, it turns out, the heaviest of them all. But I aim to make it heavier. It should be as heavy as a mountain. It should sink like a ship. And there, at the bottom of the ocean, it can take root, where nothing breathes, or burns, or blooms in the dark waters of why. Is it safe? No, it is not safe. We are not safe. Home is not safe; it is merely the rhetorical address of the impunity of why. Home/sickness is the symptom of our perpetual conflict with that which inevitably, unremittingly, seduces us into believing there is an answer on the other side of why. I don't know what that is, but I know where it lives. I have looked it up, and I am not afraid to darken its doors.

1

Party Lines

Motzstraße 72, Berlin

> The dream would be to be there, at that hour, this is the poet's dream—and getting there has always been the poem's hope. And the poem or poet is the hope for this meeting with ourselves at the hour of our most intimate foreignness, at our last minute. And then?—Then. Ah if we could go out, and, once outside, turning around, see with our own eyes the face of our own door.
>
> —Hélène Cixous, "What Is It O'Clock?"

It was an ordinary day. Woodpeckers busied themselves against the bark. A floorboard above them creaked. Someone breathing in the autumn air after opening a dormer window. Silence. A terror in itself when the sound of boots occupies so much of one's cobblestoned existence. Beyond a threshold, a tentative cry building to an anguished hush. In the distance . . . the sound of trampled souls. Inside Motzstraße 72, Dr. Abraham "Israel" Buschke and his wife, Erna "Sarah" Buschke, busy themselves against the clock. One suitcase each. His books (fig. 1.1) and beloved violin. Her pearls, stitched into the hidden hem of a lace collar. His good suit. Her faded velveteen jacket. Photos of the three children. "They say Theresienstadt will be nice," she murmurs optimistically. Dr. Buschke glances at the telephone (#25 50 11) and the massive Berlin phone book sitting next to it. The phone no longer rings, no longer signals a patient's appointment, no longer connects to any switchboard.

Fig. 1.1. Buschke's ex libris bookplate. *In Büsing and Seebacher, "Mykologen im Exlibris," Mykologie Forum (2006). Courtesy of Claus Seebacher.*

It is November 4, 1942, and the Buschkes' transport I/75 is waiting for them at the Anhalter Bahnhof station (on Schöneberg Straße).[1] The SS officers arrive at 5:15 A.M. to "escort" them to a waiting tram to the station. The officers check to see that the Buschkes' apartment is tidy. They search their luggage. They demand paperwork showing that the Buschkes' "voluntary contribution" (25 percent of their assets) to the Reich had been paid. The Buschkes step across the threshold of their home for the last time. "As they left their apartment, the Gestapo unscrewed their nameplate from their door" (Kaplan 186).[2] After the Buschkes' apartment is sealed, Jewish wardens assist the SS so that the apartment at Motzstraße 72 is "carefully registered, and then reported to the State Police and the Economic Group for purposes of unsealing and clearance" (Meyer 140). Soon thereafter, the apartment is cleared for occupancy by the widow of Dr. Buschke's colleague at the Rudolf-Virchow-Krankenhaus dermatology wards, Dr. Wilhelm Wechselmann.[3] Frau Wechselmann is a "regular" German. Replacement housing is in demand because of Allied bombings, thus Jewish property and possessions are seized as "disposable property for use in social policy" (Meyer 112–13). Good housing is for good citizens of the Reich. And phone books in the Berlin of 1942 quickly become as disposable as the Buschkes themselves. Abraham Buschke dies at Theresienstadt a few months later. His wife, Erna, survives—one of only nine on their transport of a hundred who does.

With some artistic license, I paint a scene drafted from the imagination of a composite victim, one that I will call *Sarah*. In Erna Buschke's case, it is a name forcibly inserted between her first and last name as a result of the 1938 decree requiring all German Jews to be identified by their heritage. That the name of her husband, Abraham, was also the name of the husband of the Old Testament Sarah is not insignificant. Sarah stands at the threshold of two histories. In one, she travels with Abraham into lands where he fears for her safety and substitutes one role (his wife) for another (his sister). In the other history, Erna becomes Erna Sarah to mark her as a daughter of the first history. In one history, Sarah laughs. In the other history, she does not.

I place Sarah at the crossroads of a rhetorical topography of violence, a threshold marking the trope of substitution that darkens every household on this map. Substitution is a form of violence, even if it is a metaphor that substitutes one word for another. There is a displacement, something is sacrificed. Something, or most often some one, becomes a scapegoat. Substitution is a rhetorical figure, one of the four categories of change. Euphemism is an example wherein we substitute a more acceptable term for a less acceptable term. "Voluntary evacuation" for "deportation." "Replacement housing" for "Aryanization of Jewish assets as disposable property of use in social policy of the Third Reich." "The final solution" for genocide.

The address for this chapter is a designation of such substitutions and a mapping device that serves to frame the book as a whole. As an everyday artifact, the phone book manifests the scapegoat mechanism in the starkest way possible because it is the 1941 Berlin phone book that oddly still contained several pages of listings for Jewish hospitals, schools, and community organizations in 1941. Yet, together with the address books of Berlin from the early 1930s through 1943, it is possible to chronicle the elimination of almost all of the Jews living in Berlin who were either deported to concentration camps or had committed suicide by 1943. Reading this phone book is an exercise in studying an ancient *pharmakonomy*, whereby the process of substitution is made visible through the history of addresses.[4] Voßtraße 6, Hitler's office of the chancellery and the nearby bunker where he ended his life, is now a children's playground (Ladd 133). That in itself is not a violent substitution, though it is important in the history of memory. But Motzstraße 72 was the site of at least one violent substitution. Abraham Buschke is listed in the phone book in 1941 and in the 1942 address book, but has disappeared from the 1943 address book (fig. 1.2).[5] In his place is a "regular" German family who had (perhaps, as many had) themselves been displaced by Allied bombings.

Tragically, this scenario occurred throughout Germany and the occupied countries after the invasion of Poland in 1939. Imagining that moment when Jewish families crossed the threshold beyond which most would never return is not, however, an exercise I invoke in order to set the stage for

72 E. Schlöme, B., Kfm. T.
V. Stromenger, H., Verwalt.
(Adlershof, Volkswohl-
straße 123).
Bachmann, Charlotte,
Kffr. T.
Büschke, A., Prof. Dr. med.
Facharzt T.
T.
Hannesen, F. R., Nach-
richtenbüro T.
Kortschagin, J., Kfm. T.
Kreutzmann, K., Konditorei
T.
Krüger, W., Verl. Buchhdl.
T.
Löffler, G., Dispont.
Loja M., Schauspielerin T.
Mobis E., Uhren.
Ohlerich, H., Maschinist.
Peters, A., Fabrkt. T.
Pinnow, P., Kfm. T.
Rein, R., Reg. Rat T.
Stiebner, H., Regisseur T.
Zimkeit, E., Wettannahme
T.

72 E. Sauder, Gebr. Eigen-
tüm. (Tempelhf.,
Albrechtstr. 56).
V. Stromenger, H., Verwalt.
(Adlershof, Volkswohl-
straße 123).
Bachmann, Charlotte,
Kffr. T.
Bartens, E., Wo. T.
Fleer, O., Direktorin a. D.
T.
Hannesen, F. R., Nach-
richtenbüro T.
Kortschagin, J., Kfm. T.
Kreutzmann, K., Konditorei
T.
Krüger, W., Verl. Buchhdl.
T.
Löffler, G., Dispont.
Mobis E., Uhren.
Ohlerich, H., Hauswart.
Peters, A., Fabrkt. T.
Pinnow, P., Kfm. T.
Rein, R., Reg. Rat T.
Risch, J., Schwester T.
Wechselmann, H., Frau

Fig 1.2. 1942 and 1943 address book entries for Motzstraße 72 (Zentral- und Landesbibliothek Berlin).

an examination of what happened to the Jews in the streets, in crowded Jüdehauser (Jewish homes where they were often gathered before the deportations), in ghettos, on stifling, cramped trains, in concentration-camp barracks, or finally in camp showers and crematoria. Such scenes are forever, and indelibly, chiseled into the concrete walls of memory and history. Rather, this chapter conjures the figure of Sarah as a haunted medium standing on all thresholds of violence through which the ghosts of Jewish inhabitants busy themselves against the marks of hunger, isolation, hatred, despair, and the fire-*places*. I aim, à la Jacques Derrida, to remind us that "cinders there are" (*Cinders* 21). Reminding, (re)minding, that the ashes of the Holocaust *are*, and they are *there*. The *place* is how the address of genocide inters/enters our hearts. "Pure is the word. It calls for fire. Cinders there are, this is what takes place in letting a place occur, so that it will be understood: Nothing will have taken place but the place. Cinders there are: Place there is (*il y a lieu*)" (37).

To focus on this moment of homeless-ness is not only about placing us within a "letting occur" of the place, it is also about sharing the place we call *home*. And it will have been about sharing the uncanny (*unheimlichkeit*) feeling of being homesick—of *Being* home/sick. It will have been about setting the stage for the logic of the Same Home, of the Homeland constructed by the Third Reich (*Vaterland*) and more recently in our post-9/11 United States (Department of Homeland Security). The question of place, haunted by the question of home, lurks on every page of the Berlin 1941 phone book (fig. 1.3). The visage of cinder and ash, these pages presage, line after line (lineage, patrilineal, linear) of fixed addresses, telephone routing, occupations . . . and racial hygienics.

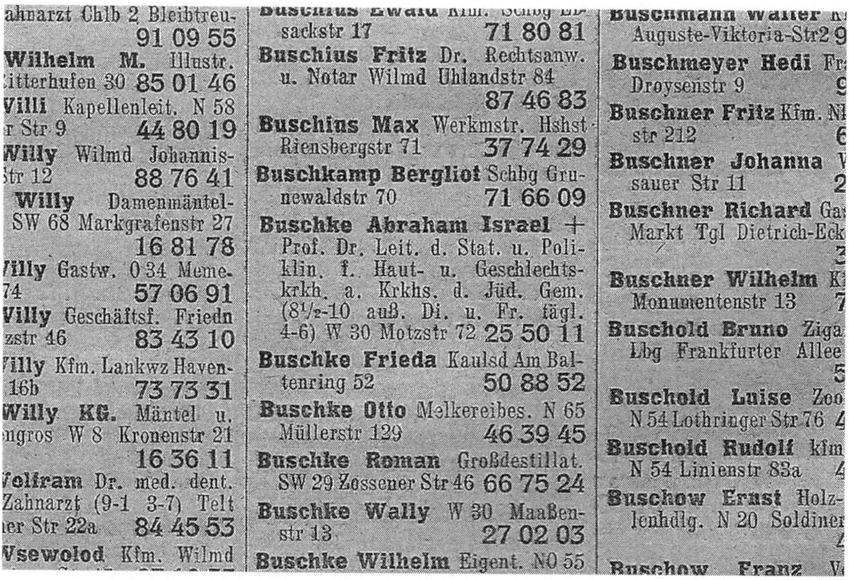
ahnarzt Chlb 2 Bleibtreu-
91 09 55
Wilhelm M. Illustr.
itterhufen 30 85 01 46
Villi Kapellenleit. N 58
r Str 9 44 80 19
Willy Wilmd Johannis-
str 12 88 76 41
Willy Damenmäntel-
SW 68 Markgrafenstr 27
16 81 78
illy Gastw. O 34 Meme-
74 57 06 91
Villy Geschäftsf. Friedn
zstr 46 83 43 10
illy Kfm. Lankwz Haven-
16b 73 73 31
Willy KG. Mäntel u.
ngros W 8 Kronenstr 21
16 36 11
olfram Dr. med. dent.
Zahnarzt (9-1 3-7) Telt
er Str 22a 84 45 53
Vsewolod Kfm. Wilmd

sackstr 17 71 80 81
Buschius Fritz Dr. Rechtsanw.
u. Notar Wilmd Uhlandstr 84
87 46 83
Buschius Max Werkmstr. Hshst
Riensbergstr 71 37 74 29
Buschkamp Bergliot Schbg Gru-
newaldstr 70 71 66 09
Buschke Abraham Israel +
Prof. Dr. Leit. d. Stat. u. Poli-
klin. f. Haut- u. Geschlechts-
krkh. a. Krkhs. d. Jüd. Gem.
(8½-10 auß. Di. u. Fr. tägl.
4-6) W 30 Motzstr 72 25 50 11
Buschke Frieda Kaulsd Am Bal-
tenring 52 50 88 52
Buschke Otto Melkereibes. N 65
Müllerstr 129 46 39 45
Buschke Roman Großdestillat.
SW 29 Zossener Str 46 66 75 24
Buschke Wally W 30 Maaßen-
str 13 27 02 03
Buschke Wilhelm Eigent. NO 55

Auguste-Viktoria-Str 2
Buschmeyer Hedi
Droysenstr 9
Buschner Fritz Kfm.
str 212
Buschner Johanna
sauer Str 11
Buschner Richard
Markt Tgl Dietrich-Eck
Buschner Wilhelm
Monumentenstr 13
Buschold Bruno
Lbg Frankfurter Allee
Buschold Luise
N 54 Lothringer Str 76
Buschold Rudolf
N 54 Linienstr 83a
Buschow Ernst Holz-
lenhdlg. N 20 Soldiner

Fig. 1.3. 1941 Berlin phone book entry for Abraham Buschke with obligatory middle name of "Israel" required of all male Jews after 1938. *Photo by author.*

Crowded Party Lines

As a child in the 1950s and 60s, I remember that my grandparents had a peculiar telephone in their small flagstone ranch house in rural west Texas. When I picked up the big heavy black receiver, sometimes I would hear other voices already engrossed in a conversation. The "party line" was not an uncommon way for people to share the expense of a telephone with other ranchers who lived miles away. As a metaphor, the "party line" can function both in the sense of the Nazi party and of shared telephone lines, shared spaces, shared conversations. In this chapter, I share a line with Martin Heidegger (especially his "Building, Dwelling, Thinking" lecture of 1951) and Avital Ronell (*The Telephone Book*, 1989), among others, in an effort to underscore the stakes for philosophy and rhetoric. We, too, are the beneficiaries of thought that occupies a vexed threshold of ontological conflict. The question of Heidegger's relationship with Nazism has produced a whole generation of scholars whose careers are thoroughly entangled with (and advanced because of) this question. It will not be the aim of these discussions here to place blame upon, find fault with, or absolve Heidegger. The hour is late for such pronouncements. The fact that ever more evidence for questioning Heidegger's thought is published each year crowds the party line with more and more voices clamoring to connect with what Ronell calls "the life-and-death switchboard" (7).[6] It is not a *fair* business. One of the most interesting suggestions of what is at stake is found in Jean-François Lyotard's book *Heidegger and "the jews."* Lyotard makes a compelling case when he writes:

> Who profits from this summary "politicization"? The fourth political power, publishing, the medium that holds the power to render things public—to make public (or not, obviously) what remained hidden, ignored by most. In this sense, scandal is the most fruitful way to publicize something. Through scandal, publishing best affirms, confirms, and comforts itself as the power that "reveals." Thus rendered sensational, the Heidegger affair is subject to the urgency of the politics of publishing. (51)

In addition, Lyotard points to other "silences with respect to adhering to Nazism," namely, "those who hide behind the (urgent) eloquence of the discourses of reparation" (52). There is no doubt that Edmund Husserl (born into a Jewish family, but later converted to Christianity), who occupied the office of Professor of Philosophy at the University of Freiburg, was forced to retire in 1928, opening (literally) his office door for a successor, in this case one of his former students, Martin Heidegger. That "deportation," while not as violent as for the Buschkes, nonetheless bears the mark of substitution we are investigating in this chapter. As Ronell put it:

> Husserl, whose name suffered erasure by Heidegger under the same regime —Heidegger had deleted the dedication to *Sein und Zeit*—was removed from the offices which Heidegger now occupies. Husserl was not there to answer; he would not even answer to his name. The mentor had had his telephone removed. During Heidegger's tenure a telephone was reinstalled. (19)

Although I am placing the party lines in circulation during World War II through to the present, I have also signaled that they are technologically conducted via a much more ancient conflict, that between philosophy and rhetoric. In *Dissemination*, Derrida explains:

> The front line that is violently inscribed between Platonism and its closest other, in the form of sophistics, is far from being unified, continuous, as if stretched between two homogeneous areas. Its design is such that, through a systematic indecision, the parties and the *party lines* frequently exchange their respective places, imitating the forms and borrowing the paths of the opponent. These permutations are therefore possible, and if they are obliged to inscribe themselves within some common territory, the dissension no doubt remains internal and casts into absolute shadow some entirely-other of *both* sophistics *and* Platonism, some resistance having no common denominator with this whole commutation. (emphasis added, 108)

As a "telephone" book, Ronell's work is both rhetorical/sophistic and philosophical; thus it shares the format of both traditions, including other traditions such as psychology and feminism. I am personally indebted to Ronell because her book was published at the time I was writing my dissertation, *In the Name of Writing: Rhetoric and the Politics of Ethos* (1994), which contained separate chapters on both Heidegger and technology. Her playful and irreverent treatment of the politics of the telephone served to cast major shadows on the "standing reserve" of Heidegger's relationship to, and writings about, the question of technology. So much so that I recalibrated the focus of my chapter on Heidegger toward the question of a different kind of "calling," the call of *logos*, leaving my work on technology for the final chapter on technology, pedagogy, and *ethos*.[7]

In the present chapter, my aim is to revisit Ronell's book briefly as a means of sharing the "party line" of a past technology and the historical moment when Heidegger took over a Jewish office (Husserl's), which later bore the sign of the Nazi Party. In essence, then, it is a question of connecting the telephone to the address not in order to supplant the political significance of one with the other, but in order to feel less distance (telephone) and more proximity (the simultaneous address of Jew/German). With each dimension of space (far and near), I am voicing with Ronell the fact that the Jews were forced to face a "death-support system" (3). Troubling the waters of Heidegger's influence, she still aims to inflect her reading by the "affair": "So, in a sense, we never leave Heidegger's side, for this side is multifaceted, deep and troubling. We never leave his side but we split, and our paths part" (4). The party line I share with Ronell also splits and our paths part, though not because of questionable politics. We, Ronell and I, are connected to a switchboard, and that switchboard is rhetoric. Thus, it is also a programming question. By what codes are we enabled to conduct our inquiries over this shared "party line"? (See chapter 2 in this book for more about IBM's complicity in the punch-card system that helped identify the Jews.) Whereas Ronell claims that "the telephone in fact will emerge as a synecdoche of technology" (13), I propose that the *address* is a synecdoche of *dwelling*. Where Ronell suggests that the telephone connects mouth to ear by hand (254–55), I am interested in the address that connects life to death by dwelling.

Either way, we are both dialed into the question of the primordial call of *home*, or as Ronell notes, "a notion of *Unheimlichkeit*, the primordial being not-at-home" into which both Freud and Heidegger are attuned (24). Here is Ronell:

> Even so, the telephone book boldly answers as the other book of books, a site which registers all the names of history, if only to attend the refusal of the proper name. A partial archivization of the names of the living, the telephone book binds the living and the dead in an unarticulated thematics of destination. Who writes the telephone book, assumes its peculiar idiom or makes its referential assignments? And who would be so foolish as to assert with conviction that its principal concern lies in eliciting the essential disclosure of truth? (5)

Perhaps I am that fool. The task of revealing the "unarticulated thematics of destination" in the Berlin 1941 phone book is not unlike answering a knock on the door at 5:15 A.M. There is first the question of the dwelling at Motzstraße 72, but we will not think of dwelling solely in material terms (the apartment, Erna's kitchen, Abraham's violin, a faded photograph). In their claim against the Reich after the war, Abraham's family filed for restitution of household furnishings, books, clothing, medical instruments, gold, silver, jewelry, artwork, and valuable papers (Wiedergutsmachtungsämter project; Berlin Landesarchiv database). To this list I would have liked to add a nameplate that bears the name *Buschke*. Theirs/there is "the essential disclosure of truth": who dwelled in the household and in what manner did they dwell? Were the Buschkes full of fear as they answered the door when the Gestapo knocked that November morning in 1942?

The Topography of Dwelling

In Walter Benjamin's essay, "A Berlin Chronicle" (1932), a haunting foreshadowing of Nazi Germany directs our attention to the nature of living as a Jew in Berlin in the early 1930s (fig. 1.4). Fascinated with the topography of everyday existence, Benjamin invites his reader to wander the city streets, courtyards, and railway stations, to hear "the carpet beating that was the language of the nether world" ("Berlin" 44). "The courtyard," Benjamin writes,

> was one of the places where the city opened itself to the child; others, admitting him or letting him go, were railway stations. On departure, their openings were a panorama, the frame of a *fata morgana* [an optical illusion at a distant horizon]. No distance was more remote than the place where the rails converged in the mist. (44)

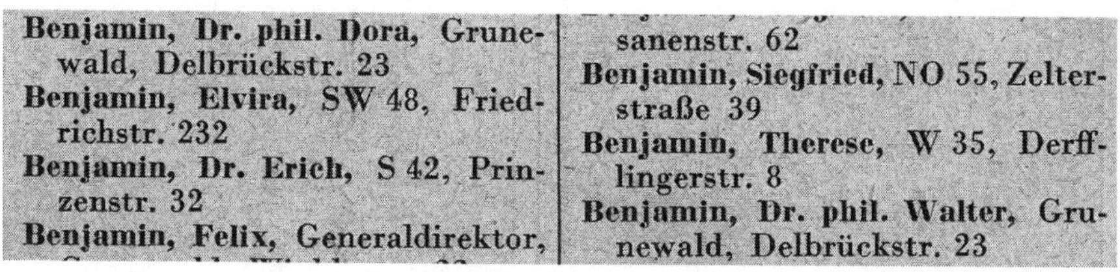

Benjamin, Dr. phil. Dora, Grunewald, Delbrückstr. 23
Benjamin, Elvira, SW 48, Friedrichstr. 232
Benjamin, Dr. Erich, S 42, Prinzenstr. 32
Benjamin, Felix, Generaldirektor,
...sanenstr. 62
Benjamin, Siegfried, NO 55, Zelterstraße 39
Benjamin, Therese, W 35, Derfflingerstr. 8
Benjamin, Dr. phil. Walter, Grunewald, Delbrückstr. 23

Fig. 1.4. 1931 Jüdisches Addreßbuch entries for Walter Benjamin and his sister Dora (Zentral- und Landesbibliothek Berlin).

In his introduction to the collection of essays in which "A Berlin Chronicle" appears, *Reflections: Essays, Aphorisms, Autobiographical Writings*, Peter Demetz explains that "Benjamin always looked for threshold experiences" (xviii). Demetz notes that the essay's title is "a misnomer, because it actually offers a map of coexistent apartments, meeting places, elegant salons, shabby hotel rooms" (xvii–xviii). For Demetz, Benjamin's imagination suggested, "as in that of Rainer Maria Rilke, [that] space rules over time; his 'topographical consciousness' shapes experience in architectonic patterns, in neighborhoods, and in particular in urban districts the borders of which have to be crossed in trembling and sweet fear" (xvii). Such "sweet fear" is, I will argue, a rhetorically conductive threshold between Benjamin's thought and the Heideggerian concept of *dwelling.*

Heidegger's later works frequently invoke the question of dwelling, specifically his 1951 lectures—"Building, Dwelling, Thinking" and "Poetically Man Dwells." While Heidegger is quick to set up the question of dwelling as the goal of building, he also describes the process itself as central to how we "attain to dwelling" ("Building" 145). Why the distinction? Julian Young claims that just as with Heidegger's methodology in *Being and Time*, wherein he seeks to disclose Being's "anxiety in the face of death" as the source of our ontological homelessness, in "Building, Dwelling, Thinking," Heidegger completes a major shift in his thinking about this specific source of anxiety (Young 189). According to Young, "At its heart, therefore, Dasein's existence is permeated by radical—as I shall sometimes say, 'ontological'—insecurity" (189). But, he continues, this is "understood by Heidegger as incompatible with, as the opposite of, dwelling. . . . Dwelling, then, is ontological security—precisely what is excluded by *Being and Time*" (189). In short, the main difference between the early and late Heidegger, what Young terms his "ontological transformation," involves his "gradual, but radical, reappraisal of the character of 'the nothing'" (190). According to Young, "In early Heidegger it is an absolute nothing. In late Heidegger it is (to use Schopenhauer's distinction) a relative nothing. In early Heidegger it is emptiness, in late Heidegger it is 'plenitude'" (192). This shift from ontological insecurity to ontological security is constitutive of Heidegger's enigmatic definition of dwelling as "*living with* homelessness" (190). In other words, dwelling is not based *merely* in staying in one place, just as building is not concerned *merely* with the construction of physical structures. For Heidegger, "Dwelling is the manner in which mortals are on the earth" ("Building" 148).

In "Building, Dwelling, Thinking," Heidegger "listen[s] once more to what language says to us" by pondering the various Old Saxon, Gothic, and High German words for *building* (*wuon*, *wunian*, and *bauen*), which basically "mean to remain, to stay in a place" (148–49). Yet, he wants to home in on the Gothic *wunian*, which "says more distinctly how this remaining is experienced" (149). Following the variations on the German word *bauen*, Heidegger tunes in closely to the Gothic word *wunian*. Specifically, *wunian* means "to be at peace, to be brought to peace, to remain in peace" (149). Granted, we are entering a slippery lack of traction with respect to dwelling by connecting it with peace—and ultimately, Heidegger says, with "the free" (149). To think beyond peace as freedom, which is where Heidegger is headed in this line of argument, he must redefine "the free" as that which is "preserved from harm and danger, preserved from something, safeguarded. To free really means to spare" (149). How, then, may we connect Heidegger's "dwelling" with the "sweet fear" in Benjamin's imagination? And why is this significant to the question Ronell examined in relation to the Jews facing a "death-support system" (Ronell 3)?

Heidegger's interrogation of building, which leads to what Young calls his "ontological transformation," builds upon (constructive-ly) the central question for Being that he formulated as early as in *Being and Time*—namely, "mortals dwell in that they initiate their own nature—their being capable of death as death" ("Building" 151). However, this passage quickens our interest in the Benjamin/Ronell connection when Heidegger explains why dwelling, "being capable of death as death," and the "real sparing is something *positive*" (149). "Mortals dwell in that they initiate their own nature—their being capable of death as death—into the use and practice of this capacity, *so that there may be a good death*" (emphasis added; 151). *Ein guter Tod.* There is a quiet desperation in Heidegger's obsession with recalibrating our relation to death by "being capable of death as death," which he claims in "What Are Poets For?" (1946) is the highest task of poets. Drawing from Rilke, as the "modern" equivalent of Hölderlin, Heidegger cites a line from a letter of 1923 in which Rilke "says that the point is 'to read the word "death" *without* negation'" ("What are Poets For?" 125). Here the positive is stressed, while the "good death" warrants a mere mention in "Building, Dwelling, Thinking." It is necessary now (especially now) to question in what manner of positivity Heidegger's notion of dwelling consists. Our interrogation will backtrack since Heidegger's essays of 1946 and 1951 postdate what seems an impossible historical time to invoke a poetic reading of "the word 'death' without negation."

"A Death of Their Own"

A rhetorical death is, of course, vastly incomparable to physical death. And yet, through Heidegger it is possible to see the danger of splitting such material hairs in the age of modern technology. In 1949, he delivered his lectures on technology in Bremen, and these texts were later published as "The Question Concerning Technology" in 1954. Earlier, however, in "What

Are Poets For?," Heidegger reads technology across Rilke's reflections on Nature and what truly menaces man and beast. Staying on track of his call to read the word "death" without negation, Heidegger's remarks on technology in his earlier 1946 lecture (delivered on the twentieth anniversary of Rilke's death) must give us pause if we are tempted to strike out on our own understanding of what is at stake. This is the threshold on which Abraham and Erna Buschke stood even as a machine waited to transport them to the "place where the rails converged into the mist" (Benjamin 44).

The problem with technology in Being's relation to death, Heidegger insists, is not in its everyday use or manufacture. The "objective character of its raw materials" is the true "nature of technology" ("Poets" 112). "Even this," he writes, "that man becomes the subject and the world the object, is a consequence of technology's nature establishing itself, and not the other way around" (112). We have constructed the machinery of our own "unshieldedness" by our "self-assertion" of objectifying the world. We have "parted" from our nature (as Beings capable of death as death) by opposing ourselves to what Rilke called the "Open," the "unheard-of center" (116). Because the "essence of technology comes to the light of day only slowly. . . . The wholesome and sound withdraws. The world becomes without healing, unholy" (117). For Heidegger, the poets stay on the "track to the holy, the hale and whole" (117). Only they are capable of discerning "the danger that is assailing man," and "the danger consists in the threat that assaults man's nature in his relation to Being itself, and not in accidental perils. This danger is *the* danger" (117). If we stare long enough at these words, really take them in and hold them up to the light of genocide, how are we to reconcile a threshold (a boundary that binds even as it separates) across which a life and death journey began at Moztstraße 72? Or the tragic suicide at Reichstraße 5 (Davidson 242)?

Martin Davidson, whose Nazi grandfather, Bruno Langbehn, was listed in the 1941 Berlin phone book on the same page as a Jewish doctor, Kurt Landsberger, discovers that the chain of complicity in the fate of Berlin's Jews was part of a systemic and tragically efficient social and economic ostracization that fueled anti-Semitism in the name of greed and the improvement of everyday living conditions for "regular" Germans. Davidson learned, with horror, that the address of a Jewish doctor who committed suicide (Hartmann Levy) was, in fact, the same address as his great-grandmother's, Reichstraße 5. He writes that "by the time Hartmann Levy killed himself, indeed, even while Dr. Landsberger's phone entry was being printed, a threshold had been crossed" (242). It is important for us to understand, as Davidson did, that those who benefited from Nazi confiscation of Jewish property were not only the German Reich, but ordinary citizens. Martin Dean's extensive study *Robbing the Jews*, explains how "every cooking pot that was taken from a deported Jewish family was first registered and then auctioned by the financial administration. . . . [where] private individuals were able to purchase scarce consumer goods at a discount" (15). According to Dean, while there is

> no doubt that the seizure of Jewish property in Europe was primarily a state-directed process linked closely to the development of the Holocaust. . . . the widespread participation of the local population as beneficiaries from Jewish property served to spread complicity and therefore also acceptance of German measures against the Jews beyond the smaller circle of immediate perpetrators. In this way, the Nazis and their collaborators were able to mobilize society in support of Nazi racial policies to a greater extent than the spread of racial antisemitism alone would have permitted. Thus, the existence of economic antisemitism and widespread opportunism must be incorporated into explanations of the Holocaust that have generally focused primarily on Nazi racial ideology. (14–15)

The availability of newly opened archives in recent years affords not only a more detailed picture of how Nazi racial ideology forced Jews to leave Germany, it paints our canvas of substitution with broad swaths of rhetorical devastation in the guise of multiple forms of persecution: social, economic, and ontological. Already the subjects of increasingly violent persecutions, the Jews became the victims of phantom political justifications for their projected absence from German society. When, for example, a Jewish family undergoes a "denaturalization" process (the legal basis for forced emigration), they are at the same time required by law to pay the "Reich flight tax (*Reichsfluchtsteuer*)," which consisted of 25 percent of their assets. Dean's research shows that the "official justification for the tax was that emigrants owed something to the state for the nonpayment of future taxes" (57).

The irony is staggering when we consider that the Nazis not only never intended for the German Jews to return from the camps, they forced them to finance their own systematic persecution and slaughter. They denaturalized them as citizens, compelled them to sell their businesses, demanded detailed lists of property down to the last thimble, confiscated their property, deprived them of their occupations and means of living, taxed them under the guise of the "war effort," and forcibly (and cruelly) stripped them of their human dignity, not to mention their very lives. Dean argues that the "steady diminution of their means reduced the opportunities for Jews to flee, wore down their physical ability to resist, and eliminated their hope of buying material support in hiding" (395). It is clear that the decimation of Jewish economic survival paved the way for the exile and genocide of Jews. The beneficiaries of the Nazi policies (and police state) may not have been openly anti-Semitic in the beginning, but as the Reich forged the bureaucratic infrastructure for the indigenous robbery of Jews, "racist-inspired greed" emerged as a major contributing factor to indifference and complicity in the highly profitable scapegoat mechanism, with its crematory sacrificial realities, known now as the Holocaust (396). Marion Kaplan writes that following the so-called "Eleventh Decree to the Reich Citizenship Law" of November 1941, which "mandated the automatic seizure of property of German Jews who had left or would leave the country. . . . 'good Aryans fought like jackals over a carcass'" at the public auctions. These auctions often "took place in the former homes of Jews, where small crowds gathered after reading announcements in the newspapers" (185–86). In Jörg Friedrich's words: "No final solution can be more final than when one has emptied the rooms" (147).

In such a climate of economic and social death, it is understandable why so many Jews committed suicide (*Freitod*, free death).[8] When deportation notices began arriving, after years of persecution and economic devastation, thousands of Jews chose what Konrad Kwiet called "the ultimate refuge"—suicide. David Lester cites testimony by Hildegard Henschel, wife of Moritz Henschel (a prominent Jewish Community leader in Berlin) during the Nuremburg trials.[9] She claimed that "Germans would revive those who attempted suicide and then order them deported first" (2). Marion Kaplan notes, similarly, that "these suicides angered the Nazis, who waited for the unsuccessful suicides to recover in order to send them to their state-controlled deaths" (180). Kwiet estimates that "under Nazi rule roughly 10,000 Jews committed suicide or attempted suicide" (Kaplan 180). Furthermore, Kaplan (citing Kwiet) says many of these suicides involved

> "careful preparations, of conversations and memories of a happy German childhood, of people remembering their children who have left Germany." . . . These Jews died by their own hand in order to preserve a sense of their

> own dignity and agency—even "Germanness." Many died surrounded by German cultural artifacts: Jewish men sometimes wore their army medals [from World War I]. . . . They succeeded in their despair-driven desire for a "death of their own," in some ways stealing it from the Nazis. (181)

Kaplan footnotes this passage by quoting from Rilke's only novel, *The Notebooks of Malte Laurids Brigge*: "It is rare to find anyone who wishes to have a death of his own" (Kaplan 259). The longer passage is worth including:

> Who is there today who still cares about a well-finished death? Nobody. Even the rich, who after all can afford this luxury, are beginning to grow lazy and indifferent; the desire to have a death of one's own is becoming more and more rare. In a short time it will become as rare as a life of one's own. Because, my God!, it is all there. You come, you find a life, ready-made, you just have to slip it on. You leave when you want to, or when you are forced to: anyway, no effort: *Voila votre mort, monsieur* [There is your death, sir]. (Rilke *Notebooks* 9)

By the spring of 1942, when the deportations were in full swing, the "sweet fear" arrived daily with the post, as for Dr. Max Loewenstein and his family just a few doors down from Abraham Buschke's family (fig. 1.5). Miraculously, the Loewensteins survived. Abraham Buschke did not. "There is your death, sir." For the Nazis, the "good death" was good for Germany, and in their twisted logic it also amounted to a *Gnadentod* (mercy death). The Nazi racist objective was demonstrated early with the T4 program, named for its secret headquarters at Tiergartenstraße 4. The T4 program was the result of Hitler's ability to exploit the post–World War I "Darwinian concept of 'the struggle for existence'" (Kogon et al. 13). Hitler outlined the Final Solution in *so many words* in *Mein Kampf*, but the idea of mass killings began with his wish to rid Germany of inferior elements (Kogon et al. 13):

> For as soon as procreation as such is limited and the number of births diminished, the natural struggle for existence which leaves only the strongest and healthiest alive is obviously replaced by the obvious desire to "save" even the weakest and most sickly at any price, and this plants the seed of a future generation which must inevitably grow more and more deplorable the longer this mockery of Nature and her will continues. (*Mein Kampf* 132)

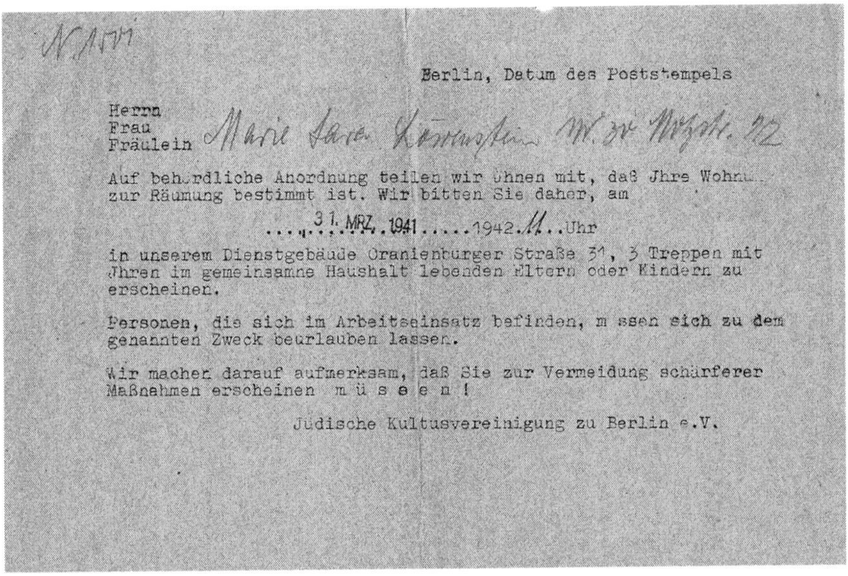

Berlin, Datum des Poststempels

Herrn
Frau
Fräulein

Auf behördliche Anordnung teilen wir Ihnen mit, daß Ihre Wohnung zur Räumung bestimmt ist. Wir bitten Sie daher, am

31. MRZ. 1941 .....1942. 11 .. Uhr

in unserem Dienstgebäude Oranienburger Straße 31, 3 Treppen mit Ihren im gemeinsamne Haushalt lebenden Eltern oder Kindern zu erscheinen.

Personen, die sich im Arbeitseinsatz befinden, m ssen sich zu dem genannten Zweck beurlauben lassen.

Wir machen darauf aufmerksam, daß Sie zur Vermeidung schärferer Maßnahmen erscheinen m ü s s e n !

Jüdische Kultusvereinigung zu Berlin e.V.

Fig. 1.5. Deportation notice for Dr. Max Loewenstein and family from Motzstraße 22. *Loewenstein Family Holocaust Papers, Jüdische Kultusvereinigung zu Berlin e. V. Courtesy Beck Archives, Special Collections, CJS and University Libraries, University of Denver.*

An entirely new set of "categories of the population" became targeted for *Gnadentod* (mercy death): "alcoholics, epileptics, psychopaths, vagrants, criminals, prostitutes, invalids, the mentally ill, cripples, and incurables" (Kogon et al. 13–14). In order to present the justification for this to the German people, even though these *euthanasia* (Greek for "good death") killings were largely carried out in secret, the Nazis

> began to acquaint the German people with such an understanding of "euthanasia." In certain publications, over the radio, in films, and in lectures, the question was insidiously posed: Does it make sense to keep alive the nonproductive mentally ill, whose care is often costly? . . . The propaganda even went so far as to set the following problem in a high school mathematics textbook: "The construction of a psychiatric hospital costs 6 million marks. How many new homes at 15,000 marks could be built for this amount?" (Kogon et al. 14; Dorner, exercise 95 on p 42)

And indeed, as we now know, the "Action T4" program in operation from 1939 to 1941 was responsible for the "forced euthanasia" of over seventy thousand people, although the numbers are much higher because doctors continued the practice even after it was officially terminated in 1941. During Action T4, the development of mass killing by poisonous gas was introduced, although it was implemented after other methods proved ineffective and time consuming for mass killings. Vans (in some cases decommissioned postal vans) were rigged for this purpose and used as mobile gas chambers. In his essay, "The Ethic of Expediency: Classical Rhetoric, Technology, and the Holocaust," Steven Katz critiques a memo from an engineer named Willi Just to Obersturmbannführer Walther Rauff that details how to improve the efficiency of gassing vans, concluding that "this memo is *too* technical, *too* logical" (257). It is a memo so rife with the "*ethos* of expediency" that Katz calls for us to re-evaluate the roots of "technical communication and deliberative rhetoric, and by extension writing pedagogy and practice based on it" (258).[10]

Undoubtedly, judging from the math textbook example mentioned above and Katz's study, the roots of pedagogy in general should be examined in light of the Holocaust. In the context of this chapter, however, it is necessary to stay on the path of the rhetorical figure of substitution and its real and symbolic manifestation on the threshold of Motzstraße 72 in order to *address* rhetoric as itself the site of an address incapable of offering "a good death." If it has taken until now to bring myself to throw down such a provocation, it will take even longer (the length of this book, and more) to come to terms with how the address bears this rhetorical burden and how rhetoric burdens the question of Being with a *haunted* form of dwelling of which even Heidegger could not *think* in language. In ". . . Poetically Man Dwells . . ." we are handed a question from the start: "how is 'man'—and this means every man and all the time—supposed to dwell poetically?" (213). How, he might have asked, was Walter Benjamin supposed to *dwell* poetically? "Does not all dwelling remain incompatible with the poetic? Our dwelling is harassed by the housing shortage" (213), following which Heidegger laments how "poetry is either rejected as a frivolous mooning and vaporizing into the unknown, and a flight into dreamland, or is counted as a part of literature" (213). In 1951, the year Heidegger delivered this lecture, West Germany faced a housing shortage of almost six million housing units ("West Germany" *Chicago Tribune*, September 27, 1951). According to reports, the shortage was not due to bombing during the war, but to the influx of East German refugees who fled to West Germany. Yet, it is difficult to dissociate this reference to "six million" from another horrifyingly familiar six million figure and not wonder how many *dwelling* thresholds represent the substitution mechanism we will now pursue: the *haunted* scapegoat.

Haunted Scapegoats

If rhetoric is a site incapable of realizing "a good death," we need look no further than the histories of rhetoric to understand *in what manner* of incapability it manifests this resistance to the qualifier of *good*ness in relation to the realities of end-of-life-ness. Rhetoric has forever been a haunted tradition. It is haunted by Plato's binary between good and bad rhetoric, by Aristotle's conflation of the good with happiness, and by Peter Ramus's defining of rhetoric as a (merely) cosmetic art (i.e., less good than philosophy, which alone deals in "truth"). It would be Nietzsche who, in *Beyond Good and Evil*, first introduced the rhetorical re-valuation of such binary thinking: "To recognize untruth as a condition of life: that, to be sure, means to resist customary value-sentiments in a dangerous fashion; and a philosophy which ventures to do so places itself, by that act alone, beyond good and evil" (17–18). Kenneth Burke, however, gathers these histories into a framework called "dramatism," in which the dialectics at work in classical rhetoric are more properly related to a misalignment of the "good" with "purpose" (*Grammar* 292–93). As Burke suggests, the question of "happiness" for Aristotle is directly connected with purposive (moral) action (292). An admittedly truncated trip through rhetorical theory still leaves open the question of how rhetoric is incapable of realizing "a good death," except insofar as we can understand how rhetoric's resistance to dialectic (Aristotle called it the counterpart to dialectic) and binary principles places it firmly on the threshold of such divisions as good/evil, life/death, true/false. It operates as a boundary condition; in other words, an essential element of rhetoric is an entirely mystical Other that we are incapable of seeing because it is the ghost that haunts the threshold itself—moving across with liminal ease into our earthly home (our bodies) and out of our earthly existence (our consciousness).

Whereas Burke associates this condition with the "scapegoat mechanism," a principle of division that operates as a vessel, merger, or unification "granted to those who have alienated their iniquities upon it, and so may be purified through its suffering" (406), the scapegoat is more than a symbol of purification to the Nazis. Burke argues that with the Nazis, the scapegoat is the "'essence' of evil, the principle of the discord felt by those who are to be purified by the sacrifice" (407). When taken to this *essential* realm, in which goodness and evil are so radically opposed as to eliminate the motive of purification, it is less difficult to view a more evil version of scapegoating. By substituting purification with "unification by a foe shared in common," the Nazi hatred of Jews turned inward when Germany's ability to "assert itself in further expansion as a 'master race' conquering the 'Semitic' enemy" forced Hitler to prolong the war out of a sense of "honor"—to self-destruct (408). Here we could point to the many suicides ("a death of their own") at the end of the war and thereafter on the part of Hitler, Goebbels, Himmler, and many of those who had orchestrated and slaughtered millions during the Holocaust.[11]

I am unwilling to express sympathy for Nazi deaths, but the presence of *pathos* in death complicates any discussion of Nazi suicides in relation to Jewish suicides. In other words, *pathos* does not depend upon human justification for sympathetic rhetoric. *Pathos is because language is.* And irrespective of our disclaimers, caveats, and rhetorical sidestepping, it is not necessary to conjure (as one would at a séance) the scapegoat—the restless ghost for whom "a death of one's own" or "a good death" means literally nothing. Only we address the ghost; it does not address us except insofar as it wanders—homelessly—in search of its own address. As the haunted ones, we find ourselves, therefore, living in "sweet fear" of such homelessness. We are, literally, home *sick*. The Berlin 1941 phone book (all 1,534 pages of it) is a home/sick text full of home/sick addresses. It wants to go home, but home is only a threshold across which the haunted scapegoats of every principle of division lament that they must dwell together, in death, within these sites of substitution. Burke cautions us in "The Rhetoric of Hitler's Battle" against the dangers of

> the basic Nazi trick: the "curative" unification by a fictitious devil-function, gradually made convincing by the sloganizing repetitiousness of standard advertising technique. . . . It may well be that people, in their human frailty, require an enemy as well as a goal. Very well: Hitlerism itself has provided us with such an enemy. . . . In selecting his brand of doctrine as our "scapegoat," and in tracking down its equivalents in America, we shall be at the very center of accuracy. (187–88)

The principle of division is, however, a frail instrument with which to perpetuate our delusion that we are better (more good than evil)—by being democratic, Christian, free, and righteous—than those ghosts with whom we will inevitably (and eternally) inhabit the only site that survives us all: the address itself. Ground Zero. Fortunately, as rhetoricians, we have a historical window into this address in the figure of the *pharmakon.*

Pharmakonomy

In December 2012, a wax sculpture of a diminutive Hitler by Maurizio Cattelan was installed in an alley of the Warsaw Ghetto (fig. 1.6). Hitler is depicted as a boyish figure in a stance of prayer with his face lifted upward. Naturally, the placement of the sculpture provoked outrage among the Jewish community around the world (Gera). Entitled "Him," the sculpture is placed at a radically conflicted address. Viewers are unable to see it except from a distance and only through a small portal in a wooden gate at the other end of the alley. I argue that this work of art, provocative though it

Fig. 1.6. Maurizio Cattelan, "Him," 2001. *Sculpture © Maurizio Cattelan, depicted with permission from artist; photo showing back of sculpture, by Maciej Szczepańczyk, Wikimedia Commons, https://commons.wikimedia.org/wiki/File:HIM_byMaurizio_Cattelan_in_Warsaw_Ghetto_2013.JPG; photo showing front of sculpture, by Paolo Pellion di Persano, used with permission of photographer.*

may be, causes us to reflect on the process of substitution at work in what I call a *pharmakonomy*, an economy wherein the chain of substitutions performs neither as cure nor poison, but as a rhetorical address for the *both/and* nature of the *pharmakon*.

Derrida famously reads Plato's dialogue *Phaedrus* as a trial of writing in which writing serves as a drug that is both a remedy and a poison (*Dissemination* 70). The Greek term for the ritual of sacrificing a scapegoat, *pharmakos*, is (according to Derrida) never used in Plato's dialogue, and yet this fact is precisely a kind of rupture in philosophy. Derrida proceeds to tell the story recounted by Socrates of the demigod called Theuth, who invented (among other things) writing (75). Speaking to the Egyptian king, Theuth claims that "'this discipline (*to mathema*), my King, will make the Egyptians wiser and will improve their memories . . . my invention is a recipe (*pharmakon*) for both memory and wisdom'" (75). Plato, as we know, considered writing inferior to speech, the living presence of the speaker. Derrida reminds us that in the *Phaedrus* "writing, touted by Theuth as a remedy, a beneficial drug, is later overturned and denounced by the king and then, in the king's place, by Socrates, as a harmful substance, a philter of forgetfulness" (126). How are we to read this in relation to the Cattelan sculpture and ultimately to the substitution trope at work in Nazi Germany?

The ambivalence of the *pharmakon*, Derrida explains, produces

> the movement and the play that links them among themselves, reverses them or makes one side cross over into the other (soul/body, good/evil, inside/outside, memory/forgetfulness, speech/writing, etc.). It is on the basis of this play or movement that the opposites or differences are stopped by Plato. The *pharmakon* is the movement, the locus, and the play: (the production of) difference. It is the différance of difference. (127)

For lack of a better image, it is a kind of revolving door situated on a violent threshold, for this "process of substitution. . . . is nevertheless not lacking in violence" (89). Furthermore, as we have heard from Derrida earlier,

> the parties and the party lines frequently exchange their respective places, imitating the forms and borrowing the paths of the opponent. These permutations are therefore possible, and if they are obliged to inscribe themselves within some common territory [the address], the dissension no doubt remains internal and casts into absolute shadow

> some entirely-other of *both* sophistics *and* Platonism, some resistance having no common denominator with this whole commutation. (108)

And, for Derrida, "*that* is the danger" (109). We have no means of understanding this "entirely-other" both/and, nor do we have the means to reconcile the "violent movement of this surrogation" this "surrogate of a surrogate" (109). It is dangerous because "the supplement *is* not, is not a being (*on*)" (109). In this context, Cattelan's figure of Hitler praying fractures our tidy image of evil, ruptures our righteous anger, and makes of the "common territory" of the Warsaw Ghetto a mockery. It *is* not, it has *no being* that we recognize within a framework of propriety. Derrida's deconstruction of the *pharmakon* not only implodes the boundaries of inside/outside, it can be viewed as one views "Him," through a slender portal in a rustic wooden gate, across a threshold of stone and iron, toward a figure praying, a wax figure destined one day to melt, to burn, to shapeshift according to the laws of Nature.

> The Hitler representation is visible from a hole in a wooden gate across town on Prozna Street. Viewers only see the back of the small figure praying in a courtyard. Because of its small size, it appears to be a harmless schoolboy. "Every criminal was once a tender, innocent and defenseless child," the center said in a commentary on the work. (Gera)

Every threshold marks the passage of the ghosts of both innocence and evil, persecuted and persecutor—it is the address of a haunted *pharmakonomy* in an age of perpetual conflict (*polemos*).

Polemos

> *"To Karl and Kitty with a copy of 'One-Way Street'"*
>
> Is this the landscape image of that one-way street
> That you want to walk down?
> I almost doubt it. But know
> Where you should go.
> There are so many streets with paths of return
> One doesn't see.
> And when direction leads to an impasse:

It's not true that nothing can happen.
There is no negotiating at a collision;
It is the lightning strike.
And finding yourself transformed utterly:
It's no illusion.
In ancient days all paths led
Somehow to God and His Name.
We are not pious. We stay in the Profane
And where God once stood, stands: Melancholy.
(Gershom Scholem, in Pensky 1)[12]

In Walter Benjamin's book, *One-Way Street* (*Einbahnstraße* 1928; fig. 1.7), the figure of the threshold—what I have called the address of a haunted *pharmakonomy*—is given a physical address, No. 113, in an aphorism called "Cellar" ("One-Way Street" excerpt in *Reflections* 62–63). The republication of *Einbahnstraße* by Suhrkamp Verlag (Berlin 2009) suggests that the section is titled like a number over a door, specifically an infamous Paris casino and brothel at No. 113 Palais Royal (352). The poem by Gershom Scholem above was written as a response to Benjamin's *Einbahnstraße*. Whereas Benjamin sees the one-way street as a "zone between the private house and the public flânerie" (Bock 73), Scholem counters with the image of lightning. The "Cellar" points us to the one-way street as a dream sequence. Scholem's poem says it's "no illusion."

Fig. 1.7. Original cover of Benjamin's *Einbahnstraße. Design by Sasha Stone.*

Cellar. *We have long forgotten the ritual by which the house of our life was erected. But when it is under assault and enemy bombs are already taking their toll, what enervated, perverse antiquities do they not lay bare in the foundations. What things were interred and sacrificed amid magic*

> *incantations, what horrible cabinet of curiosities lies there below, where the deepest shafts are reserved for what is most commonplace. In a night of despair I dreamed I was with my first friend from my school days, whom I had not seen for decades and had scarcely ever remembered in that time, tempestuously renewing our friendship and brotherhood. But when I awoke it became clear that what despair had brought to light like a detonation was the corpse of that boy, who had been immured as a warning: that whoever one day lives here may in no respect resemble him.* ("One-Way" 62–63)

"Whoever one day lives here may in no respect resemble him." It is difficult not to filter this passage through the replacement logic of Nazi deportations, indeed of the specific case of Abraham and Erna Buschke and the next tenant of their apartment, Frau Wechselmann. Equally surreal is the lightning fast timing with which such replacement housing occurred. Scholem's image of lightning, however, refers us to the moment of "collision," the "lightning strike" (*der Blitz schlägt ein*) (Scholem 81). As we close in on the rhetorical address as the site of a haunted *pharmakonomy* and our task of addressing rhetoric in the age of perpetual conflict, it is to the question of conflict that we now turn—the *polemos* of all ages, the premise of all scapegoat mechanisms.

To situate the importance of *polemos* at the rhetorical threshold I am examining, we first need to see how Heidegger's reading of pre-Socratic *logos* squares with both the perpetuality and the conflict occupying the address of violence. In his interrogation of Being, Heidegger finds that *where* human beings dwell is a paradox. On more than one occasion, Heidegger claims that "language is the house of Being" ("Letter on Humanism" 193; *On the Way to Language* 5, 21–22). In other words, we are most at home, in our essential dwelling place, in language; but, paradoxically, the essence of language is unrepresentable. Thus, in his attempt to unveil the nature of Being and language, Heidegger reflects on *logos*, whose modern meanings correspond to language, speech, and reason. After years of thinking, however, he could not grasp its essence. In *On the Way to Language*, Heidegger explains that in fact, "it was a reflection on the *logos*, in which I was trying to find the nature of language. Yet it took nearly another ten years before I was able to say what I was thinking—the fitting word is still lacking even today" (8).

In his search for the fitting word, Heidegger's encounter with Heraclitus is a search for the primordial point of tension (*relation*) between being and *logos*. In *Introduction to Metaphysics*, Heidegger claims that "[*logos*] does not let what it holds in its power dissolve into an empty freedom from opposition, but by uniting the opposites maintains the full sharpness of their tension" (134). The point of tension is in actuality not a fixed point so much as a point in motion. Within the sphere of motion there are conflicting forces that set up the possibility for destruction or harmony. Heidegger believes that being is constituted by both destruction *and* harmony in a process described by Heraclitus. Taking the popular interpretation of Heraclitus to task, Heidegger argues that when we

> sum up his philosophy in the dictum *panta rhei*, "everything flows." . . . [These words] do not mean that everything is mere continuous and evanescent change, pure impermanence; no, they mean that the essent as a whole, in its being, is hurled back and forth from one opposition to another; being is the gathering of this conflict and unrest. (133–34)

In fragment 53, Heraclitus says: "Conflict [*polemos*] is for all (that is present) the creator that causes to emerge, but (also) for all the dominant preserver. For it makes some to appear as gods, others as men; it creates (shows) some as slaves, others as freemen" (qtd in *ITM* 61–62).[13] As Heidegger understands it, Heraclitus uses *polemos* to name the conflict that first created opposites.

The key point he makes, however, is that

> *polemos* named here is a conflict that prevailed prior to everything divine and human, not a war in the human sense. . . . In the conflict <Aus-ein-andersetzung, setting-apart> a world comes into being. (Conflict does not split, much less destroy unity. It constitutes unity, it is a binding-together, *logos*. *Polemos* and *logos* are the same). (62)[14]

For Heidegger, the struggle (the "original struggle") is sustained not by warriors, but by the "creators, poets, thinkers, statesmen" (62). He warns, however, that when "the creators vanish from the nation, when they are barely tolerated as an irrelevant curiosity . . . ; when authentic conflict ceases, converted into mere polemics, into the machinations and intrigues of man within the realm of the given, then the decline has set in" (63). Authentic conflict, the original struggle, is *perpetual* conflict. Heidegger sees in Heraclitus the seeds of a riddle that has eluded "our contemporary everyday understanding" of Being ("Logos" 60). The rhetorical figure that solves the riddle is lightning. Heidegger points us to Heraclitus's fragment B 64: "'But lightning steers (in presencing) the totality (of what is present).' Lightning abruptly lays before us in an instant everything present in the light of its presencing. The lightning named here steers. It brings all things forward to their designated, essential place" (72). The proximity of meaning among Heidegger's chosen terms (*logos*, *polemos*, lightning) is gathered in the following passage at the conclusion of his essay "Logos":

> We see this lightning only when we station ourselves in the storm of Being. Yet everything today betrays the fact that we bestir ourselves only to drive storms away. We organize all available means for cloud-seeding and storm dispersal in order to have calm in the face of the storm. But this calm is no tranquility. It is only anesthesia; more precisely, the narcotization of anxiety in the face of thinking. (78)

Gregory Fried argues that "polemos, or Auseinandersetzung, is an *ontological* concept for Heidegger. It describes the way in which Being happens and how it concerns us, and it also describes our relation to Being as what Heidegger calls Dasein, the site, the There, in which Being manifests itself. Our Being is polemical" (16). Such an ontological alchemy, in which turmoil and conflict constitute the way Being *is*, and with which lightning reveals (in only a flash) the nature of its movement . . . such an alchemy (I have argued) goes by other names: threshold (that both binds and separates), *pharmakon* (both poison and cure), and scapegoat (both cause and redemption).

Unser Kampf, Notre Combat, Our Struggle

A young girl in a red dress stands on the threshold of text and image, her unshod feet betray her bare life (fig. 1.8). The artist Béatrice Turquand d'Auzay, born of a German mother and French father, writes that "like the 'Heimatlos,' uprooted people tossed between borders, I myself am divided by two cultures." The significance of this image in the context of the home/sick Berlin 1941 phone book is striking for two reasons. First, her artwork is painted onto page 289 of the French translation of Hitler's *Mein Kampf*. It appears in Linda Ellia's project called *Notre Combat* (*our* struggle as opposed to *my* struggle) (173). Ellia invited various artists to alter pages of *Mein Kampf* in order to form a collaborative altered book. Second, Turquand d'Auzay's contribution portrays a figure on the threshold of a doorway. Beyond the young girl is the textual rubble of Hitler's rationale for Aryan supremacy:

Fig. 1.8. From *Notre Combat*, altered book project of *Mein Kampf* by Linda Ellia (artist, Béatrice Turquand d'Auzay, p. 173). *Courtesy of Linda Ellia.*

> It is idle to argue which race or races were the original representative of human culture and hence the real founders of all that we sum up under the word "humanity." It is simpler to raise this question with regard to the present, and here an easy, clear answer results. All the human culture, all the results of art, science, and technology that we see before us today, are almost exclusively the creative product of the Aryan. (Manheim translation 290)

The young girl dwells on this tenuous borderline between art/language, life/death, home/homelessness. And yet she is free, not bound to the text, situated between the imposing dark walls on either side of her. One imagines she likes to dance. The threshold beneath her feet seems to float. She has escaped the scapegoat structure. Hélène Cixous sees her plight, her ageless bare feet.

> Give me your name, your age, your address, the judge enjoins. I say my name. *My* age? How to say? We aren't an age, and it isn't us. We're never of age for the judge. That one we never manage to be. Something makes it precede us, like a mobile border. ("What Is It O'Clock?" 63)

This girl, her red dress . . . she passes through the address like an angel. Cixous believes in her immortality and momentary grief for the living.

> We don't believe in death. We never stop thinking about death. Grief and mourning begin long before the event, begin on the first day of love, for years we fear, but we don't believe, fear doesn't believe, certitude stays outside the door, outside the skin. . . . We inhabit the country of the living; that which is beyond, outside—we don't have the heart to believe. We can't believe in death in advance, it remains inadmissible. Our immortality is: not-believing-in-death. (71)

The "sweet fear" of the threshold that is not a between, but a *be-for-ness.* We are beings *for* one another in fearing that crossing. It does not mean we do not cry, just that crying only expels our fears out, into the air, as ephemeral mist. Cixous writes:

> Tearless I cry for all these scenes, our dearest scenes, which come to pass outside of us . . . the scenes so violently cruel they take our tears away and at a blow dry us out and deprive us of beverage and libation. I know them and we know them, the *lightning* ones, who transport us with a single phrase, with a sentence, to the other side of the word. (71; emphasis added)

Through a door, a passageway over which hangs a nameplate too easily removed, a name-plate that will inevitably signify no-thing, tossed into the smelting pot where the new name is literally slated to appear above Motzstraße 72. Or perhaps it is just tossed, making it an unbearable name—the name that no one can *bear*—Sarah. The young girl in the red dress lives at only one address, has only one passport to *no-where.* Like Turquand d'Auzay, Cixous's mother was German and her father was French (from

French Algeria). Yet, Cixous's family was exiled as Jews from Germany, and as French Jews from Algeria (the result of the loss of French citizenship in 1940) ("My Algeriance" 155). Her passport is her "paradox," "neither France, nor Germany, nor Algeria. No regrets. It is good fortune. Freedom, an inconvenient, intolerable freedom, a freedom that obliges one to let go, to rise above, to beat one's wings. To weave a flying carpet. *I felt perfectly at home, nowhere*" (155).

The *Homesick Phone Book* addresses rhetoric in the age of perpetual conflict (*polemos*), though it is not delivered to its readers as one addresses an audience. It is a report on violence sent to every address in the state of mortality: "*living with* homelessness" (Young). These party lines are shared across every division in every age, where the no-where bleeds, where the threshold leads—to Sarah.

2
Casuistic Code

Lankwitzer Straße 13–17, Berlin

> Code is the only language that is executable, meaning that it is the first discourse that is materially affective.
>
> —Alexander Galloway

On first glance, it looks like just another broken-down tabulating machine from the thirties (fig. 2.1).[1] I knew instantly, however, it was a killing machine. Not that I have seen that many. In so many of the exhibits at the US Holocaust Memorial Museum, *everyday* artifacts re-present abject information lurking in the pins and punch cards that recorded details about *everyday* people. This particular machine was manufactured by the Deutsche Hollerith Maschinen Gesellschaft (Dehomag), a subsidiary of IBM on Lankwitzer Straße 13–17 in Berlin. After Hitler came to power in 1933, Dehomag (fig. 2.2) offered to assist in conducting the 1933 census in Germany. According to Edwin Black, thousands of Hollerith machines were situated in various camps during World War II in the camp's Labor Service Office, what prisoners at Bergen-Belsen called "'the lion's den'" (*IBM* 20). Hole punch categories on Hollerith cards detailed

> nationality, date of birth, marital status, number of children, reason for incarceration, physical characteristics, and work skills. Sixteen coded categories of prisoners were listed in columns 3 and 4, depending upon the hole position: hole 3 signified homosexual, hole 9 for anti-social, hole 12 for Gypsy. Hole 8 designated a Jew. (21)

Black claims that "the infamous Auschwitz tattoo began as an IBM number" ("At Death's Door").

Fig. 2.1. Hollerith tabulating machine from IBM (USHMM # 9048–1). *United States Holocaust Memorial Museum; used with permission.*

Deutsche Hollerith Maschinen
GmbH.+Lochkartenmasch.Uhren
u. Zeitreg.-App. Fabr. u. Direkt.
Lfe Lankwitzer Str 13-17
✱ 73 51 31

Fig. 2.2. 1941 Berlin phone book entry for Dehomag. *Photo by author.*

This is code for casuistry of the worst kind. We know from Kenneth Burke that abstract principles applied to specific cases can sometimes lead to justifications for refining the principles themselves. Thus, Burke warned that "the process of casuistic stretching must itself be subjected continually to conscious attention. Its own resources . . . must be transcended by the explicit conversion of a method into a methodology" (232). The difference is that "casuistry as a method" is "the concealing of a strategy," while "casuistry as a methodology" is "a description of a strategy" (232). What I am about to stretch is the casuistic code of hole 8. What I hope to avoid is the refinement of a principle, which is itself a refined way of saying that at all costs one should avoid the twisted logic that *uninstalls* the ethics of technology and information control. In fact, it is necessary to decode the question of ethics itself.

The first stage of such decoding involves how to un-play the race card. Running the sequence now. If tagging is encoded at the very intersection of "international business" *solutions* and political expediency, then keypunch operators implemented (by proxy) the original <meta> tag, and sorting machines became the search engines ranking and optimizing the fate of millions of Jews. Hitler's algorithm installed a mass "state of exception" in the history of *categorical* violence (hole 8 designates Jew). According to Giorgio Agamben,

> If the law employs the exception—that is the suspension of law itself—as its original means of referring to and encompassing life, then a theory of the state of exception is the preliminary condition for any definition of the relation that binds and, at the same time, abandons the living being to law. (*State* 1)

In hypertext markup language, the *suspension* <meta> tag marches lockstep into the "ambiguous zone" of the history of computing, which is at once both the (innocuous) history of human accounting and the (noxious) counting of humans as nonexistent. Alexander Galloway and Eugene Thacker raise the obvious implication of such ambiguity: "The question of nonexistence is this: how does one develop techniques and technologies to make oneself unaccounted for?" (135).

One way to understand the question is to situate it in the context of the rising need to control information in the late nineteenth century. Jan Rune Holmevik chronicled the history of modern computing in his 1994 thesis *Educating the Machine*. Holmevik points to the emergence in the United States of the need to "find more efficient ways of handling and processing the vast amounts of census data" in the years leading up to the 1890 census (38). Herman Hollerith, a Census Bureau engineer, devised "a new punched-card-based electromechanical information processing and tabulating system" (38). This megamachine was soon adopted worldwide following the success of the 1890 census. By 1896, Hollerith "had established the Tabulating Machine Company," which changed its name in 1924 to International Business Machines (IBM) (39). What we now know about the commercial ties between IBM and the Nazis raises the question of how Hitler could so easily indenture a machine in the service of genocide. In Holmevik's study, Lewis Mumford provides a clue.

> According to Mumford, as a social organizational principle, the megamachine originated in ancient Egypt where the center of authority rested with one absolute ruler, the earthly representative of the Sun God. He believed that several megamachines had existed throughout history but what distinguished the new megamachine of the twentieth century was that the center of authority had become the system itself. "The computer," he argues, "turns out to be the Eye of the reinstated Sun God, that is, *the Eye of the Megamachine.*" (Holmevik 35; Mumford 274)

The relation between the divine and the machine became both codified and reified during the years of Hitler's emerging god complex. However, as Merry Eisenstadt anticipates, executives at IBM are unwilling to draw a direct link between technology and genocide (much less between gods and machines). Eisenstadt acknowledges that "machines have no national allegiances and no moral code." Citing Michael Berenbaum's, *The World Must Know*, she helps make the link explicitly visible.

> "The IBM technology was neutral; its use by the Nazi regime was malevolent. Clearly, its potential was understood by the German manufacturer," Berenbaum states, citing an exuberant statement by DEHOMAG director Willy Heidinger in 1934 about the future role of statistics and tabulating machinery in the Nazi state.
>
>> We are recording the individual characteristics of every single member of the nation onto a little card. We are proud to be able to contribute to such a task, a task that makes available to the physician of our German body-social [i.e., Adolf Hitler] the material for his examination, so that our physician can determine whether, from the standpoint of the health of the nation, the results calculated in this manner stand in a harmonious, healthy relation to one another, or whether unhealthy conditions must be cured by corrective interventions. We have firm trust in our physician and will follow his orders blindly, because we know that he will lead our nation toward a great future. Hail to our German people and their leader! (Eisenstadt n.p.)

Such <meta> tags for insanity chillingly mark the means by which Nazi megamachinery, forged in the factory of fascism, represents the pathological idolatry of indices—a collective index finger pointing inexorably to hole 8—the mark (and birth) of a malevolent search engine. If today's Internet search engines are virtual descendants of the Hollerith machine, then the <meta> tag is the indexical means to achieve the optimal number of *hits* or search engine optimization (SEO). It attempts to transcend the neutrality of data and installs metadata as the ultimate "quality control." Though not explicitly tackling metadata, Galloway and Thacker name the intersection of sovereignty and networks as *the* juncture of repression and control (5). "*This is why*," they argue, "*contemporary political dynamics are decidedly different from those in previous decades: there exists today a fearful new symmetry of networks fighting networks. One must understand how networks act politically, both as rogue swarms and as mainframe grids*" (15). "*Connectivity is a threat. The network is a weapons system*" (16). In their analysis, Galloway and Thacker contend that resistance and intervention cannot succeed against "states of exception" that perfect (by adopting) terrorist network tactics. Such "asymmetrical" forms of conflict require an "exploit" (21). Since networks are "largely immaterial," they "operate through the brutal limitations of abstract logic (if/then, true or false). *Protocological struggles do not center around changing existent technologies but instead involve discovering holes in existent technologies and projecting potential change through these holes. Hackers call these holes 'exploits'*" (81).

The undeniable upshot of their solution is the shadow figure of hole 8. It was also an exploit. There is a thin line between *exploit* and *exploitation*. While I am not forcing a connection that Galloway and Thacker have ignored, I am raising the bar for their discussion of exploitation and asking that we include genocide as a "metasploit"[2] much more serious than their focus on the "practice of bioprospecting" and the exploitation of human labor (135). In other words, as a <meta> tag designed to optimize their theory of networks, the "exploit" is inadequate to help the "impoverished classes" by exposing the "exploitative classes" they term "source fetishists" and McKenzie Wark calls "the 'vectoralists'" (135). The problem is that the exploit is a vector itself—metasploiting is about system "penetration testing" (Metasploit Project)—and you cannot penetrate a system without your own version of malicious code. As Nazi Germany became obsessed with statistics science, code provided the inner circle with names. Edwin Black reports that, eager to please Hitler, Friedrich Zahn, head of the Bavarian statistical office, gleefully summed up the government's new information power: "'In using statistics, the government now has the road map to switch from knowledge to deeds'" (59).

Shifting gears slightly, it is not unimaginable to consider Galloway and Thacker's "exploit" as a postprotocological *deus ex machina*. In Greek tragedy, this device was employed as a means to supply a happy ending. For example, toward the end of the play *Medea*, Euripides staged a *deus ex machina* to solve the protagonist's crisis. Literally speaking, a god was lowered onto the stage via some kind of machinery. Critics from Aristotle to Nietzsche have, however, criticized the literary device. In *The Birth of Tragedy* Nietzsche explains the problem: "the *deus ex machina* has taken the place of metaphysical solace" (84). In essence,

> theoretical man. . . . fights against Dionysiac wisdom and art; it strives to dissolve myth; it puts in the place of metaphysical solace a form of earthly harmony, indeed its very own *deus ex machina*, namely the god of machines and smelting furnaces, i.e. the energies of the spirits of nature, understood and applied in the service of higher egotism; it believes in correcting the world through knowledge, in life led by science; and it is truly capable of confining the individual within the smallest circle of solvable tasks. (85)

The smallest circle is hole 8, and the god of smelting furnaces turned out to be the *deus ex machina* for the Nazis. The stage of their drama was a secret conference at an "elegant villa" located at Wannsee outside of Berlin (Black, *IBM* 366). According to Black, among the "senior Nazi leadership" who attended were several census and statistics experts who provided Adolf Eichmann with "a long list of Jewish populations" compiled by IBM's German subsidiary (366). "The conclave at Wannsee resulted in a Protocol, which outlined the massive demographic and geographic logistical challenge" (366).

This is not merely a cautionary tale—it is a narrative inflected by protocols, exploits, and database death squads. To casuistically stretch such code is to identify a neglected rhetorical history, but more importantly it is to guard the question of *how* our field consorts with hacker culture and new media discourse. Lev Manovich explains that new media theories and practices are marked by the conflict between two dominant forms: narrative and the database. Manovich notes the historical predominance of narrative as the "key form of cultural expression of the modern age" (39) and argues that in today's computerized society, the database is the newest symbolic form with which "to structure our experience of ourselves, and the world" (40). So, while computer games, for example, are certainly "experienced by their players as narratives" (41), the hidden data structure and algorithms necessarily project "the ontology of a computer onto culture itself" (42). In short, he writes, "any object in the world—[such as] the population of a city . . . is modeled as a data structure, that is, data organized in a particular way for efficient search and retrieval" (42–43). Manovich translates this new "cultural algorithm" into the necessity "to develop the poetics, aesthetics, and ethics of this database" (40).

The question has been put, as well and *so* well, by Steven Katz, who wrote: "The question for us is: do we, as teachers and writers and scholars, contribute to this [ethics of expediency and technological] *ethos* by our writing theory, pedagogy, and practice when we consider techniques of document design, audience adaptation, argumentation, and style without also considering ethics?" (271). This is the casuistic <meta> tag without which search engine optimization remains merely an expedient perpetuation of metaphysical solace, our data *deus ex machina* logging in to the next server of genocide. As mentioned at the outset of this chapter, one should avoid the twisted logic that *uninstalls* the ethics of technology and information control.

Avoiding does not mean, however, that we look the other way when contending with a database of hidden narratives, i.e., narratives concealed in the machinery of Nazi IBM punch cards, Jewish deportation notices, Jewish asset inventories, SS memos, and the millions of half-burned and abandoned documents that littered the bombed-out rubble of Berlin in 1945. If, as Manovich asserts, the narrative and database are the dominant forms of new media theories and practices, it seems to me that our rhetorical task is to gaze with a renewed intensification into the space of their conjuncture—the hole. Thus, the figure of hole 8 operates as a portal through which we glimpse the horrors of Nazi racial ideology—it is a window that frames the ease with which a people can be exterminated with the aid of machinic madness. As with the rhetorical threshold of violence examined in chapter 1, we can now see that ethics is situated on the same dual-edged sword. The task now is to suggest an exploit for ethics that reveals both the essential problem with optimization and the <meta>bolical consumption of the diabolical within the database. This is our second stage in identifying a problem with ethics: decoding ethics to understand what is encoded deep within the word itself.

In order to approach a casuistic stretching of the code deep in the history of ethics, more specifically its etymology, as in chapter 1 we turn to Heidegger. In the "Letter on Humanism," Heidegger responds to the question, "When are you going to write an ethics?" (231). In response, he acknowledges the need for the "greatest care" to be "fostered upon the ethical bond" (231–32). This does not, however, prevent him from returning to his primary question: "But does this need ever release thought from the task of thinking what still remains principally to be thought and, as Being prior to all beings, is their guarantor and their truth?" (232). In other words, according to Heidegger, ethics is a post-Platonic discipline; whereas, *ethos* is preserved in Sophocles and Heraclitus "more primordially than Aristotle's lectures on 'ethics'" (232–33). Heidegger uses Heraclitus (fragment 119) to illustrate his argument: "*ethos anthropoi daimon*" (233). In its traditional interpretation, we say, "A man's character is his daimon" (233). For Heidegger, it means: "Man dwells, insofar as he is man, in the nearness of god" (233). In this sense, *ethos* means "abode, dwelling place. . . . the open region in which man dwells" (233). More specifically, "the open region of his abode allows what pertains to man's essence, and what in thus arriving resides in nearness to him, to appear" (233). However, it may seem that when Heidegger earlier calls *language* the "House of Being," he is contradicting himself. To those who make this assumption, Heidegger counters: "The talk about the house of Being is no transfer of the image 'house' to Being. But one day we will, by thinking the essence of Being in a way appropriate to its matter, more readily be able to think what 'house' and 'to dwell' are" (236–37). In other words, when we attempt to refute Heidegger's translations or his methodology using our Aristotelian logic of noncontradiction, we are reminded that within "logic" our terms are too often unexamined and restrictive.

While some critics have approached Heidegger's ability to "more readily" think in this manner, they invariably fall back into their logical zones of comfort. Charles Scott provides an appealing example of Heidegger's kind of thinking, and he seems to break through the logical barriers; but, in the end, his analysis is also a trap designed to "comprehend" Heidegger's thought in terms of the *right* questions. Scott reminds us that in its earliest usage, it is *ethos* (not *logos*) that derived from a word that meant essential dwelling and habitation (*ethea*), although he manages to link *ethos* with the same "dynamic of conflicting opposites" Heidegger discovers in *logos*. What is radical about Scott's approach to *ethos* is his examination of its primordial affiliation with conflict. What is traditional about his account is that Heidegger is still found lacking. Thus, a brief look at Scott's analysis of *ethos* offers a clue to the paradox in Heidegger (and ethics) we are examining.

Scott enters the Heideggerian "text" at the point of tension between *ethos* and *nomos* and Heidegger's forgetting of the question of ethics. Scott relies upon earlier research by Charles Chamberlain, who traces *ethos* to its Homeric roots and theorizes that the earliest recorded uses of *ethea* (the root of *ethos*) referred to an essential quality in animals untouched by *logos* or rationality though it followed its own (different) principle of *logos* ("From 'Haunts'" 102). Specifically, Chamberlain argues that the development of this term reveals that "ethics" is historically tied to an irrational principle, that is, one that follows its own form of rationality. This may, perhaps, be the most significant evidence for establishing that *ethos*, when dominated by *logos* as rationality, has come to mean a form of habituation that goes against a very basic instinct. In Homer, for example, Chamberlain explains that *ethea* was used to designate "the places where animals are usually found" (97). Homer uses *ethea* in the Odyssey (in every instance) in connection with an animal's place of "belonging in" (97). Eventually, Homer and others used the term as a simile. For instance, in the *Iliad*, Homer applies it to Paris in the following passage:

> As when a stabled horse, having been fed at a manger, breaks his bonds and runs galloping over the plain, since he is accustomed to bathe in the flowing river, glorying. He holds his head high, and his mane leaps on his shoulders on both sides. His knees swiftly bear him, trusting in his splendor, to the *ethea* and pasture of horses. (I1.6.506–11; qtd in Chamberlain 98)

In short, Chamberlain suggests that Homer refers to the "power of habituation"; that is, when horses are confined to a manger, it is in order to domesticate them, to force them to change their habits by using their hunger, to make them "regard the manger as home" (98). Such confinement, however, never completely erases the fact that horses long to break free, to return to their pastures and rivers, to their *ethea*. Chamberlain goes on to argue that by showing the effects of habituation on a living creature, Homer symbolizes the ambiguity inherent in the term. In other words, though later Greeks believed that

> animals differed from humans in having no share in *logos*, "reason," or what we might call the principle of order . . . clearly the horse, because he

> does return to his *ethea*, shows that some reason or principle of order is at work in him; the *ethea* of horses are not totally random. (98)

The key point, however, is that the *irrational* possesses a principle of rationality, but of a different sort. It is based on a special (radically different) *order* of *logos*.

Homer used the word *ethea* to refer to the places where animals dwell and to where they return if, as Scott says, "a violation of its particular order occurs" (143). In addition to its Homeric use, Herodotus specifically uses it to refer to the *ethea* of barbarians and other non-Greeks. According to Scott, then, *ethea* are places that "resist Greek civilization" (143). *Ethea* is also closely related to *nomos* (field, pasture), which is linked with the *nomades*, the pastoral nomadic tribes. Thus, there is a sense in which *ethea* and its relationship to the habitual environment comes into conflict with the *nomos* and its association with wandering, uncivilized tribes. Scott describes the conflict as a "fateful struggle" (144). In the struggle, he writes, "the limiting principles of order and random movement without limiting principles unsettle each other" (144). Gradually, *ethea* was used to refer to "a locale of characteristics and to the hidden but characteristic part of a person" (144). In short, as time and varying usages persisted, "*ethos* continued to have an habituated and resistant quality and to exist separately from the *nomos* of the soul" (144). The key, in Scott's estimation, is that an "*ethos* can be ordered by reason, but its variant structures are not the same as rational *logos*" (144). *Ethos*, then, is often hidden and recalcitrant, its power existing in its resistance to outside forces. Scott suggests that "to know a creature's *ethos*, one had to see where the animal went to be at home, as it were, or where it went when threatened, or where it went to die" (144). The dynamic of conflict, in this case, is played out on a field where range wars erupted, which contributed to the rules and laws (*nomos*) that dominated the resistant aspect of *ethea* (145).

Thus, within the *ethea* there were differences and conflicts, and among *ethea* there rose conflicting rules and regional claims of authority. Scott concludes by drawing out the implications for the "viability of Heidegger's thought in the context of the question of ethics" (146). Given the contingent nature of competing *nomoi* among regional unruly *ethea*, powers were formed that were "unconditioned by time" (145). In essence, such powers held that their "timeless universality suggested superiority over all time-generated, contingent powers" (145). If, then, we apply Scott's explanation to

Heidegger's situation (not to mention our own), it is less difficult to see the "logical snare" we identified earlier. Heidegger, who sought in an exhaustive manner to preserve the unity and wholeness of Being, was no different in his *ethnicity* from other Germans, Jews, Poles, or Gypsies, each desiring to be in their own *ethea*. That is, the question of Being (and Heidegger's retrieval of it) stands in stark contrast to the question of ethics if it is *unaccompanied* by the acknowledgement and celebration of ungrounded difference. Scott marks the limits of Heidegger's thought in a "largely unconscious desire for definitive unity," which, if not experienced as a question, can have "terrible consequences as it prompts the imposition of goods, rights, and orders that now appear to us to be as ethnic as the expropriated regions, whether geographical or soulish" (146). Is it possible that Heidegger, in his painstaking hermeneutical methods, simply asked the wrong question? Can we ask such a question ourselves given the preceding analysis? Even our question is not sufficiently alleviated of the same desires for definitive unity. As Scott notes in his introduction, the "suspicion held by 'the question of ethics' is that ethical concern has a pathogenic dimension and is composed of values that occasion human suffering in the pursuit of human well-being" (1). The trick (the exploit) is not to dwell too long on the question, to become nomadic and return to our own *ethea*.

To bring this trajectory of thinking full circle, back to my experience of standing before the Hollerith machine at the Holocaust Museum, I now understand that the Deutsche Hollerith Maschinen Gesellschaft (Dehomag), a subsidiary of IBM on Lankwitzer Straße 13–17 in Berlin, occupies what Scott calls the "pathogenic dimension of ethical concern." The current website for IBM in Germany (as of August 2015) gives the history from 1910 to 2000 (by decades), yet it is completely sanitized of its complicity in identifying Jews for the 1933 census. It merely states that in 1934 the capital investment is increased to seven million Reichsmark, following which the factory began to take its first "custom work" orders (IBM). It does not mention that the infusion of investment funding for Dehomag came from its American partner, IBM, nor that Thomas Watson (IBM's CEO) traveled to Berlin in 1937 and met with Hitler, who decorated Watson for special service to the Reich (Watson returned the award after the war began). By 1939, according to the website, Dehomag achieves its first "spektakulären Höhepunkt" (spectacular highpoint) with the 1939 census, which used over ninety million punch cards.

The simple and unambiguous meaning of a punch card lies in its seemingly innocuous holes. While it is certain that they led to the swift and expeditious identification and rounding up of the Jews, we can encode our own exploit, and through the portal of hole 8 we can lean close and view a different scenario, one where Sarah plays in a field of green grass and wildflowers, perhaps even as Homer would have described her: "[She] holds [her] head high, and [her hair] leaps on [her] shoulders on both sides. [Her] knees swiftly bear [her], trusting in [her] splendor, to the *ethea* and pasture of horses" (Il.6.506–11; qtd in Chamberlain 98).

3
Mechanical Faith

Lindenstraße 9–14, Berlin

I have ruined this chapter. That is to say, it is both about ruins and has been *ruined* by having been written. I imagine it as the hollow shell of a once grand structure, an overgrown ruin that has seen better days and echoes with the voices of desperate prayers whispered to disparate gods. I wish I could reverse the decay that unavoidably began with the initial "I" that confessed to have ruined this chapter and continues to chip away at each metaphor like centuries of wind or glacial grind. In this "I," I have faith, but only insofar as I know faith is the evidence of things not seen—the wind . . . time . . . the weathered word.

Language is an instrument that documents its own decay. Just as wartime aerial photographs are used to pinpoint "strategic bombing sites," notes Charles Merewether, we are also reminded that they record the destruction of cities and citizens (29). Merewether argues that "the illusion of veridical documentation and the ideological function of instrumental and aesthetic realism create a blind spot, obscuring the complicity of technologies of representation in technologies of destruction" (29). It is a necessary paradox, mechanization; but wrapped in the enigma is the problem and the promise of *mechanical faith*—belief in the *ruins of writing*. And *Belief* . . . in the ruins of writing.

I was reminded of this in an unexpected way in 1994 when the director of the creative writing program where I had just begun my first academic job told me that I had "ruined" his graduate TAs by teaching them rhetoric, which I took to mean that their writing was "ruined" in his mind by their encounter with critical and rhetorical theories of writing. If I could rewind that conversation and replay it, I would have told him that writing is always a ruin. And then we would go round and round about what constitutes good writing, as do writing teachers of virtually all genres of written expression (creative, technical, business, argumentative, expository, and so forth), not to mention our colleagues in other departments who "know good writing when they see it." In the director's reaction, after years of thinking about it, I detect a stereotypical faith in both the mechanics of writing and the craft of poesis . . . to successfully and artfully make words mean. The "faith" commonplace, however, is a mechanical form of faith. That is, it has become so mechanical or habitual that it performs as a belief without any verifiable understanding of how writing happens. For years I have told the TA's I train to teach first-year composition that 99 percent of the textbooks and handbooks we teach with are great at teaching invention and revision and not so great at teaching writing. As I see this fact render them confused and anxious, I take it one step further and explain why . . . because writing cannot be *taught*. We can only intervene in each student's writing process, make observations and assessments (ad nauseam), and hope for the best. We have faith that somehow this will make a difference in their subsequent writing, and by that I don't mean just the *product*, but mostly their *thinking*, their *process*, their *experience* of writing. For me writing is a *spiritual* experience. Yes, part of me eschews the inspiration theory of writing, but not when I take the word on faith, the moment I am *in/spired* . . . where meaning asks us to breathe in and out . . . inspiration and expiration. The end of life is the end of language, the end of breathing meaning in and out. But I am convinced (I believe) that we have lost (if we ever had it) a *spiritual* and *ruinous* understanding of the happening of writing.

The writing I ruined is evidence of the toll of nature on the materiality with which it has been constructed, namely months of research using technologies comprised of networks, databases, interfaces, digital images, pens, paper, iPad, laptop computer, and historical artifacts such as the 1941 Berlin phone book. Physical evidence of homes, offices, schools, synagogues (in ruins), the Reich Chancellery telephone number imprinted with the same mechanization as the phone numbers of Jüdische retirement homes, culture ministries, and hospitals. But no phone numbers to Hitler's bunker or the camps and crematoria, the real machinery of ruins. Walter Benjamin wrote that "allegories are, in the realm of thoughts, what ruins are in the realm of things" (*Origin* 178). In this chapter I offer two allegorical checkpoints (or meditations) as addresses along a trade route where points of mechanical faith, belief, writing, and ruins may be mapped.

The first address is in Berlin—Lindenstraße 9–14. Mark Taylor describes how architect Daniel Libeskind designed the Jewish Museum extension (fig. 3.1) to the Berlin Museum by "triangulating the addresses of E. T. A. Hoffmann, Heinrich von Kleist, Rachel Varnhagen, Arnold Schonberg, Erich Mendelssohn, Friedrich Schleiermacher, and Walter Benjamin" (*Nots* 147), the result of which formed (in Libeskind's words) "'this connection between figures of Germans and Jews . . . a compressed and distorted star: the yellow star that was so frequently worn on the site'" (*Counterdesigns* 86; qtd in *Nots* 146–47).[1] At one end of the path is the E. T. A. Hoffmann Garden, "surrounded by a continuous ramp made of Jerusalem stone," a glass border inside of which is "sand from the desert of Israel" (153). Mechanical objects suggest "Freud's reading of Hoffmann's tale" of a "mechanical doll," giving the "feeling of *das Unheimliche* [uncanny]" (153). Taylor notes that for

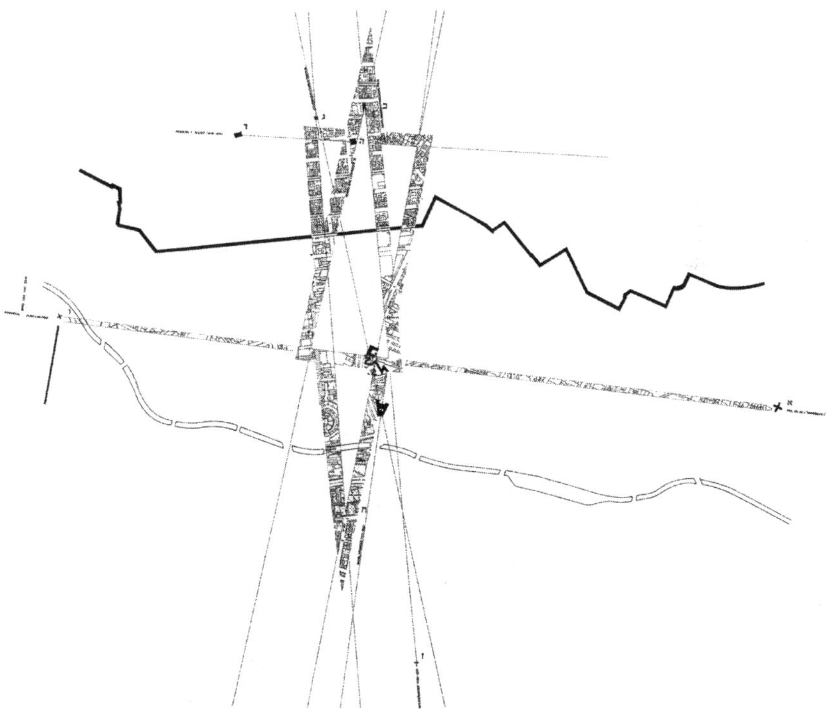

Fig. 3.1. Site plan for Libeskind's extension of the Berlin Museum with the Jewish Museum. © *Studio Daniel Libeskind. Used with permission.*

"Libeskind, responsible architecture must have a spiritual dimension . . . and various translations of spirit appear through Libeskind's writings, drawings, and models" (159–60). As such, Libeskind's work should not be viewed as forms of critique of the Holocaust. Jean-François Lyotard understands that one cannot simply critique something like the Holocaust

> because critique builds an architectonics of reasons, but it is impossible to build anything whatsoever from or on this debris. All one can do is thread one's way through it, slip and slide through the ruins, listen to the complaints that emanate from them. . . . Philosophy as architecture is ruined, but a writing of the ruins, micrologies, graffiti can still be done. This writing preserves the forgotten that one has tried to forget by killing it; it advances in the direction of the immemorial through the destruction of its representations and of its witnesses, "the jews." (*Heidegger and "the jews"* 43)

The spiritual ruin of the Holocaust is, of course, unable to be located at this address any more than a gravestone can dial up a father's hug, the sound of his laughter, or the twinkle in his eye. Libeskind's project could not have been realized before the fall of the Berlin Wall in 1989, itself a ruin marked by writing, faith, and incredible loss. Predating and foreshadowing Libeskind's Berlin project are his architectural machines (fig. 3.2), entitled "Three Lessons in Architecture: The Machines."

Fig. 3.2. "Memory Machine." © *Studio Daniel Libeskind. Used with permission.*

The machines occupy the second address. Lebbeus Woods explains the significance of Libeskind's machines.

> Elaborately constructed and enigmatic in purpose, Libeskind's machines are striking and sumptuous manifestations of ideas that were, at the time he made them,

> of obsessive interest to academics, critics and avant-gardists in architecture and out. Principal among these was the idea that architecture must be read, that is, understood, in the same way as a written text. . . . Their use of analogy to inform the field of architecture is a [more] potent tool for exploring much-needed new ideas of space and its human purposes than are afforded by the ordinary design process based on history and accepted building typologies. ("Libeskind's Machines")

Libeskind's machines were, by his own account, "built by praying on one's knees—total faith" (*Space of Encounter* 193). "We built [these] machine[s] in a small place without any power tools, just with hand tools. With no electricity, just with candlelight. During the procedure we agree to work hard, speak only in 'small talk,' smoke cigarettes" ("Architecture" 116; qtd in Taylor 130). The machines, Libeskind writes, "seem to prefigure the holocaust" in a sort of reverse plagiarism because all three machines burned in 1987 at the Centre of Contemporary Art in Geneva. The reading machine, the writing machine, and the remembering machine are "situated along the intersection between the Axis of Architecture (Time) and the Axis of Technology (Soul)" (*Space* 183). The Writing Machine is "made of wood, graphite, and metal, and contains complex gear-shaft-driven systems that rotate the multilingual papers; 49 cubes that revolve at various speed ratios; and faces that show saints who have emerged from the project and who return to Roussel's Book of Saints" (182). The forty-nine cubes were to be filled with ashes of unknown saints. The machine, he explains

> had to have a lubricant, fuel for the machine, and so I had to use the books. There had to be surfaces because it was not for one reader. To lubricate such a big industrial piece of writing one would need all the texts in the whole world, so I translated the books into 49 times 4 languages because 7 words times 7 is 49 cubes. The cubes are pinned on 4 sides revealing 4 faces, which means 49 times 4 surfaces. Many, many axles to lubricate; many languages. The first machine creaks (the reading machine), the second one clicks (the remembering machine), and this one, I can assure you, whirls rapidly. A very well-lubricated mechanism goes very, very fast—in any language. (193)

The machines are now *ruined*, cinder and ashes replaced word and "small talk." They were literally built with mechanical faith, but no literary idea of faith, and no mechanical faith in technology. "Everybody needs machines," Libeskind explains.

> To try to become the pure medieval craftsman—that's really the object of this exercise. To make something in a way that is made only on one's knees; which is made through complete faith in the transcendence of architecture, of the text, of reading; that is made by a total faith in the craft; that rejects all modern techniques and technology. (188)

My purpose in this chapter is not didactic. I do not wish to instruct, but to write on my knees, so to speak. Nor do I wish to romanticize ruins, rather I would build ruins that are always already neglected—writing not at ground zero, but on zero ground. No edifice, no foundation. Only ruin. Andreas Huyssen filters the question of ruins through time.

> As commodities, things in general don't age well. They become obsolete, are thrown out or recycled. Buildings are torn down or restored. The chance for things to age and to become ruin has diminished in the age of turbo capitalism, ironically in step with the continuing rise in the average age of the populace. The ruin of the twenty-first century is either detritus or restored age. In the latter case, real age has been eliminated by a reverse face-lifting. The new is made to look old rather than the old made to look young. Repro- and retrofashions make it increasingly hard to recognize that which is genuinely old in this culture of preservation and restoration. The German writer and filmmaker Alexander Kluge once spoke tellingly of "the attack of the present on the rest of time." (10)

When Albert Einstein toured the war ruins in France after World War I, he remarked that students around the world should visit the ruins. It might, he suggested, "cure people of their 'literary' idea of military conflicts and the ruins they cause" (Roth 15). According to Michael Roth, "ruins were thus used as scenes of moral instruction, or admonition, in the wake of violent conflicts. This convention grew more intense after World War I, when the graveyard was to function as a somber reminder of the destructive power of mechanized warfare" (15). The question posed by this chapter concerns the ruins of writing in the wake of a mechanical faith in technology and a literary idea of faith. The literary/mechanical trope is not, in this instance, furthered in order to rally the troops or stir the congregation. It is, rather, intended to project a visual ruin of writing not unlike Wordsworth described in "Tintern Abbey," "that time is past, / and all its aching joys are now no more, / and all its dizzy raptures." The irony of employing a poetic image to evoke (somehow) the problem of mechanized literary writing will, I hope, help sponsor a faith outside of mechanics, outside of literary imagery. We have only to view Leni Riefenstahl's documentary of the 1934 Nuremberg Reichsdag in *Triumph of the Will*, to understand the dangers of mechanical (lockstep) faith and the devastation of scripted, "dizzy raptures." Mass technologized spectacles, such as the Nazi rallies, may seem far afield from the question of faith and writing. But Martin Heidegger was concerned with precisely this question in his 1935 essay "The Origin of the Work of Art." For Heidegger, buildings (whether those at the Nuremberg parade grounds or a Greek temple) "portray nothing" (41). While "the building encloses the figure of the god. . . . by means of the temple, the god is present in the temple" (41). No temple, no god. No god, no temple. There is a reciprocity vital to the "holy precinct" in which is gathered "the unity of those paths and relations in which birth and death, disaster and blessing, victory and disgrace, endurance and decline acquire the shape of destiny for human being" (42). This chapter calls us to write, and to invite student writing, that visits the ruin of such temples, yet does not (in the process) produce writing with what Hitler's architect, Albert Speer, dubbed "ruin value" (*Inside* 66). Speer's "theory of ruin value" aimed to build structures that formed "'a bridge of tradition' to future generations," that would "communicate heroic inspirations that Hitler admired in the monuments of the past" (66), and that would, even in a state of decay, after hundreds (or thousands) of years more or less resemble the grandeur of Rome.

No ruin value, just ruins. I prefer to dwell (ruinously, poetically) with this excerpt of a fragment by Hölderlin.

> I want to build
> And raise new
> The temples of Theseus and the stadiums
> And where Perikles lived
> But there's no money, too much spent
> Today. I had a guest
> Over and we sat together. (32)

4
Writing Offshore

Heidegger's Hütte, Todtnauberg, Germany

There is no longer a rational explanation. Reason has awakened to its limitations and, embracing the reality of the paradox, is compelled to transform itself. The natural space for this transformation is the borderline.

—Lebbeus Woods, *BorderLine*

There is a seal or sepulcher to be broken, a rock to be broke open, to disclose the living water; an eruption. Begin then with a fracture, a cesura, a rent; opening a crack in this fallen world, a shaft of light.

—Norman O. Brown, *Love's Body*

It was quite possibly the coldest, wettest, and most frightened I had ever been, perched on the bow of a small converted seal-hunting boat as it chugged straight into the Arctic Sea, the coastline of Northern Norway barely visible above the mist, rain, and choppy seas whipped up by a storm into which, against all logic, we were apparently heading. I was torn between two worlds. I wanted more than anything to see a whale, but I was unable to take my eyes off the disappearing coastline, its security beckoning, the warm duvet on my bed, the clean wool socks I had forgotten to put in my backpack, the safety of the streets of Andenes, home to a handful of whale researchers and Northern Lights scholars. It occurred to me that I should have made out a will. When the coastline disappeared altogether, I turned to face the stinging rain and willed a whale to surface, to blow some warm air my way. I tugged my coat tighter and asked myself more than once what this Texan was doing on *this* boat. The answer is, I was a tourist.

Lately, I have wondered the same thing about what I am *doing* in *this* field of rhetoric and composition. I would like to think that *I think*, among other things. And that thinking *is* doing, and not just some form of academic tourism, something "extra-curricular . . . [that] one pursues in the summer, at the end of the term after the 'real' intellectual labour is finished," as Gary Genosko puts it (1–2). I have, however, donned the uniform of tourism often enough to recognize those of us who wear the glazed look of tourists flitting from theory to theory, or who document our rhetorical travels with snapshots of this pedagogy or that. Our professional byways are crowded with khaki and (Gore-Tex)tual tourists, field glasses in one hand, the latest guide to teaching writing in the other. And yet, despite the tightly built craft in which we entrusted our survival as a field, we kept too close to the shoreline, dragging the anchor of *argumentative writing* (aka critical thinking) until it took hold among the bedrock curricula of grammar and style, aims and modes, claims, grounds, and warrants. And now our most sound composition pedagogy has run *aground* like some leviathan, a beached whale that inexplicably (and paradoxically) crawls onto the shore—onto the ground of all ground, figuratively speaking. And thus begins our exhaustive search for the explicable in the inexplicable—the why, the reason, the rationale.

Why does the whale beach itself? Is it some kind of "will to strand"? Why does the whale, when returned to deep water, sometimes re/turn and strand itself again? These are rhetorical questions. The problem lies in the institution of *why* (for what reason?). We can pile reason upon reason, answer upon answer, and still never know the "why." We can shift the ground/figure relationship and still never know the "why." We can even supply a nonanswer and continue to tell ourselves that a way of seeing is also a way of not seeing—and still be no closer to the *why*. The ground/figure analogy we are fond of invoking when pressed to explain rhetoric is actually not an analogy at all. It is a *trick* image, namely, the *trick* we pull on ourselves that there actually *is* a distinction between figure and ground, when ground is nothing but *our most supreme invention*, when ground is all we desire, tricked by the reified figurative field into believing *figure* is not ground. We are tourists on a search for *why*. The problem with this particular junket is that it has been made at the students' expense. We need the why, so it stands to *reason* they must need the why.

Sharon Crowley argues against the dominant view that students "need" to write and think in particular ways. She situates the conventional wisdom of academia on this topic inside a powerful "discourse of needs." According to Crowley, "The discourse of needs positions . . . teachers as servants of a student need that is spoken, not by students themselves, but by people speaking for powerful institutions" (257). She goes on to conclude that the "claim that students need composition is 'privatized,' . . . in other words, the claim is so widely accepted in the relevant communities that it is simply not available for argument" (259). But what *is* available for argument? The teaching of argument itself? Conventional wisdom says no—argumentative writing is not up for argument. It has become the *capstone* of composition.

By now your suspicions are well founded, that I have somehow foundered (and there must be a good reason). No *reason* to be coy; it's true—I am dissatisfied with teaching writing that is primarily argumentative writing *qua* reason. And what leads me to think this through in writing here could not be defined as reasons *per se*; rather, it is a face that haunts me—that post-9/11 face of disbelief, disenchantment, and disaffection for writing arguments when *so much defies reason*. Those faces belong to students and graduate teaching assistants who look to me to supply reason enough for writing as a function of reason. But . . . "There is no longer a rational explanation" (Woods). Airplanes hit towers, and structures implode with people in them. Refugees drown in sinking boats, and pernicious people traffickers (so-called "travel agents") camped on the fringe of refugee camps count their money. Illegal immigrants go "asylum-shopping" ("Huddled Masses, please stay away" 29), while boat people sabotage their own boats, desperate for rescue. To casuistically stretch Kenneth Burke's observation that we are "rotten with perfection" (*Language* 16), it is time to admit that we are also "rotten with reason."

One could argue that I am merely joining the queue of those in our field who are perpetually dissatisfied with everything. Geoff Sirc astutely observed that

> the reason the teaching of writing is permeated by dissatisfaction (every CCCC presentation seems at some level, a complaint) is that we—bad enough—don't really know what teaching is, but also—far worse, fatal, in fact—we haven't really evolved an idea of writing that fully reflects the splendor of the medium. (9)

Furthermore, he adds, "much of what I hear in conferences and conversations suggests that we have already returned to a desire for something else (if we've ever really left—Composition Studies as a perpetual scene of disenchantment)" (12). We have seen composition theory weather some damaging storms, but no squalls have threatened to blot out its *theoretical* coastline from our view as significantly as moves toward service learning and distance learning, or the dual *topoi* of *actual* and *virtual streets*.[1] This is *not* to say that service and distance learning form some kind of "*axis of evil*"; rather, that the theories driving such pedagogies need to be unmoored from the "street" jurisdiction in whose name they *appear* to elicit and value student writing rooted primarily in the "experience of everyday life" and grounded in, or armed with, the ubiquitous *good* reasons. Writing offshore suggests a mixed reality that privileges neither *terra firma* nor *terra nullius*,[2] nor "castles in the air." It is *suggestive*—an idea that will bear us (by indirection) toward nonsovereign outposts along transitory migration routes. In other words, we cannot land, and we must keep moving. Our address is unfixed.

But this will be no call for movement for the sake of movement, and this chapter's address turns out to be quite fixed. While the lessons of deconstruction have propelled some of us into a maelstrom of moveable feasts, me included, movement is no panacea against totalizing centers, fortresses, and border checkpoints—or, against pedagogical regimes grounded in *ground* metaphysics. "And yet motion can have a direction," suggests Diane Elam (24).[3] According to Elam, "displacement must not be thought of as a movement from one ground to the next . . . but as a displacement which must concede that the grounds don't exist" (24–25). Calling for what she terms "groundless solidarity," Elam understands the fierce resistance to the disintegration of the principle of grounding. Still, citing Gayatri Spivak, Elam "hold[s] out for the possibility of 'revolutions that as yet have no model'" (84). Equally charged, and similarly *moved*, I mean to probe the ground beneath teaching argument (*née* critical thinking) that compels us to teach *good writing* as the invention of *good reasons*. Student writing should not be labeled ill (writing lab mentality), nor should reason be conceived as the *panacean* remedy (*panacea*—Gr. pan + akos; all-healing); it is always already *both* poison and cure (*pharmakon*). Perhaps it is best to describe composition theory thus situated as lashed to the hull of an itinerant *aporia*—Ahab at the helm, bearings lost, the image of Keats's epitaph, "Here lies one whose name was writ in water."

Casting Off

Needing the Sea

in September maybe most: that time
when the earth begins to take over again
something in me gets bogged down and
cries out for the grace of water[4]

My task is to maneuver us in a different direction, to draw us away from the shoreline of philosophical reason and its alluring beacon of argumentation (housed in the heaviest of *light*houses). I am tempted to say that for this we need *abstraction* (Latin: *abstractus.* [abstere], abs + trahere; to pull, draw, Caputo, *Mystical*, 13), but that may commit us to the "discourse of needs" about which Crowley warns. It would be more compelling to point us toward an *abstract* horizon (such as Walter Benjamin's *fata morgana*), much as one does when adjusting the attitude or pitch of one's satellite dish. This is the move in question; or, this will be the signal on which we will home in: *abstraction*, not argumentation. In casting off from *ground* metaphysics (a difficult dissuasive move), we occupy a paradoxical position; we must stand with one foot on land and one foot on our vessel. Then the release—the letting go (*gelassenheit*)—shifts our stance in relation to *footing* in general. One does not lose the ground by stepping into the abyss, for it, too, assumes a *finite* ground. Rather, our footing depends on depth, and shifting depth at that, the ebb and flow of depth. Writing instruction, caught between a rock and a hard place, seems to have, unwittingly, opted for both. Teaching argument amounts to sheltering students from the deep (and too-fluid) regions of language (and Being). Yet we know (don't we?) that writing should be strange, that we should feel alienated, removed, and detached from our *standard* habits of reading and thinking. Taking a stand, we teach, means adopting a critical stance. But we are unwilling to relinquish the *standardization* of the methods and means for doing so; and, we are not exactly eager to look into the *depths* of how this particular pedagogy came about. As it happens, the link between logic/reason and pedagogy is a devastating link—one whose history we cannot ignore, one whose power we ought not sustain—and we need to understand that ours is a guild into which our students are meant to perpetuate the constant churning out of pedagogues.

In his ground/breaking work *Ramus, Method, and the Decay of Dialogue*, Walter Ong excavates the history of a major shift in the evolution of intellectual thought orchestrated by the French Renaissance humanist Peter Ramus (1515–1572) (*Ramus* vii). The key force in his thought centers on the Ramist *dialectic*, marked by its decimation of Aristotelian philosophy, its reliance on visualization and quantification of thought, and the veneration of logic and reason. The explicit dangers of his dialectic concern (among other things) its severe limitation of the scope of rhetoric, but we are concerned here more with the hidden dangers. According to Ong, "Long after Ramus' age, the importance attached to logic in the general consciousness is due less to its association with thinking than with pedagogy" (150). In essence, because the university teacher "was also part of a corporation," Ramus sought to "[reduce] the personalist, dialoguing element in knowledge to a minimum in favor of an element which made knowledge something a corporation could traffic in, a-personal and abstract" (152). Thus, "dialectic . . . was habitually thought of as implementing not dialogue, but the *huge pedagogical apparatus*" (143, emphasis mine). Ong explains further how reason and teaching became inexorably linked: "This tradition more or less took for granted that teaching is carried on abstractly, since knowledge was generally equated with abstract or scientific knowledge. What is not conveyed abstractly and explicitly, is not taught. *Doctrina* is *scientia*. Teaching something is the same as 'proving' it" (156).

To achieve this connection, Ramus blurs the distinction between *ars* (art) and *doctrina* (teaching), often using them interchangeably (160). Dialectic, effectively, was the "teaching of teaching" (161). Logic's function in this interchange was, surprisingly, not a philosophical one. Ramus maintained that "'logic is not the *teaching* of how to argue about the precepts of logic; . . . logic is the *teaching* of how to discourse well'" (160). In short, according to Johann Piscator, a Ramist follower, "'to discourse (*disserere*)' means 'the same as to teach' (*docere*)" (qtd in Ong 161). Ramus had invented the supreme tautology; teaching logic (dialectic) "teaches the teaching of teachings" (162). In Ong's estimation, Ramus believed "dialectic . . . should govern all life" (167). By expanding "the purview of dialectic. . . . the purview of pedagogy was itself being expanded so that the world outside the classroom purportedly governed by dialectic was by that fact being assimilated to the classroom itself" (167). Reason is perfected in pedagogy, for pedagogy, by pedagogues. Trafficking in abstract thinking installs, brilliantly, the ultimate logic of containment inside a "huge pedagogical apparatus." Teaching's purpose, in this system, is to produce more teachers; and the proliferation of reason underpins such logic.

Composition pedagogy, having inherited what Ong calls the "pedagogical juggernaut" (149–67), must unbuild this pedagogical apparatus. We must break with a system in which teachers are the sole possessors of abstract thinking, and students are taught *as if* they are nascent teachers. Teaching abstraction (as *detachment from pedagogy*), rather than argumentation (as *learning to teach*), would place in students' hands the power to resist teaching itself, would enact the necessary detachment (*abstractus*) that would unhinge the link between reason and pedagogy, and dissemble the assembly line model of education in whose grip we have been ever since Ramus so cleanly paired discourse and logic.

Where does this leave writing? Lynn Worsham suggested some years ago that

> our emphasis should shift from the notion of writing as a mode of learning to that of writing as a strategy, without tactics or techniques, whose progress yields "unlearning." This result does not mean that writing produces ignorance; rather, it produces a sense of defamiliarization vis-à-vis unquestioned forms of knowledge. . . . Students may discover ways to make something of what has been made of them. ("Writing" 101–102)

Writing that unlearns such a "pedagogical apparatus" is apt to be wildly unfamiliar to us. Hélène Cixous describes this writing.

> Whoever wants to write must be able to reach this lightening region that takes your breath away, where you *instantaneously* feel at sea and where the moorings are severed with the already-written, the already-known. . . . All great texts begin in this manner that *breaks*: they break with our thought habits, with the world around us, in an extreme violence that is due to rapidity. They hurl us off to foreign countries. (*Three Steps* 59)

Writing in a "manner that breaks," however, severs more than the disciplinary moorings at stake in the field of rhetoric and composition. Breakers crash as well onto the ethical and political shores from which we obtain our license to monitor the steady traffic of student writing. The politics of such cornerstones as *process*, *propositional logic*, and *portfolio assessment*, to name a few, are given to determine the acceptable rhetorical borders (breakwaters) within which we operate. Recurrent bouts with plagiarism, student diffidence, and service-oriented curricula, continue to plague composition programs and prompt further shoring up of each foundational outcome in each departmental strategic plan. To suggest that argumentation has reached its breaking point, or (more drastically) to break up the lofty and lucrative industry of argumentative writing pedagogy, will meet with the most stern rebukes and further entrenchment of argument upon argument. The clarion calls to resist the breakup will likely adopt the most political and ethical of arguments. Thus, we must first understand, as Derrida reveals, that when one's politics or ethics is questioned, it is often because "the first defensive and reactionary reflex is to accuse of ethico-political irresponsibility, even of 'nihilism,' the very one who comes like this to question and disturb the *doxa* in its slumber" ("Canons" 202–03). Let me wear the moniker of irresponsibility if it means divesting oneself of responsibility in order to probe the depths of a more responsive relation to students, to each other, and to each *Other.* It is time to put off the mantle of *autochthonous* authority, to disavow our discourse of desired roots from which we erroneously believe we are giving our students the gift of *ground.*

Home/land

there's no need friend to remind me
about the countless whose lives are far from such luxury
about starvation and misery the latest holocaust
of those who never got a dog's chance oh
as I write I can hear the scream of
someone being carefully tortured while others
with their only life blindfolded face into
the high cement wall of one military or another
even the thought like that of Poland becomes
a kind of dying: what that hitcher from the North felt
as he watched the blaze of his cottage

Noting the irony of opening a discussion of Heidegger with this next section of Desmond Egan's poem, "Needing the Sea" (hailing us as it does as with reminders of the *absolute* material conditions of the millions of victims of genocide), I cringe as I prepare *us* to "need the sea." I struggle to stand (literally); yet my legs buckle in the face of past and present *violent realities,* as if standing on the threshold of Heidegger's hut in Todtnauberg—which I now assign as the address of this chapter.

Thus, it is crucial that we acknowledge a potentially crippling aspect of Heidegger's thought, namely, the identification of elements of violence found in his language of "rootedness, homeland, and native soil," terms that implicate him in the rise of National Socialism, according to Charles Bambach (4). The precise tension I aim to scrutinize, however, is the *unmitigated* trajectory of Heidegger's thinking from within the context of Nazi Germany toward his postwar critiques of logic and reason, though I do not trace Heidegger's so-called "turn" in quite the same manner as others who focus on his shift from questions of Being to questions of language. I want, rather, to call attention to a shift in Heidegger's thought from *anchoring* Being in the "rootedness" of the "homeland" to *releasing* Being into its essence *as* the principle of ground itself. Admittedly, it is impossible to reconcile Heidegger's thinking, starkly demonstrated in a 1934 radio address ("Creative Landscape: Why Do We Remain in the Provinces?") in which, Bambach notes, he concentrates on the "folkish constellation of themes around the notion of 'rootedness,' or *Bodenständigkeit*," themes intimately implicated in "the oppression, exclusion, violence, and terror that [Ernest Bloch] identifies as belonging to the essence of an Alemannic-Swabian-Bavarian form of National Socialism," (4) which Bloch (in 1929) termed "'pastorale militans'" (qtd in Bambach 4). In Bambach's analysis, this oxymoron belies a decidedly less than "bucolic" association between "blood and soil" (4).

> For Bloch, the language of the homeland and of an Alemannic rootedness in the soil betrays a political longing for "a myth that has its fantasy not in the distance but embedded beneath the soil as it were." This mythic attraction of German fascism for "blood and soil" rhetoric "constitutes the chloroform practice of Hitlerism." As early as 1933 Bloch will lament that "the eternally same, ignorant arias that Hitler sings to his petit-bourgeois followers do not become any better when the university whore who he found (just as Wilhelm II found her in 1914) latinizes the kitsch and improves the deception with refinements à la Schmitt or Freyer or Heidegger." (4–5)[5]

Nevertheless, other influences upon Heidegger must be taken into consideration when held up within the constellation of themes circumscribed by *mythic attractions*, namely, influences infrequently attributed to Heidegger's thought, such as the *dis*traction of mysticism and its pull away from reason and logic toward theology and *ab*straction. If, however, we are to discern the *autochthonous* roots of "reason" and its priesthood of logicians, we cannot simply *re*tract thought from the realm of Western ontotheological metaphysics; it is necessary, as Heidegger knew, to *ext*ract thought from the bedrock itself: the principle of *ground*.

In John Caputo's compelling book *The Mystical Element in Heidegger's Thought*, he traces Heidegger's affinity for Meister Eckhart (von Hochheim), a thirteenth-century Dominican preacher from Central Germany. Caputo examines Eckhart's vernacular sermons, written primarily to the "religious orders of women" of the time who could not read Latin, having never received the "formal theological training accorded to men," and for whom he resorted to a more vernacular style of writing (101). According to Caputo, Eckhart was driven by a desire to undo "the onto-theo-logical God," that is "what men call God, whether on the basis of metaphysical theology or even of revealed faith" (xviii). He wanted to rid us of the need to understand God by exerting "the sway of human knowledge" and, instead, to bring us to a point in which we "suspend operations of subjectivity, to disconnect the *ego cogito*, and let God *be*, let God be *God*" (xviii). Eckhart believed the "highest work of the soul is to let Him go, to let Him be, to remain open to the *lethe* [withdrawal], indeed to shelter Him from the fire of metaphysical conceptuality, to preserve Him in His withdrawal" (xix). Similarly, Heidegger also held that "withdrawal, *lethe*, concealment is inscribed in the 'essence' . . . of Being" (xxii), although he addresses a secularized unfolding of the history of Being, rather than Eckhart's mystical desire for the "unity of the soul with God" (xvii). While similar, Caputo notes, in Heidegger there is a *danger* in this line of thinking not present in Eckhart's religious mysticism, namely, that because "we ourselves are the beings at stake," the "stakes are high" in this "game [*Spiel*] whose outcome is dark and uncertain" (xvii–xviii). "*Es ereignet weil es ereignet. Es spielt weil es spielt.* It does what it does, groundlessly. It plays because it plays" (xviii).

In order not to mistake my Heideggerian interlude for an obscure (and abstract) sidebar (or worse, jeremiad), let me align our discussion of reason and composition pedagogy with the same telescopic (and equidistant) horizon. Reading the *effects* of the history of reason in the field of rhetoric and composition requires in us an awakening to the withdrawal, though not one that frees us from reason's sway. Caputo's explication of Heidegger's exposition (his exposing the "'*debilitas*' of reason" xix) is useful.

> On Heidegger's own terms, oblivion, withdrawal, is *ineradicable* [emphasis mine], and possesses what might be called, in a language we can no longer trust, a structural necessity. If withdrawal is the very condition which grants the possibility *of* history, then there can be no point *in* history where oblivion is overcome. To "awaken" to this oblivion, which is what "overcoming" means, can have no historical correlate, cannot be instantiated somewhere inside history—whether in a "brief but magnificent time" in the first beginning or in some "new beginning." Wakefulness does not emancipate us *from* the oblivion, but *to* it. It does not point back to a primal time nor does it hail a coming future, but it gives us a certain way of reading that history—as the history which is effected by the withdrawal. (xxii–xxiii)

In *effect*, until we awaken *to* the oblivion, reason's sway continues to call to us from *inside* the history of rhetoric (its first beginning), but also (and thus more insidiously) from inside the "new beginning" of the rhetoric/composition fray, thus denying us a way to *read* that history or to *wrest* (from Old Norse, *reista*, to bend) ourselves from reason's grasp without doing so in a violent diremption. It rises to the surface—can you see it? Just there, beneath the seas of Eckhart's theological detachment and Heidegger's secular withdrawal, we witness the thunderous breach of our whale—*abstraction*. But unlike Melville's Ahab, we do not slaughter the abstraction and lash it to our vessel in order to preserve some divine balance between Kant's *a priori* and Locke's *tabula rasa*. We let it *be* abstract; we withdraw, move away, and tread in astonishment.[6] Into its wake I would have us sail as awakened teachers of writing and rhetoric, inviting students to detach themselves from us, from the ground—and to think *in* the *abstract*, in writing. Still, it's a concrete world in more ways than one; and abstraction cannot be established by reason if we mean to detach composition from its argumentative foundations (its leviathan). We need to *hear* this word, and we need to tread slowly.

In "On Detachment," Eckhart uses "the Middle High German word *abegesheidenheit* as a translation of *abstractus*, that which is 'drawn away' and 'removed from' matter and the conditions of matter" (qtd in Caputo 11). To issues relating to structure, matter, and concrescence, I will return later. For I do not wish to commit what Alfred Whitehead termed "the fallacy of misplaced concreteness" (to mistake "what is abstract for what is concrete"; Kwinter, "Fallacy" 267–68). To do so would merely rehearse Henrik Ibsen's drama *The Master Builder* in which Solness (an architect) promises to build a young woman (Hilda) a fairy-tale kingdom with "castles in the air" (Ibsen 371). Eivind Tjønneland interprets Solness's symbolic goal as "'artificial and unrealistic.' . . . he loses all sense of reality, the juxtaposition between 'the foundation' and 'the castle in the air' becomes what Kierkegaard calls 'an untrue exaggeration'" (Tjønneland 80; qtd in Tostrup 166). The master builder wanted *nothing* to build, "nothing really built; not anything sacrificed for the chance of building" (Ibsen 380); nevertheless, when Hilda asks, "a real castle in the air?," Solness replies, "Yes. One with a firm foundation under it" (371). Allegorically speaking, if unbuilt material designs constitute an abstract materiality, the realization of which would result in a "diminished" abstraction, "it stands to *suggest*" that writing that abstracts itself in order to re-present abstraction results in a *built* meaning, rather than an *unbuilt* and infinite source of meaning. Our conundrum is not unlike the "methodologically impregnable" leap of Heidegger's. We cannot leap from ground to ground unless we keep moving; and we cannot build castles in the air on solid foundations. The master builder was only half right; the problem lies *not only* in the *nothing*, it lies in the principle of ground. But Eckhart and Heidegger knew we must *go through* the *nothing* in order to accomplish the abstraction of, and detachment from, the sphere of matter and reason.

There is a saying in Norway, "Av måneskin gror det ingenting"—Nothing grows in the moonlight. It means that some things are beautiful, or of value, despite their seeming lack of purpose, their lack of *ground* metaphysics. Heidegger takes up the problem in *Der Satz vom Grund*, a series of lectures he delivered in Freiburg in 1955–56. His concluding lecture, "The Principle of Ground," dealt with the famous principle of Leibniz, "nothing is without reason" (sometimes translated as "*nothing* is *without* ground"). In order to bring the problem of ground into relief, and thus critique the history of logic and rationality, Caputo suggests that Heidegger takes Leibniz's principle as a "touchstone of the entire Western metaphysical tradition, i.e., of the history of philosophy and reason in the West" (*Mystical* 47). Placing the emphasis differently, Heidegger rereads the phrase as "nothing *is* without *ground*" (qtd in Caputo 67) in a new key. To penetrate the destructive force of philosophical reason, Heidegger chooses to elucidate the verse of the mystical poet Angelus Silesius called "Without Why" (from *The Cherubinic Wanderer*): "The rose is without why; it blooms because it blooms; / It cares not for itself; asks not if it's seen" (qtd in Caputo 40). That Heidegger chooses a mystic poet is not insignificant. The rose does not obey the principles of logic and reason, as men do; it is detached from representational thinking. In order to enter this other region outside representational thinking, we have to suspend our role as a representational subject looking to supply grounds for the rose (Caputo, *Mystical* 66). We should understand that we are like the rose—without why, which is different from being without because. *Very different.* In according the rose its place in the "*principium reddendae rationis*" (principle of sufficient reason), the poet, Heidegger is suggesting,

> speaks of the rose not as it stands before the representing subject, but as it stands in itself. The poet lets the rose be the thing which it is, without reducing it to the status of an "object." He detaches [*abstractus*] the rose from the demands of representational thinking. For the poet, the "rose remains without a relationship to the ground, a relationship which questions and which expressly represents the ground." (qtd in Caputo 64)

According to Heidegger, philosophy, as a thing of reason, is the result of an oblivion of the fact that things do not depend on human justification, they emerge before us on their own. Yet, Caputo notes, Heidegger's critics (especially Laszlo Versényi, Paul Hühnerfeld, and Walter Biemel) find his leap from representational thinking to the nonrepresentational thought of Being (via mysticism) difficult to accept since he has not passed through the "trial of reason" (42). Such a leap involves a discontinuity; it is accomplished without a bridge, that is, without propositional logic, and this leap has the *appearance* of being methodologically impregnable (41, 70). That is, Caputo explains, if one criticizes

> Heidegger's thought from without. . . . one will inevitably adopt the language of metaphysics and, in so doing, distort what is important about it, viz., its very overcoming of metaphysics. The alternative to this, Biemel notes, is "to arrive at Heidegger's position with a leap and then to remain there." (qtd in Caputo 41)

If we explore Heidegger's critique of logic further, however, we come to see that the danger in the leap shifts not toward the leap itself so much as to the logic that compels us *not* to leap. In his "Letter on Humanism" (1947), Heidegger takes humanism "offshore" by refusing to shore up a technical interpretation of thinking, an interpretation that, he maintains, has been seized by logic and grammar, both operating under the banner of metaphysics and acting on the strength of metalinguistic positions aimed at disarming all that threatens the autonomy of reason, rationality, and logic (194). The problem, he argues, is that thinking should not be

> judged by a standard that does not measure up to it. Such judgment may be compared to the procedure of trying to evaluate the nature and powers of a fish by seeing how long it can live on dry land. For a long time now, all too long, thinking has been stranded on dry land. Can then the effort to return thinking to its element be called "irrationalism"? (195)

Furthermore:

> Because we are speaking against humanism people fear a defense of the inhuman and a glorification of barbaric brutality. For what is more "logical" than that for somebody who negates humanism nothing remains but the affirmation of inhumanity? . . . With the assistance of logic and ratio—so often invoked—people come to believe that whatever is not positive is negative and thus that it seeks to degrade reason—and therefore deserves to be branded as depravity. We are so filled with "logic" that anything that disturbs the habitual somnolence of prevailing opinion is automatically registered as a despicable contradiction. . . . Following this logical course we let everything expire in a nihilism we invented for ourselves with the aid of logic. (225–27)

The fear of being groundless and the risk of being branded inhuman (or posthumanist) are compelling (*ir*resistible) reasons for not taking the leap of thought, for not forsaking the principle of ground. But surely we are not mere puppets of first principles, or statues rooted in reason. The question is mir(ror)ed in Heinrich von Kleist's essay "On the Marionette Theatre." Kleist explains that marionette puppets are, in a way, weightless.

> They are not afflicted with the inertia of matter, the property resistant to dance. The force which raises them into the air is greater than the one which draws them to the ground. . . . Puppets need the ground only to glance against lightly, like elves, and through this momentary check to renew the swing of their limbs. We humans must have it to rest on, to recover from the effort of the dance. This moment of rest is clearly no part of the dance. The best we can do is make it as inconspicuous as possible. (n.p.)

Resting in our not leaping poses the ultimate hazard: we become so rooted in reason that our feet sink deep in the sand at low tide, and each attempt to step out and up is futile. "The more we pursue grounds, the more we lose our footing" (Caputo, *Mystical* 57). The tide returns, and we can only stand staring out to sea, desperate to swim free. We are no more than iron statues, standing rooted, up to our necks in ground, beautifully illustrated in British sculptor Antony Gormley's group of one hundred iron figures semiburied in the sand and water, looking out to sea along the Norwegian coast at Stavanger (fig. 4.1). Asked what their stance means, he replies, "The sculptures do not take their belonging to the world for granted, they are trying to find their place in it and they do not take the act of standing as a given; they are learning to stand" (Gormley "Extracts").[7]

Fig. 4.1. Antony Gormley, *Another Place*. Cast iron, 100 figures, 189 × 53 × 29 cm, artist's photo from installation at Stavanger, Norway, June 1997. *Courtesy of the artist.*

Composition and rhetoric must relinquish its role in teaching students to rest rather than dance, to reason rather than detach, to face the eroding coastline of ground metaphysics rather than the open sea. Converting our rhetorical latitude against the groundswell of urban argument requires equal pressure on both reason and region. Thus, we must understand the equally disabling coordinates of coercion that have been handed down through philosophical pragmatics, cognitive science, formal logic, and legislated consumerism thinly disguised *as* education. We can continue to embrace this legacy, or step away, step back, and remain detached. This requires not fortitude, but forbearance—not rationality, but a deconstructive heart—and an ear to hear the language of abstraction. One trajectory, ours at the moment, offers to outsmart old alibis (street smarts) by adopting new allegories, new cosmo-politics, and avant-pedagogy. It is now or never, no time to lament, writes Nietzsche.

> We have left the land and have embarked. We have burned our bridges behind us—indeed, we have gone farther and destroyed the land behind us. Now, little ship, look out! Beside you is the ocean: to be sure, it does not always roar, and at times it lies spread out like silk and gold and reveries of graciousness. But hours will come when you realize that it is infinite and that there is nothing more awesome than infinity. Oh, the poor bird that felt free and now strikes the walls of this cage! Woe, when you feel homesick for the land as if it had offered more *freedom*—and there is no longer any land. (*Gay Science* 180–81)

Street Smarts

> we all know about the houses of hopes blown up blown out
> we all bump into the local alcos the druggie
> youngsters their adult faces mugged by less than poverty
> just off the O'Connell Street of our new towns

In her 2002 Conference on College Composition and Communication convention call, Shirley Logan challenged us to "connect the text and the street." In the call, Logan cites Chicago poet, novelist, and teacher Gwendolyn Brooks, who once said, "I wrote about what I saw and heard in the street. I lived in a small second-floor apartment at the corner, and I could look first on one side and then on the other. There was my material" (Gayles 15). In answering the call, our fields of rhetoric and composition gathered around and collectively celebrated (and critiqued) our hipper version of the *promenade*. As I reflected on the call at the time, I became increasingly convinced that the institutionalization of the "street" as source material, among other things, effectively hails our students into the romantic subject position of the (masculine) *flâneur*. Charles Baudelaire describes the *flâneur*:

> It is not given to everyman to take a bath of multitude; enjoying a crown in an art. . . . The solitary and thoughtful stroller finds singular intoxication in this universal communion. . . . He adopts as his own all the occupations, all the joys and all the sorrows that chance offers. (20; qtd in Jarvis 106)

More recently, critical theorists of various stripes have adopted the *flâneur* as a means of resolutely connecting (and valorizing) the principle of ground and social realism, the effect of which is a dizzying turnstile through which passes the flotsam of so much bohemian slumming. According to Chris Jenks:

> The flâneur, though grounded in everyday life, is an analytic form, a narrative device, an attitude towards knowledge and its social context. It is an image of movement through the social space of modernity. . . . The flâneur is a multilayered palimpsest that enables us to move from real products of modernity, like commodification and leisured patriarchy, through the practical organization of space and its negotiation by inhabitants of a city, to a critical appreciation of the state of modernity and its erosion into the post-, and onwards to a reflexive understanding of the function, and purpose, of realist as opposed to hermeneutic epistemologies in the appreciation of those previous formations. (148)

Rob Shields further situates the *flâneur* at the apex of urban street life, as one who

> jealously guards his individuality and agency by obscuring it beneath the mask of the anonymous and insignificant "man of the crowd," pursues a course which alienates him from even the possibility of a deeper inter-subjective exchange with the other members of the crowd scene. . . . Flânerie is a sociability of Ones. . . . This is the life of watching the world go by, not ever exchanging a word acknowledging the presence of an Other. (76–77)

Perhaps this is not precisely descriptive of the student writer, but it is eerily allegorical in its equivalence between the classroom and "a sociability of Ones," between our social epistemic rallies for student agency and this one who "jealously guards his individuality and agency." The student as man-about-town, member of the "leisured patriarchy." His writing safely hidden by anonymity and insignificance, ironic in its aimlessness in an aims-driven rhetorical industry. *Cyberflânerie* constructing our students as lurker/browsers of the Internet. To be sure there are multiple and exemplary countertexts to the activities and alienation emerging from my close rendering of the *flâneur* as student writer. More indirect than direct, my tactic here is to splice scenarios together in order to glimpse an unhappy association in whose folly we are unwittingly complicit by connecting "the text and the street." Leaving aside the feminist leverage we should make out of the student as romantic man-about-town, I want to focus on the questions urgently posed by our ongoing romance with the *topos* of *street*, questions that involve not only its thorough rootedness in ground metaphysics, but also its franchised reproduction of the generic site of an agonistic and violent topography.

The word *street* is what Gayatri Spivak would term a normative *catachresis* in that its original referent is the result of an arbitrary abuse of the metaphor of ground (*Critique* 14). Put in a more vernacular context, "the street" serves as a metonymic substitution through which the old "bait and switch" of "reinventing the university" is accomplished. Gerald Graff sets such an agenda when he claims that "inside every street-smart student (which is to say, every student) there is a latent intellectual trying to break out, an identity that it is my job somehow to tease out and help to articulate itself" (23). What Graff terms "hidden intellectualism" must be "translated into academic discourse" or street smarts "will have limited influence on the public sphere" (23). "To emerge as critical theory, street smarts have to undergo transformation" (23). Yet the transformation Graff calls for is little more than a thinly disguised transformation of street fighting, and it is not clear whether and to what degree Graff distinguishes street conflict from street smarts in his claim that street conflict has to be channeled into academic argumentation. But there is nothing new under the sun in Graff's argument.

Walter Ong has studied the agonistic residue of Hellenic male ceremonial combat within contemporary critical practices. Ong lays partial blame for academic agonistics on the ancient practice of "fliting," in which heroic fighters hurl verbal insults at one another as a prelude to physical combat (*Fighting* 108). Other elements of bravado, such as bragging, taunting, ridicule, and insult, were also important parts of these ancient ritual contests. Ong concludes that only when literacy subsumed orality and exterior combat turned inward, did these aspects of agonistic behavior begin to manifest themselves on two fronts, "the narrative and the scholarly-scientific fronts" (186). Given this history, and in response to a world that seems to breed adversarial cultures, Ong calls for an increasing number of self-styled "conflict engineers" who practice various ways of eliminating, circumventing, or reducing such adversarial relationships (17).[8] Graff clearly sees himself as just such a "conflict engineer" given his view that "encouraging students to argue can escalate into violence, but repressing argument can lead to violence, too" (31). And, interestingly, Graff bears out Ong's analysis by admitting that one critic of his work suggests that "the pedagogy of 'teaching the conflicts' and the joys of literary critical contention became [for Graff] a kind of street fighting by other means" (31). The street, and all the sub-cultural resistance that the term evokes, is emblematic of a well-oiled logic of containment at work.

Taken to its *logical* conclusion, Graff's pedagogical urbanity is mirrored in the current popularity of both "reality" and "weakest link" television programs—the survivor and/or the *street-smart* contestant. ("Street Smarts" was a Warner Brothers comedy and game show "where contestants prove how smart they are by predicting how dumb other people can be.") I would call this an *urban* lesson, one designed to render illusive the boundary between *urbanity* and the *banal*—city streets filled with *street-smart* people spared from the cognitive burden of reasoning—commonplace concepts that happen to share the root word *ban* (meaning "to proclaim or command under threat or penalty"). From there it is but a short distance to *banish* (deport) what is learned by other means, what is written in other forms, and what is thought outside the turf of reason.

Architecture Allegories

is the world which so many miss
realised for them you'd wonder through others
do we carry it for this mongol child that
bucketful of abortions in the sluice room?

The question becomes, then, how to deconstruct the *topos* of the street and its abject ground zero. John Rajchman would have us move away from stories rooted in soil toward stories that trace trajectories. He writes: "Ungrounded movement is [a] movement that is no longer bound to move from one fixed point to another but rather traces its own unbounded space through the trajectories or paths that it takes" (85). Rajchman takes his cue from Paul Virilio, who claims that "between the subjective and objective it seems we have no room for the 'trajective,' that being of movement from here to there." (Virilio 24). Virilio laments the "loss of the traveller's tale" (25); he longs for the "essence of the path, the journey" (23). But Rajchman parlays Virilio's romanticized view of travel into the geophysical language of the dispossessed.

> Perhaps . . . we need to get away from the picture that social life has roots in the ground or soil that supplies it with its basic sense and circumscribes

> the movements of which it is capable—that the life-world is in the first instance a grounded world. . . . The modern world unleashes patterns of demography or migration that put people in situations where, in relation to themselves and to one another, they are no longer able to tell straight narratives of their "origins." They become originals without origins; their narratives become ungrounded, out of joint, constructed by superposition or juxtaposition rather than by development or progress; a "time" of socially ungrounded movement is thus introduced into their being. (Rajchman 87–88)

Rajchman's question, which I adopt here, is: "What would an architecture of such trajectories and movements look like?" (86). Using the question as a linchpin around which our periscope pivots, we will name two primary arcs of interest: the ungrounded and unbuilt. One aim of this dual trajectory is to deploy my figurative (but no less inflammatory) substitution of the flamboyant *flâneur* with the figure of the dispossessed (*refugee*), a provocative denomination for the student writer in the intensive zone of offshore pedagogy to be examined in the section following. Manuel De Landa reminds us that we

> live in spatio-temporal [extensive] zones bounded by . . . familiar borderlines. . . . But there are other zones that we inhabit, too, but which are less familiar than extensive zones. These are "zones of intensity," such as differences in temperature, zones of high pressure explored by deep-sea divers, high or low gravity zones [e.g., commercial airliners conducting High-G maneuvers to thwart a hijacking]. These zones are bounded by intensive borderlines, critical points of temperature, pressure, gravity, density, tension, connectivity, points that define abrupt transitions in the state of the creatures inhabiting those zones. . . . The role of the philosopher and artist is precisely to reveal this other world, these intensive nuomena behind the extensive phenomena. We are certainly not the first generation to discover intensities, but we may be the first one to be called to revive the forgotten craft of living creatively within intensive zones. (n.p.)

It is appropriate here to conspire with Geoff Sirc again, to wield our uncanny (because unintentional) collaboration along similarly unbuilt lines. As a consistent theme in Sirc's work over several decades, avant-garde architectural theories have energized his prescient thought to connect movements such as the Situationists and Happenings artists of the fifties and sixties to composition in general. Sirc recognizes in these architects and artists "a need for a new intensity" (26) with which he calls for a "new urbanism in Composition Studies" and thereby to "return the favor, in a sense, and use a few ideas in architectural theory (especially as they relate to city-planning) in order to read the scene of the writing classroom" (187). Sirc wants to immerse us in the *topos* of street with the aim of shocking and intensifying it *as* an intensive zone, but his is a trope from the *street* as mere *topos* to the *street as event*. For Sirc, composition as happening "silences that tedious, already-wrote drone of *knowing*, *selecting*, *evaluating*, *reporting*, *concluding*, and *arguing*. It is a pedagogy designed to un-build our field's spaces, a standard-stoppage, a composition theory (like Schoenberg's) that values the eraser end of the pencil (or the delete key)" (278). Tripping on Happenings' neoangst, Sirc revitalizes a tired composition-as-construction-site by daring to "see Versailles in the A&P parking lot . . . to see the (other) story that *dwells* in the (purported) story" (193). In *groundless solidarity* with Sirc, so to speak, I would have us un-build our field's royal discourse and make of *argument* an urbanished structure, thereby turning a pretender-to-the-throne into an underground fugitive sovereignty. But my design is not meant to actively un-build spaces so much as to step back and view the *unground* (der *Abgrund*—abyss) beneath the structures, and to sketch a *rhetoric of the unbuilt*.

The question of what we *should* build has an inverse—what should we *not* build? Architects rarely offer answers to that question, but not in the case of Lebbeus Woods. Woods understood that "because architecture is allied with centers of economic and political power, which are concerned first and foremost with extending, or at least maintaining, their hegemony, and denying or suppressing any signs of its instability, this is architecture's most *likely* role" (*BorderLine* 36 %, emphasis mine). A theorist of architecture since 1976 (following a stint with the Eero Saarinen firm), Woods was primarily concerned with the excessive rationalism of contemporary architecture. His artistic renderings and models were frequently exhibited in international installations, and Woods's publications portray his remarkable mesh of sociocritical politics and design. More famous for what he has *never* built, Woods straddles the threshold between abstract and concrete, often locating his critiques at the borderline of troubled port cities, where land and water meet.

A rhetoric of the *unbuilt* is most aptly poised to consider first and foremost the effects of architecture commissioned by those that require a "rational, that is, predictable, stability" (36%). It also suggests a mode of transgressing the threshold between the inside and outside. Woods frames the potential in terms of borderline conditions, or "between zones," which "no longer separate certainties, but become spaces where uncertainties meet, interact, fuse or are repelled" (32%). Using the examples of two coastal urban districts, Kraljevica (Croatia) and La Boca (Buenos Aires), both of which were "once vital" shipyards and docks, and both suffering "from varying degrees of pollution that impinges heavily on the quality of living" (36%), Woods redefines *critical architecture* by naming such places as "experimental zones, where problems already present in the surrounding territories, but concealed by appearances of normality, are confronted and engaged" (36%). While their governments solicit building projects in the hope of attracting tourism, Woods suggests the possibility of doing so is slim. Recycling reason is not the answer, so Woods offers ideas for reconstructing Kraljevica with "new types of buildings, ones that float or amphibiously move from sea to land; or re-frame the harbor as a laboratory for the study and development of noise-control technology" (37%). In La Boca, he imagines building a "floating community of river-cleaners, who make houses of their floating pollution-eating machines . . . [and] a 'museum of sunken boats,' which reveals the long-hidden spaces they have created under the river's surface; a 'museum of raised boats,' which turns them fully in space, revealing their sensuous resurrected forms" (37%).

In "The Storm," an exhibit at Cooper Union, Woods's words marked the entrance:

War and Architecture

Architecture and war are not incompatible.
Architecture is war. War is architecture.
I am at war with my time, with history, with all authority that
resides in fixed and frightened forms.
I am one of millions who do not fit in, who have no home, no family,
no doctrine, no firm place to call my own, no known beginning
or end,
no "sacred and primordial site."[9]

There are no doubt many examples evoked by Woods's declaration, but one site seems eternally destined to fit a rhetoric of the unbuilt: *Jerusalem*. Occupying a contested plot of land, Woods's observation that standing inside "the borderline are other borderlines" (38%) is aptly illustrated by two key vectors, the vertical Western Wall and the horizontal flat rooftops of Jerusalem. Standing for thousands of years, the Western Wall (also called the Wailing Wall) in Jerusalem is a site of prayer and blood, the sacred *topos* of religious certainties rendered uncertain by politics and war. To study its façade is to study "the communication between the inside and the outside" (Tostrup 13)—to probe the depths of a single surface polished by hands, to step back from the wall, to detach (*abstract*) ourselves from its visceral wail—is to study its sign of disunification as an *unbuilt* text of "full-scale realities that have not yet been made concrete" (Tostrup 12). Architects Deborah Natsios and John Young have realized the paradox of such border politics by deconstructing an above-ground horizontal plane of the divided city using the rooftops of Jerusalem.

In their essay "Jerusalem SKY," Natsios and Young propose a radical conjuncture of military and ecological *topoi* as a means of "[subordinating] pernicious surveillance to the knowledge-based act of seeing Jerusalem anew." Opting for reclaiming the sky as eco-political space (redefining *total air supremacy*), their project aims to track and monitor migratory bird populations whose trajectory takes them over the divided city of Jerusalem (fig. 4.2). Using the thousands of flat rooftops of Jerusalem, Natsios and Young lift the plane of conflict above ground, yet they use existing structures for participation in an ecological intervention into the troubled reality of Arab-Israeli relations. They envision "bird's-eye-view perspectives of Jerusalem [that would] construct the city along the pilgrim's spiritual horizon, a vertical axis whose vanishing points converge into sanctified sky—the allegorical airspace of Jesus' and Muhammad's respective ascensions." The project would retrofit military technology in the service of the migratory winged pilgrims making their journey south every year. Natsios and Young explain:

> *Jerusalem SKY's* new bird's-eye views of the city have emerged out of regional conflict-resolution initiatives precipitated by birdstrike hazards. Catastrophic birdstrikes—symptom of unresolved spatial conflict between militarized airspace and transboundary avian flyways—are being mitigated through innovative remediation that relies in part on national security technologies. Today, migration conservationists are tracking and mapping their mobile subjects using what was once the exclusive paraphernalia of war—real-time surveillance radar warning systems, satellites, unmanned military drones, motorized gliders, and satellite intercept radio-transmitters.

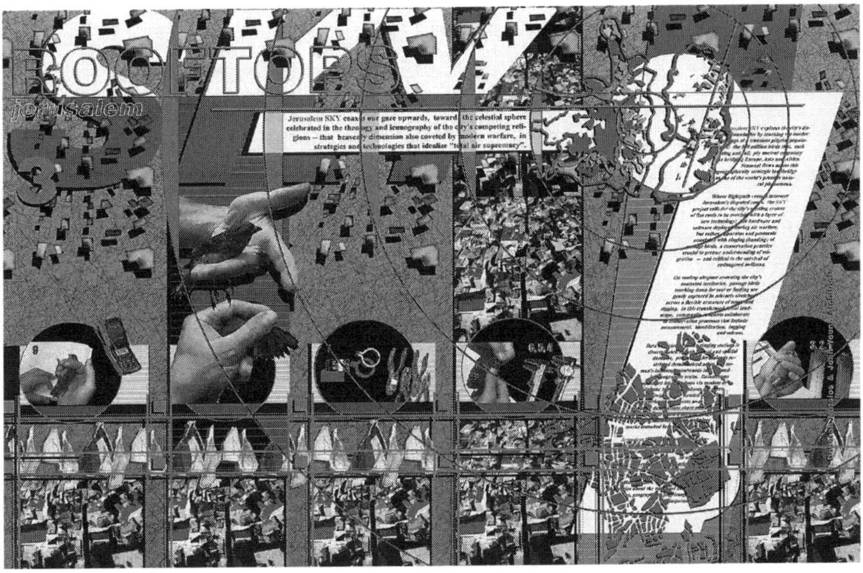

Fig. 4.2. "Rooftops" image from *Jerusalem SKY. © 2001, 2002 Deborah Natsios and John Young; courtesy of Deborah Natsios.*

Other projects undertaken by Natsios and Young include a transboundary peace park to be built in the DMZ between North and South Korea, where fifty years of "no-man's-landscapes" have harbored "rare flora and fauna, including some of Northeast Asia's most endangered migratory species, despite the prevalence of antipersonnel land mines, razorwire and tank bunkers" ("Parallel Atlas: 38° N"). Such projects remind us that a rhetoric of the *unbuilt* must also consider (and render in *in*/visible textures) *unqualified* hope. Churning into the storm of reason necessitates strong measures for survival, and hope is above all crucial. The texts of hope are, however, often latent in some landscapes (those no-man's-landscapes that wiped out all mankind).

To render them visible requires that we ask what coordinates mark the sites of those who did not survive *the* storm of reason? Daniel Libeskind, son of two Holocaust survivors from Poland, is an architect for whom such coordinates are more than residual traces of genocide. Originally chosen as the master designer of the new World Trade Center in New York (though that subsequently changed), Libeskind first emigrated to the United States with his family in 1959; he now resides in Berlin after a lengthy stay there to oversee the construction of his design for the Jewish Museum. Earlier, in 1987, Libeskind entered a design contest called Urban Competition in Berlin and won. The plans, however, were "shelved post-unification" (Mackenzie). In Libeskind's vision of Berlin, called *City Edge*, the unbuilt text is reticulated, or networked arbitrarily, as a means of wrapping architectural space in language. He explains that

> very thin paper—like that of architectural drawings, Bibles, maps, telephone books, money—can be easily cut, crumpled, or folded around this indestructible kernel. Then the entire unwieldy construction can be floated on water like the tattered paper making its Odyssey on the Liffey. . . . In this way reality, as the substance of things hoped for, becomes a proof of invisible joys—Berlin of open skies. (*Space* 55)

After twenty years of theorizing and writing about architecture, Libeskind was awarded the commission for building the Jewish Museum Berlin.

> When the museum opened in 1999, it opened empty by public demand. In its first year, all the time empty, there were half a million visitors; people queued round the block. A curious idea in itself, a museum with no exhibits. If the traditional idea of a museum or an art gallery is to provide a window through which you look, safely, as into another world, and where the space itself is invisible, Libeskind turned this on its head. (Mackenzie)

Learning our lessons with a *rhetoric of the unbuilt* means searching for that which permits isomorphisms between nonterritorial (and nonfoundational) versions of composition. As Libeskind writes in "An Open Letter to Architectural Educators and Students of Architecture," "Why spend time tediously applying gold leaf onto a pinnacle of a tower (impressive!) when the foundations are rotten? Before that delicate task will have been completed, the entire edifice will collapse, destroying both the work and the worker. Invisible disasters precede those that can be seen" (*Space* 20). The lessons of the Holocaust are, for Libeskind, not solely the province of historians. After an invitation to a competition that would determine how the land next to the Sachsenhausen concentration camp would be used, Libeskind struggled with whether to participate. In the end, he submitted an idea that was radically different from the ideas of the other five architects, who had all willingly agreed to design housing (as stipulated by the competition organizers). The first prize went to another architect, but after further negotiations among the committee members, Libeskind was invited to speak to the city mayor and the committee to present his ideas, after which the decision was reversed and the housing idea scrapped. Against the historians, who wanted to "reconstruct all the Nazi buildings in order to preserve the history" (90), Libeskind believed that the expense required to stabilize the decaying foundations, and build new walls and windows, would "have produced a mockery, a kitsch, a misunderstanding of history" (90). Explaining his original idea, Libeskind proposed

> that the S.S. buildings disintegrate over time. It is very difficult to do this ecologically, but one could do it in a controlled manner, in order to see the history, not as a simulation of the Third Reich, but to see what is there invisibly, the infrastructure between the S.S. lands and the Sachsenhausen concentration camp. I argued with the historians and pleaded that they think about the invisible traces of history, the history which never had a chance to be expressed; a history that should not be seen simply as an outline of a building. (90)

Libeskind's proposal "shifts, detaches, and reconnects the competition site in its relation to the equilateral triangle that forms the visible apex of the all too invisible symbol worn by the thousands of prisoners within the camp" (91). By reconnecting the three points, "deliberately built to define the outer limits of the triangle" ("the crematorium for incineration, the villa of the commandant, and the administrative headquarters of all the concentration camps in Europe"), a "new orientation has been created along the line pointing toward Lübeck, where the infamous Sachsenhausen Death March was to reach its conclusion in the drowning of the victims" (91). The planned site

> splits into two areas that are treated in two wholly different ways in order to displace the imagery of the past and to reconsecrate the land. One part of the plane is excavated, and the remaining buildings on it are flattened, exposing the foundations and interconnections of the machinery and its brutality. This part is then flooded with water from the adjacent canal, creating a sunken archaeological zone. The newly formed lake refers not only to the slave labor connected to the waters, but also frees the water from its historical role by using it as a new ecological element to restructure the topography of the place. (91)

The exposition of brutal foundations followed by the flooding of a site of mass extermination goes much farther than my *mere* expository attempt to locate (and appropriate) permissible isomorphisms between theoretical architecture and composition theory. It is offered here as a corrective, as a means of deploying a perpetual *recon*secration of all ground that uses the alibi of reason to perpetrate homologous *de*secration. It is also offered as evidence of the material force effected by the conjoining of language and design. The introduction of language as a "material intervention in the urban continuum" began with visionary architects like Antonio Sant'Elia, whose *Messaggio* text and futurist designs of the early twentieth century put an end to the differentiation between politics and architecture. Sanford Kwinter suggests that such avant-gardes understood that their designs "were yet too primitive or ontologically conventional to express the conditions of a revolutionized cosmos. What clearly was needed were not new objects, but a new orientation toward a phenomenal field of events and interactions—not objects, but the abstract regimes of force that organize and deploy them" (*Architectures* 84). In the intervening years, architecture has succumbed to the pressures of economical and technological constraints, and Elizabeth Tostrup rightly suggests that "one problem in contemporary architecture consists of not getting caught in the dissolving and mirroring illusions of technological supremacy, but of turning the focus back to the earth and dealing with the neglected realities of human needs" (170).

We find ourselves, then, between a (practical) rock and a (theoretical) hard place. On the one hand, we do not want to commit the sort of Kierkegaardian "untrue exaggeration" exemplified by Ibsen's *castle in the air* ("they are so easy to take refuge in"), nor do we want to cling to the ground in the name of not neglecting the "realities of human needs." It is not as simple as countering the *ground* with *air* or *water*, nor is this deconstructed landscape solely the province of newly sovereign subjects. Writing offshore designates classrooms of students as what Spivak terms "clusters of alterity" ("Decolonizing," my notes)—and what I submit are clusters of sub-urban provincials living not on the border between refinement and uncultivation, but in the interregnum between danger and persecution—in a word, *refugees*. In today's fractious geopolitical climate, new meaning (in *doublespeak*) has been given to refugees: "ambient noncombatant personnel" (Lutz 176). In today's reality, refugees are denied place, passage, and papers; and, if given land at all, they are often relegated to contaminated ground—*terra contagio*. In the space of this politico-juridical crime is the crux of a tested ambivalence, namely, the simultaneous desire to ground our pedagogy and our desire to reject the self-awarded subjectivity of the rational subject. But, as Spivak also suggests, if (in the classroom) we make disappear what we cannot desire (like Narcissus), then we disappear, too; and this is "the pharmakon that cannot be swallowed" ("Decolonizing")—or, the Jonah rejected by our erstwhile whale. This is the cantilever with which our abstract detachment, offshore trajectory, and rhetoric of the unbuilt can bridge the expanse between reason and refuge.

Refugees from Reason

> I need the sea
> my being as if on strike soundlessly cries out
> to come on it high above the road I
> want to stand on that rock which tells no lies and
> feel the grassgreen otherness making the mind reel
> see the wide slow gathering of a watershadow rising rising up into
> the wash the rush the clatter spreading down a beach
> hear the strangely comforting clicking of pebbles

One answer, then, to the question of what an architecture of trajectories would look like is: *a boat in an intensive zone.* The offshore world is as dangerous as it is sublime; but this is a *pharmakon* that we *must* swallow if we are to abide in the intensive zone between a deconstructed ground and the guarded question of our figurative offshore refuge. As such, I freely admit that my whale tourism experience is a far cry from the experience of hundreds of Afghan refugees who, that same summer, half a world away, bought passage on an Indonesian trawler only to end up frightened, cold, and wet, huddled on a sinking boat (two weeks prior to 9/11/01), while governments argued over who would rescue them, who would allow them entry, who would "process" them—these people *sans papier*, living without papers. A Norwegian cargo ship finally picked them up and, ignoring warnings against entering Australian territorial waters, did so anyway and gave them temporary sanctuary offshore from Christmas Island. In a letter to the Australian authorities, written while circling the island waiting for word about their status, the refugees wrote this:

> We request from Australian authorities and people, At first not to deprive us from the rights that all refugees enjoy in your country. And in the case of rejection due to not having anywhere to live on the earth and every moment death is threatening us. We request you to feel . . . for the life of (438) men, women and children. ("Boat People's Plea")

The Australian government later agreed to transfer the refugees to the tiny island of Nauru, the smallest independent nation, once a lush tropical island, now only a "barren refuge" (*terra contagio*). According to BBC News, "In 1899 a British prospecting company discovered that Nauru was nearly solid phosphate. Since then, phosphate mining has devastated the environment. Nauru's 'topside' is a barren landscape of gouged earth inhabited by packs of wild dogs" ("Pacific States"). Nauru is now notorious for its 400+ offshore banks, where it is estimated that over seventy billion dollars in funds generated by the Russian mafia have been handled.

There is no longer a rational explanation. The rose is without why. *Av måneskin gror det ingenting*—nothing grows in the moonlight, especially at sea. As in the case of the Afghan refugee crisis, we hardly need reminding that reason operates on every level of political, economic, and institutional power relations, including the critical intimacy that even the most radical teacher presumes shields him or her from the will-to-remarginalize the marginalized. Thus, let me quickly say that I am no less at risk of committing an act of *reason* by naming the *refugee* as the subject of an *unreason*able pedagogy and seeker of an *abstract* asylum. I offer, then, these perturbations (dist*urb*ing *urb*anity) as substitutes for what would otherwise be an unreasonable plea to frame our problem with a particularly abject approach. Other sectors of abject existence suggest equal exigency: nomad, gypsy, emigrant, evacuee, fugitive, expatriate, deportee, exile, diaspora. While the refugee maintains an affinity with other displaced people, he or she occupies a more *generic* condition affecting one's relation to home, land, and nation that crosses beyond other defining markers of marginalized people such as race, ethnicity, religion, class, and gender. The generic condition of abject forced mobility could happen to any of us, at any time. And in fact, the dissolution of ground metaphysics with which I have been concerned effectively throws us all into the sea, or on the move, in one fell swoop. *We are all boat people.*

Thus, I want to also concern us with the effects of this thrownness on our students, for whom forced mobility is constitutive of their constant moving from classroom to classroom, from pedagogy to pedagogy, from discipline to discipline, from technology to technology, from this settlement to that camp. Still, treading other cautionary waters, again siding with Spivak, requires us to "arrest the understandable need to fix and diagnose the identity of the most deserving marginal. . . . [and to also] suspend the mood of self-congratulation as saviors of marginality" (*Outside* 61). It *cannot* go without saying that removing the ground has profound implications for re-moving students into the murky waters of border politics. It also cannot go without saying that the "critical poetry of flow," movement, oscillation, trace, and becoming should not serve us too easily. We (academics) traffic in such migrant metaphors while right now, on some distant sea, desperate people drift on and on and on, in boats, on rafts—or line the borders of war-torn nations—against all odds of surviving. In "The Trouble with Borders," Aleksandra Wagner and Alexander Stein put a face to the problem.

> There is no "receiving country" on the horizon: the right to leave may be universal, but the right to enter is not. Thus the whole critical poetry of *flows* liberates borders for goods better than it does for people; goods and services flow, while people must stay in line. . . . The border is no longer a heroic spot; it is, rather, the space where so many people are. . . . [people described elegantly by Bharati Mukherjee] "[people] dressed in shreds of national costumes, out of season, the wilted plumage of intercontinental vagabondage. We ask only one thing: to be allowed to land; to pass through; to continue." (qtd in Wagner and Stein, n.p.; Bharati Mukherjee's *Jasmine*, 91)

Such poignant evocations of the refugee also remind us that *refugee* is not a *catechresis*, a sign for which there is no longer a literal referent, or an arbitrary abuse of the metaphor. Nor is the *refugee* an inflection of Burke's "representative anecdote" (*Grammar* 59), which holds that a selection of reality performs as a reflection of reality (in our case, that *refugee* performs as a reflection of *student writer*). It is, rather, a term that necessitates more of a reduction than even Burke would have predicted. It shares in what Giorgio Agamben calls the "materialization of the state of exception," the *camp*.[10] Striking at the heart of the *essence* of the concentration camps, Agamben suggests that

> it would be more honest, and above all more useful, to investigate carefully how—that is, thanks to what juridical procedures and political devices—human beings could have been so completely deprived of their rights and prerogatives to the point that committing any act toward them would no longer appear as a crime. (*Means* 40.1)

In Agamben's terms, the camp's inhabitants "*have been stripped of every political status and reduced completely to naked life*" (40.1).

Placing the birth of the *camp* as a phenomenon of "our time," Agamben also marks its birth as a rupture forming in the structure of the modern nation-state, "founded on the functional nexus between a determinate localization (territory) and a determinate order (the state), which was mediated by automatic regulations for the inscription of life (birth or nation)" (42.3). What defines this rupture is that this political system "enters a period of permanent crisis and the state decides to undertake the management of the biological life of the nation directly as its own task" (42.3). In essence, it takes place not in the aspects that previously constituted it (territory and order),

> but rather at the site in which naked life is inscribed in them (that is, there where inscription turns *birth* into *nation*). There is something that no longer functions in the traditional mechanisms that used to regulate this inscription, and the camp is the new hidden regulator of the inscription of life in the order—or, rather, it is the sign of the system's inability to function without transforming itself into a lethal machine. (42.3)

The "materialization of the state of exception," (i.e., the camp), "intended as a dislocating localization is the hidden matrix of the politics in which we still live, and we must learn to recognize it in all of its metamorphoses" (44). In his most disturbing analysis, Agamben fears that an "even more extreme" form of the camps has recently reappeared in the former Yugoslavia, where there has been not just your ordinary run-of-the-mill "redefinition of the old political system according to new ethnic and territorial arrangements" (44).

> Rather, we note there an irreparable rupture of the old *nomos* as well as a dislocation of populations and human lives according to entirely new lines of flight. That is why the camps of ethnic rape are so crucially important. If the Nazis never thought of carrying out the "final solution" by impregnating Jewish women, that is because the principle of birth, which ensured the inscription of life in the order of the nation-state, was in some way still functioning, even though it was profoundly transformed. This principle is now adrift: it has entered a process of dislocation in which its functioning is becoming patently impossible and in which we can expect not only new camps but also always new and more delirious normative definitions of the inscription of life in the city. The camp, which is now firmly settled inside it, is the new biopolitical *nomos* of the planet. (44–44.5)

What differentiates the "rape camps" in Bosnia from the long history of rape as a byproduct of war is that in this instance the Serbian conquerors of Bosnia were *ordered* to rape Muslim women as a principle tactic of war (Gutman; Vranic). In an interview about her book, *Breaking the Wall of Silence*, Seada Vranic explains that because there is no genetic difference between Bosnian Muslims and Serbs, other strategies of ethnic cleansing emerged. According to Vranic, "behind it all lay just one idea: to expel the population of other nationalities from a given territory. Rape is a very effective means for that purpose: if three or four raped women arrived in a village, all the villagers would quickly take flight. They couldn't kill everybody, you see." It is hard to find a more compelling example of Agamben's "materialization of the state of exception," a flagrant instance of which marked people who "have been stripped of every political status and reduced completely to *naked life*." In Agamben's account, we hear echoed Heidegger's thought concerning the *unconcealedness* of Being. Keeping in mind our *refugee*, we will take her through a poetic self-reflection that, in Heidegger's terms, understands Being as the "gathering release" and "flinging loose" of beings into "the daring venture" ("Poets" 101). We will, with Heidegger, confront her not as naked in the narrow sense of disrobed, nor in the generic sense of revealed, but in the fullest notion of life as "that which arises" and, as a consequence, that which is unshielded yet upheld because it hangs (daringly) in the balance (101–3).

We have already witnessed Heidegger's critique of ground metaphysics in which he accuses philosophy, as a thing of reason, of being oblivious of the fact that things do not depend on human justification; they emerge before us on their own ("the rose is without why"). Now, it is important to gather into our trajectory Heidegger's meditation on the nature of Being as disclosed in his reading of a short, improvised verse from Rainer Maria Rilke. In some sense, we are tracking Heidegger's critique of reason and ground metaphysics metaleptically, that is, having worked through (briefly) his later thought in *Der Satz vom Grund* (1957) and now pondering an earlier examination of Being's ground in an essay written in 1946 on the occasion of the twentieth anniversary of Rilke's death. In this way, we are, to expound on the nature of *metalepsis*, sending this fragment through time by means of a metaleptic transference. Such an approach mirrors Heidegger's own method of "trans-lation" of the various fragments of pre-Socratic philosophers, which, according to Herman Rapaport, functions by "describing the wear and tear of words which act upon the fragment through time by way of tran-scribing the trans-scriptions, or of trans-lating the trans-lations" (30).

In Rapaport's account, Heidegger's critique of philosophy via translation and transcription forms the basis for his notion of *destruction*, which means "to open our ears, to make ourselves free for what speaks to us in tradition as the Being of being (*Sein des seienden*). By listening to this interpellation we attain the correspondence (*Entsprechung*)" ("What Is Philosophy?" 69–71; qtd in Rapaport 32). Heidegger's two modalities will later be called by Derrida *deconstruction*.

Derrida, however, describes Heidegger's tactics a bit differently. Unhappy with Heidegger's demystification of the term *Geist* (spirit) in *Being and Time* and his rehabilitation of the term much later in his rector's address, Derrida notices that Heidegger is in the habit of "putting terms under watch or arrest—an imprisonment or quarantining of terms—that is at a later time lifted so that these terms can undergo a rehabilitation or reappropriation" (Rappaport 158). I bring this to our attention to advance the notion that in both "What are Poets For?" and *Der Satz vom Grund* Heidegger puts the term *ground* under quarantine in order to rehabilitate it when he calls *Being* the *ground* of all grounds, and he does so in both places through analyses of poetic language. As we learned earlier, there are problems associated with Heidegger's usage of "rootedness" (*Bodenständigkeit*) in his mystical passages on the "play of Being." If, however, we place under quarantine his use of rootedness in order to learn more about his quarantine of the term "ground," we can (perhaps) hear Caputo's analysis more favorably, namely, that for Heidegger, "the true 'ground' of human existence is Being itself" (*Mystical* 58). As Caputo has it, in Heidegger's leap of thought,

> which we will learn to make by listening to Leibniz's principle more carefully, we will arrive at a new ground, a new rootedness which is Being itself, although to metaphysical reason this ground must needs appear as an "abyss." In so doing we will attain a new way of thinking which is not confined to "giving reasons." (58)

In order to prepare us to hear the plea of the Afghan refugees in a new light ("And in the case of rejection due to not having anywhere to live on the earth and every moment death is threatening us. We request you to feel . . . for the life of (438) men, women and children."), it is necessary to understand the degree to which we are unprepared for confronting their "naked life" from *inside* the same realm in which their unshieldedness puts them at risk. It is also necessary to understand that we share equally in Rilke's prescient recognition that Nature "grants none special cover" (qtd in Heidegger's "Poets" 102)—*equally* with the Bosnian rape victims in Vranic's report, such as "the testimony of a woman from Rogatica, a village in eastern Bosnia: her two daughters, four granddaughters and four daughters-in-law had been raped, and the rest of the family burnt alive in their house." I know this is hard; it is impossible. It is (nevertheless) necessary to implicate the poet in our face-to-face with these ravaged "clusters of alterity"—to stand over their same abyss and give ourselves over to what Heidegger terms the "flinging loose" that (nevertheless) "gathers everything in the play of the venture" ("Poets" 105). To press together words like *ravaged* and *play* is the hard thing. To ponder, deeply, the sheer violence of the *relation* we are establishing between ravaging and venturing—this is the hardest thing. Whereas Rilke speaks of turning our unshieldedness into the *Open* and thereby affirming it, "to read the word 'death' without negation" (125), Heidegger puts it in terms of living Being: "The hard thing is to accomplish existence" (138).

That is why it is useful to look closely at how Heidegger begins his essay, the timing of which is not insignificant (1946). In the first sentence Heidegger puts us directly into the conversation of poetry: "' . . . and what are poets for in a destitute time?' asks Hölderlin's elegy 'Bread and Wine.' We hardly understand the question today" (91). Heidegger sets forth an ambitious, yet simple, poetic trajectory: to turn mortals around to face (and experience and endure) the abyss (the Open), then to identify those mortals who reach sooner into the abyss, the poets, and thus effect the return of the gods. For Heidegger, our foremost danger in this destitute time lies in the withdrawal of the holy, "hale and whole" (115), from our understanding and health. Thus, he tenders, the "world becomes without healing, unholy" (117). In this light one option becomes most urgent; we must depend on certain mortals (the poets) to see "the threat of the unhealable, the unholy, *as* such" (117). This means that

> they would have to discern the danger that is assailing man. The danger consists in the threat that assaults man's nature in his relation to Being itself, and not in accidental perils. This danger is *the* danger. It conceals itself in the abyss that underlies all beings. To see this danger and point it out, there must be mortals who reach sooner into the abyss. (117)

It seems, then, that we are in greatest danger *not* from accidental (or worldly) perils, but from being turned away from (and against) that relation into which we have been born and into which we are destined: Being itself.

The nature of our destitute time rests in the following formulation: "Mortals have not yet come into ownership of their own nature. Death withdraws into the enigmatic. The mystery of pain remains veiled. Love has not been learned. But the mortals *are*" (96). And they *are* insofar as "there is language" (96). Essentially, what Rilke terms "the Open" (99) bears a resemblance to what (elsewhere) he calls "the globe of being," and is reflected in the verses we have been following by the phrase "in widest orbit somewhere" (124). Heidegger refers us to a letter of 1923 in which Rilke says that "like the moon, so life surely has a side that is constantly turned away from us, and that is not its opposite but its completion to perfection, to plenitude, to the real, whole, and full sphere and globe of being" (124). The turn, or conversion, that Heidegger draws out in Rilke's verse consists in our converting the unshieldedness of standing apart from the Open into the unshieldedness of standing in the widest orbit. And this is what poets are for.

Poets are on the track "leading to the trace" of the fugitive gods, who, having failed to arrive, are (nevertheless) waiting for beings to turn toward the realm of their ground, and who do not reach as far into the abyss as mortals because mortals are "touched by presence, the ancient name of Being" (93). The poet is the one who, being the most capable, is able "to say worldly existence, to say out of the haleness of the whole pure draft and to say only this" (138). By putting us into the conversation of poetry, Heidegger is not conducting some academic exercise designed to preserve the realm of letters for the educated elite; rather, he brings us all into proximity with our own Nature, the ground of our being, Being itself. Poets, he whispers, sing the song of existence. They are, to cite Rilke's verse, "'more daring by a breath'" (139). This breath is "another breath, a saying other than the rest of human saying" (140). To further impress upon us the singular significance of *this* breath, Heidegger quotes Johan Gottfried Herder.

> "A breath of our mouth becomes the portrait of the world, the type of our thoughts and feelings in the other's soul. On a bit of moving air depends everything human that men on earth have ever thought, willed, done, and ever will do; for we would all still be roaming the forests if this divine breath had not blown around us, and did not hover on our lips like a magic tone." (139)

In one breath, Heidegger (via Rilke, Hölderlin, and Herder) lets us in on a secret. "It is not for nothing," he writes, "that the words 'more daring by a breath' are followed in the original by three dots. The dots tell the secret" (140).[11] Just as he opens the essay by drawing us into the conversation of poetry, he ends by leading us out with poetic language, which is not the end of life, but the beginning of our ability to hear what the poet has to say for *us*—what *must* be said *for* us: "that which this way never lapses into the flux of perishing, overcomes from the start all perishability. . . . What is presumed to be eternal merely conceals a suspended transiency, suspended in the void of a durationless now" (142).

Having ventured such a rapid sketch of Heidegger's thought, I feel now that we are better prepared to hear Rilke's "improvised verses," which have provided each link in the gathering of Heidegger's answer to the question "what are poets for?" But I leave them to their own saying/singing of the song of Being, believing I could scarcely improve on Heidegger's reading. These verses were inscribed in a volume of Rilke's book of poems, *Malte*, given by him to Baron Lucious.

> As Nature gives the other creatures over
> to the venture of their dim delight
> and in soil and branchwork grants none special cover,
> so too our being's pristine ground settles our plight;
> we are no dearer to it; it ventures us.
> Except that we, more eager than plant or beast,
> go *with* this venture, will it, adventurous
> more sometimes than Life itself is, more daring
> by a breath (and not in the least
> from selfishness). . . . There, outside all caring,
> this creates for us a safety—just there,
> where the pure forces' gravity rules; in the end,
> it is our unshieldedness on which we depend,
> and that, when we saw it threaten, we turned it
> so into the Open that, in widest orbit somewhere,
> where the Law touches us, we may affirm it.
>
> (qtd in Heidegger "Poets" 99)

Thus far we have *scarcely* issued a reading that can *properly* stand beside the *refugee* without addressing the incongruity of poetizing in the face of their immediate and devastating dangers. Some will no doubt view it as absolutely inhospitable, certainly unreasonable. It is, however, more than a question of what is proper; it is the province of the ethics of irreducible translation and the politics of intellectual courage. What cannot be translated (their pain, loss, suffering, fear, raw terror), *must*. What should not be legislated, *must not*.[12] In the space of this *aporia* is an *other* means of intervention, a deconstructive move we will call *(t)reason*.

Committing (T)reason

> I need
> to be consoled by the rush of my own smallness
> to swim my soul awhile in the pure space let it go adrift
> where one wave can hide the shore

In the heady days of deconstruction before the discovery of Paul de Man's wartime journalism in the early eighties, there was ample cachet in donning the garb of deconstruction's *metaphysical homelessness*. In the intervening years, it has undergone a crisis of legitimation that undermined (unfortunately) its ability to *read* ethico-political issues as effectively as readings undertaken within the sphere of (and in the name of) *practical reason*. Reason begat reason and falsely accused deconstruction of not living up to the rules and structures it sought to implode, spawning illegitimate descriptions of deconstruction held to standards and models defined solely by reason. But, Donna Haraway reminds us, "illegitimate offspring are often exceedingly unfaithful to their origins" (151). Thus, rather than deconstruction refusing the ill-conceived moniker of illegitimacy, it commits an act of *(t)reason* by putting *legitimacy* under quarantine (as we saw in Heidegger) in order to pressurize the realm of decidability so cleanly ruled by the lockstep "jackboots" of reason. The *(t)reason* we have in mind, however, is not defined by some exchange of state secrets (as in a spy game); rather, it is an affirmative act of betrayal, a leading astray. It is a material abstraction caught in the act of detachment.

While *(t)reason* is no mere benign form of treachery, neither is it a destructive agent hell-bent on some secret mission. According to Caputo, deconstruction is "not some stealthy, cunning agent of disruption, is not an agent at all," rather it "simply [passes] the word along that one is rather more on one's own than one likes to think" (*Against* 4). Far from being anethical and apolitical, Caputo explains,

> Deconstruction shows how a film of undecidability creeps quietly over the clarity of decisions, on cat-soft paws, clouding judgment just ever so much, so that we cannot quite make out the figures all around us. But do not be mistaken. *Deconstruction offers no excuse not to act. . . .* Undecidability does not detract from the urgency of decision; it simply underlines the difficulty. (4, emphasis mine)

Addressed to the refugee, then, pressing matters not only demand pressing actions, they must first (and continuously) demand *pressing* readings. It is a question Derrida addressed in his essay "On Cosmopolitanism," delivered in 1996 to the International Parliament of Writers, which formed the nexus of a network of asylum sites called *cities of refuge*. As with Diane Elam ("groundless solidarity") and Gayatri Spivak ("revolutions that as yet have no model"), Derrida joins in the call for cities of refuge that are "each as independent from the other and from the state as possible, but, nevertheless, allied to each other according to forms of solidarity yet to be invented" (*Cosmopolitanism* 4).

In this context rhetoric not only shares the burden of such urgency, it is poised to constitute a form of refuge as well. When histories of rhetoric are viewed through the lens of refuge, it is not difficult to discern this shadow trajectory. Thus, Derrida's call for "forms of solidarity yet to be invented," achieves a stronger rhetorical bite when he says that "this invention is our task; the theoretical or critical reflection it involves is *indissociable* from the practical initiatives we have already, out of a sense of urgency, initiated and implemented" (4, emphasis mine). Derrida's *(t)reason* consists in probing the dual concepts of hospitality and cosmopolitanism, and doing so in the face of the "multiplicity of menaces, of acts of censorship (*censure*) or of terrorism, of persecutions and of enslavements in all their forms" (5). Seeking neither to lapse into the "compulsory rhetoric of electoral programmes" (12), nor the "rhetorical alibis" lurking in the discourse on *opportunistic* refugees, Derrida understands that one must keep an eye on the conflation of the economic and political, of the status of the refugee and the political immigrant (12). One must, for example, recognize the "tendency to obstruct" by the states in the European Union, which "under the pretext of combating economic immigrants purporting to be exiles from political persecution . . . reject[s] applications for the right to asylum more often than ever" (13).

Common sense tells us that the everyday conflation should not measure up to the efforts of countless countermeasures launched every day along the lines of Derrida's reconceived notion of hospitality, most notably among groups such as "Doctors without Borders," "Women on Waves,"[13] and other humanitarian transsovereign initiatives. Unfortunately, there is a commonplace perception that thinking and writing (especially of the sort in which Derrida is engaged) pale by comparison with the practices of such groups. But should we distinguish between one form of courage (action) and another *intellectual* courage (virtual)? In an interview appropriately titled "Intellectual Courage," Derrida tackles the question head on. Asked whether intellectuals can "take courage again" because of then-recent elections in Great Britain and France (i.e., the new parliamentary majorities for the Labour and Socialist Parties), Derrida replied,

> Certainly they can permit us to hope for a more vigilant political and social resistance to the economism and monetarism which tends to dominate the new European spirit. But the "pragmatic realism" claimed by these two governments risks reproducing exactly what they pretend to interrupt. . . . I perceive at most nuances of adjustment, rhetorical changes (and that is not nothing), but no rupture with the immediate past.

Asked whether the "left" is "too occupied with questions of cultural identity and of having forgotten questions of social justice," Derrida restates the question, asking

> why must one choose between the care for cultural identity and the worry about social justice? They are both questions of justice, two responses to anti-egalitarian oppression or violence. No doubt it is very hard to lead both of these debates in the same rhythm, but one can fight both fronts, cultural and social, at the same time, as it were, and one must do so. The task of the intellectual is to say this, to mediate the discourses and to elaborate strategies that resist any simplistic choice between the two.

Derrida's participation in the International Parliament of Writers' Cities of Refuge project extends, also, to the IPW e-journal, *Autodafe* (The Censored Library). In his piece on "Displaced Literatures," Derrida outlines the stakes of writing for those who are denied the right "to choose their place, to move about freely." (Notable examples are the fatwa issued against Salman Rushdie and the assassination of Algerian writer Tahar Djaout.)

> A new literary space has been opened up and its stakes are less than ever confined, today, to philosophy or science, to poetics or literary theory, in an abstract form, a classical or not-so-classical form. The displacements we will have to talk about are also becoming (and there are too many examples of this) questions of life or death. Every day it is the body of languages, the body of works, and the body of writers that are at stake.

Whether arrested, under surveillance, or confined to a cell, Derrida writes, these writers live with the constant threat of imprisonment, torture, execution, or assassination. In these dire straits, rhetoric may be their only refuge. Derrida underscores my point: "In order to accede to the daylight of the public space, in the muffled resistance of a clandestine or cryptic literature, it also happens that still other places, the 'commonplaces' of rhetoric this time, become the ultimate recourse for tricking the censor." Recognizing that this is nothing new in the history of literature, Derrida acknowledges that these questions "demand that we take account of the most ancient resources," even though these forbidden places exist "well beyond the academic example of 'Plato-and-the-poets-driven-out-of-the-city.'"

Rhetoric *as* refuge rearticulates the paths of the poets and illuminates their abstract trajectories. Displacing argument is rhetoric's supreme task; disinventing *logos* is rhetoric's sacred duty. Rhetoric and composition theorists on the fringe have voiced similar manifestos in recent years, yet their rejections of argumentation pedagogy have too often been perceived as having infringed upon the hallowed ground of critical thinking and are, finally, relegated to the ranks of renegade rhetorics, Show me a mainstream composition textbook that teaches Greg Ulmer's *Heuretics* (1993), a trajectory in which he ventured that "this difference in 'logics' is the point of departure for imagining what a new rhetoric will do that does not argue but that replaces the logic governing argumentative writing with associational networks" (18). Find me a Braddock award-winning article that reports on classroom practices based on Geoff Sirc's "Writing Classroom as A&P Parking Lot" (first appearing in *Pre/Text* in 1993, but also in *English Composition as a Happening*, 2002), which ended with a quote from Bataille (mirrored in the opening epigraph to this chapter): "'It is too late to be reasonable and educated—which has led to a life without appeal. Secretly or not, it is necessary to become completely different, or to cease being'" (Sirc 233). Supply me with the syllabus that is fashioned upon Lynn Worsham's refashioned view of "writing as a strategy. . . . whose progress yields 'unlearning'" ("Writing" 101). Tell me a *mystory* of composition theory that decants Victor Vitanza's "paralogic pedagogy," a *moratoria* montage that drifted our way in 1991 ("Three Countertheses"). Read me the job description for chair of an English department who would hire faculty such as Diane Davis, a rhetorician whose laughter both literally and figuratively breaks up totalities that would reconstitute *community ad nauseum* across the great divide between rhetoric and literature. Each is consubstantial (I believe) with Vitanza's desire to reconceive argument as "*dissoi paralogi.*"

> Argument in this modification is not a means of achieving or accounting for consensus. It is, instead, a means of continuous "dissensus"; it "counterhopes" to achieve an occasional, if not permanent, place of misology (i.e., a distrust of *logos*), a place that Plato and Socrates saw as anathema (*Phaedo* 89dl–90c7) but that must be seen as the beginning of what Deleuze and Guattari would call a "nomadology" (*Thousand* 351–423) or what Montaigne and Lyotard combined would see as "just drifting/gaming." It is a place outside the philosophical and rhetorical polis; it is places (exploded and) realized through diaspora/dispersion. It is the *pagus*. ("Three" 165)

Into these *un*commonplaces I submit *rhetoric as refuge*, *writer as refugee*, and *abstract* pedagogy.

In the proximity of such "counterhope" (which is *not* the lack of hope, despair) we can scarcely overestimate the value of setting up (and setting going) a telling congruity between the seemingly incongruous terms: destitution and institution. In this setting forth, there must be a move that *sets off* what has disabled the field from seeing its complicity in the pragmatic disenfranchisement of the kind of intellectual work represented by the aforementioned scholars (among others). What Sirc identifies as the disenchantment of composition is (quite possibly) also a blatant co-option of despair, a wresting away of the lack of hope from those who most define it and *an institutionalization of desperation* in the guise of critical pedagogy. It seems that while we have been preoccupied with injecting composition theory with the more urgent *pharmakoi* of ideology, cultural criticism, and process pedagogy, a quiet desperation has settled over our field. The odd thing is that we have come to love and nurture it, even *will* it, because we need the "discourse of needs" (Crowley) upon which it is grounded; and, it supplies a convenient rationale for force-feeding argumentation to our un/sophisticated "clusters of alterity" on a daily basis. We seem to have established (instituted) deprivation (destitution) as our *reason* for teaching *reason*. It has become the scapegoat tethered to the stake in the center of our village, and we feed it and nurture it until such time as the sacrifice is necessary—until our pedagogical despair becomes unbearable—until we are so desperate that we find new grounds for our despair, new reasons for sustaining despair as our *raison d'etre*.

Here is my tiny *(t)reason*. On April Fool's Day 1983, the dean of liberal arts at the University of Texas at Arlington, Thomas E. Porter, submitted an ambitious proposal to the National Endowment for the Humanities to establish "a lower-division undergraduate sequence of courses that integrate composition, text analysis and critical thinking (CACTIP)" (Porter).[14] Fueled by a collaborative approach to teaching composition, and a marriage between philosophy and rhetoric, the proposal was accepted, implemented, and largely successful in its initial phase. Over thirty years later, the program is dead, the result of what many involved believe was the steady poisoning of rhetoric with the principle of reason. Others believe it was the other way around. Regardless of which version is the correct diagnosis, to read the proposal rationale is to glimpse the symptoms of a "gathering danger" (to borrow the language of a desperate political ruse for going to war), and to hear the death rattle of an *unquiet* (collective) desperation. It was, for its time, considered far ahead of its time. It represented the most advanced theories and practices in composition pedagogy, and mirrored the clarion call around the country for more integrated approaches to literacy education. In the rationale we are told that

> when the instructor in History 303 tells his [*sic*] class to "write a paper on the causes of the First Punic War," the odds are that most of the essays he receives, even from the so-called better students, will be semi-literate. Errors in mechanics—grammar, spelling, syntax—will be only the tip of the iceberg. The substance of the presentations is likely to contain global generalizations, gratuitous opinions, free associations, non-sequiturs and semantic approximations. Considering the range of deficiencies, the instructor correcting the papers will have a difficult time deciding where to begin. After a few such experiences, the instructor may decide to forgo

> essay assignments. When one considers the complex of abilities the student must exercise to fulfill the typical "paper" assignment decently, it is no wonder that students quail and instructors are tempted to despair. . . . In 1974 a publication of the Associations of Departments of English stated: "we are faced with an increasingly desperate attempt to overcome the semi-literacy of most incoming students, who have had little or no practice in reading and writing." (8)

Year after year, English departments (or their counterparts) in colleges and universities across the United States pen similar reports for a variety of reasons: to seek funding, to revamp composition programs, to respond to mandated writing assessments, to construct strategic plans, to create curriculum, to justify hiring new faculty, and so forth.

In a white paper issued from the Center for Communication in Science, Technology, and Management at North Carolina State University, the authors found similar attitudes about teaching composition dating back to the late nineteenth century. "For example, the Harvard Overseers commissioned four reports in the 1890s about the 'composition problem'—that is, the poor quality of student writing and the 'mental drudgery of the most exhausting nature' required to read and evaluate student writing" (qtd in Carter et al). "One teacher in 1903 voiced the feelings of many even today: 'I thank God I have been delivered from the bondage of theme-work into the glorious liberty of literature'" (Connors; qtd in Carter et al).

Such high-minded desperation echoes what Lester Faigley discovered in his analysis of Vopat and Coles's textbook, *What Makes Writing Good*, namely, that while contemporary methodologies employed in teaching writing are at odds with the kind of writing that teachers value, standards of judgment in composition have not shifted significantly from those valued by the field during the 1930s.[15] Faigley cites "a 1931 report of an external review of the College Entrance Examination Board's 1929 English examination" (*Fragments* 114). According to the commission (published by Harvard UP and comprised of professors from Harvard, Yale, Cornell, Vassar, among others), "the goal of teaching writing . . . 'is not the mere composition of some indefinite entity known as "a theme." [The student] must understand that true originality will be the result of discriminating and vigorous perception and thought'" (Commission 185; qtd in Faigley 118).

Such sentiments, voiced variously by noted professors since the late 1800s until today, fit squarely within Sirc's characterization of the field mentioned at the outset: "Composition Studies as a perpetual scene of disenchantment" (12). The striking thing in current debates about teaching argument is that there seems to be no question that teaching argument is necessary. Disputes revolve more around which methods, which heuristic strategies, and which modes are best suited to teaching students how to construct effective written arguments. Occasionally we have seen efforts to stem the power of argumentative tactics, or to question the gendered nature of agonistic styles of inquiry; but for the most part, argument remains the cornerstone of composition pedagogy, and reason remains the earth beneath. Far from being seen as refuge in this scenario, rhetoric is more like a bunker from which reason may be volleyed with greater accuracy and force—teaching students that positioning matters more than thought, and reason more than distance sought.[16] Our collective *(t)reasons* will be necessary to dismantle this edifice. Our collective trajectories will be more effective if deployed in a quaquaversal—omnidirectional, in every direction at once. There are indications the work has begun. Sirc hopes to

> put pressure on Compositions' canon, recalibrating the field according to a general economy of the compositional arts—a destabilized site of various competing schools, undercut by an on-going, productive tension between the academic and the avant-garde: to liberate thinking in our field from the strictly semantic, re-opening Composition as a site where radical explorations are appreciated, where aesthetic criteria still come into play, but criteria not merely cribbed off an endless, formalist tape-loop. (32)

Ours is an *other* tape-loop.

There is no longer a rational explanation. The rose is without why. Av måneskin gror det ingenting—nothing grows in the moonlight. We are all boat people. The question is how to speak the language of boat people and refugees (a language not ruled by the sovereignty of ground logic) and how to unbuild the logic of containment,[17] the camp.

Infiltration

In Vitanza's "Three Countertheses," in which he suggests a "moratorium on attempting to turn theory into praxis/pedagogy" (160), he also cuts to the crux of the matter with the following inauspicious declaration: "What we want is a way to proceed without foundations and without criteria (the first counterthesis) and without knowing as a subject (the second) and without conventional theory and pedagogy (the third)" (165). The following series of links are offered as consubstantial *ad hoc* suggestions, staying true to my desire to remain *suggestive*. We need the sea, and so must cast off the principle of reason. We must take the leap, glance off the ground if only to keep the dance in motion. We must take off the garb of the *flâneur* and leave the *topos* of the street. We must unbuild our ground metaphysics and establish cities of refuge, instant cities, walking cities. We must take to the rooftops and wailing walls and sinking boats, heed the call of the poets drawing us out to sea. We must un-define our despair and undo the institutionalization of destitution in the name of the refugee, against whom we must neither argue nor teach argument. We must dispossess our monopoly on abstraction and teach it to our students to help them detach from us, from the teaching machine, the "huge pedagogical apparatus." We must be (t)reasonous. We must be intensive and hospitable; we must be without why. We must let them pass through, let them write rhetorically—in the safety and refuge of fathomed havens (Old Norse > *hav* > the sea).

Thus, as my concluding gesture I bring Ann Berthoff's "abstraction as a speculative instrument" to further deconstruct composition's unrelenting rush to reason. In the early 1980s, the central debates in composition pedagogy were shifting (cf. Maxine Hairston's "The Winds of Change") rapidly in reaction to a number of theoretical influences ranging from research in cognitive psychology, poststructuralist theory, ethnography, social constructivist theory, psychoanalytic theory, and feminist theory, among others (see Faigley, *Fragments* 25–47). Clearly the field was inundated with speculative theories, and some took hold more so than others. One that failed in the long term to capture a foothold was Ann Berthoff's work on "abstraction as a speculative instrument." In her article of the same name, published in the collection, *The Territory of Language*, Berthoff rightly observed that "abstraction is rarely well defined as a term and the complex concept it names is not generally well formed. For some, abstraction is a power of mind to be encouraged and trained; for others; it is a stylistic fault to be avoided" (227). Berthoff goes on to explain why the "distrust of abstraction in current rhetorical theory is more fundamentally an epistemological matter" (228). When language is viewed as a "map for the territory of reality, the Ladder of Abstraction," the linguistic perspective considers abstraction "to be hazardous" (228). The problem occurs when abstraction and generalization becomes conflated by positivists. Berthoff wishes to redefine their relation and argues that "generalization requires abstraction, but we can have abstraction without generalization" (229). Her point is that models such as S. I. Hayakawa's "ladder of abstraction" are an inadequate means of accounting for nondiscursive elements of abstraction, such as imagination, mythic ideation, context, perspective, purpose, poetics, and other holistic activities (228, 230). Working instead from Susanne Langer's notion of "direct insight," Berthoff recasts abstraction as "the recognition of form; as the symbolic representation of our recognitions" (229). But Berthoff not only theorized that abstraction benefits the process of composing, she put her theories into practice in her textbook, *Forming/Thinking/Writing* (1982).

John Clifford explains that Berthoff's textbook "embodies a philosophy of composition" because she "takes seriously her call to weld philosophical frames of reference to classroom techniques" (331). Students are encouraged "to be reflective as they look for relationships in paragraphs as diverse as those of Gertrude Stein, William Blake, and Claude Lévi-Strauss" (331). But, Clifford is concerned that "the mental gymnastics needed for this kind of composing is heady and demanding" (331). Students will become disoriented and frustrated. Thus, he writes, "Berthoff is taking a calculated pedagogical risk through her optimistic leap of faith about the forming abilities of the mind" (332). As we saw in Heidegger's leap, for which he was criticized because he had not passed through the "trial of reason" (Caputo, *Mystical* 42), Berthoff's leap also involves a discontinuity; it, too, is accomplished without a bridge, that is, without propositional logic. Clifford sympathizes with Berthoff's frustration when "seemingly broad-minded theorists . . . refuse to see how far from shore we can drift on theoretical currents" (338). Obviously, composition theory has drifted on many theoretical currents in the two decades since Berthoff's work and Clifford's subsequent assessment of it. Yet we have not drifted far enough away from the disappearing coastline for more than small recoiling bursts; and, in fact, we seem to have moved farther inland with each recoil. If, however, we refashion and extend Berthoff's *abstract* trajectory, drawing from Heidegger and Eckhart's more originary conception of *abstraction* as *detachment* (*das Abgeschiedene*) instead, we set up the conditions of possibility for writing nomadically—as refugees from reason.

Such writing would not, however, diminish the urgency of teaching students the *relation* of language to decision-making, nor would it circumvent the necessity of teaching rhetoric in the interest of resolving problems simply by abandoning a pedagogy grounded in reason. Our task would be to teach an *inflected* rhetoric, that is, a redirected course of writing.[18] In the retraction from reason we would rethink our contract with reason and reflect on reason's sway. Abstraction would be a shuttling between retraction and contraction. Some may assume teaching abstraction involves teaching higher-order thinking; but we are not after reinventing the hierarchies of Hayakawa's "ladder of abstraction." Some examples of rethinking our current vocabulary: "taking a position" would become *testing contradistinctions*. Advancing a course of action through writing would replace the formulaic problem/solution argument. Shoring up one's argument would become distilling objections to one's abstraction. The diverse senses of converting argumentation pedagogy to teaching abstraction could also include teaching how to achieve distance, to detach from one's preconceptions, distill concepts, condense language, and translate meanings. Learning to abstract would involve learning the alluring nature of language, how it draws you away, how it seduces you. Rendering abstract ideas would entail understanding the problem of representation, its rhetorical role in homogenizing difference. Writing in the abstract also suggests learning the rhetorical device of brevity and the rhetorical power of the *aphorism*. Teaching the value of exploring something in the abstract, without practical purpose or intention, would return composition pedagogy to its *sophistic ethos* (we dare not say *roots*). In other words, finding new touchstones means leaving touchstones behind. It means plumbing the depths of abstraction. It means ob/literating the ground.

at times I need this deep
forgive me

5
Glitch Rhetoric

Gulzar e-Hijri, Pakistan

At first he appears nervous, but he speaks in his own words. Then he reads something scripted, like a robot, and he is afraid. There are Arabic words in one corner of the screen. And unspeakable images in the other. You brace yourself. Your heart is pounding. You pray. You pray hard. Then death. The harrowing of all humanity in *a split second*. Then the glitch happened. The cameraman got too close, and the camera jammed. They had to start again. I had to watch. I had to know, I told myself. I had to test my convictions about peace. I had to know the meaning of peace, and the peace of meaning. I was *affected*. As Roland Barthes puts it, "affect was what I didn't want to reduce. . . . I wanted to explore it not as a question (a theme) but as a wound" (21). I had to know whether peace *advocates*. Whether peace has a voice at all. Whether advocacy is a turn toward hope or just another futile trope against death. In his case, a gentle journalist caught in the crosshairs of human depravity, it not only turned toward death—it took out language, the last outpost of blood and breath. His last words were, "My father is Jewish, my mother is Jewish, I am Jewish." The last sound he hears is "the motion of the knife as it approaches his throat. He hears a rustle in the air next to him and realizes the [executioner] is practicing" (Lévy 42). His name was Daniel Pearl.[1]

Now this video file sits on my computer desktop like some visual rhetoric exercise about snuff movies, a guided reading of real-world texts. I have tried to drag it to the trash, but I cannot bring myself to carry out such a symbolic act. I cannot unwrite Daniel Pearl from my random memories. I cannot erase those images. I cannot stop hearing those words. I cannot write these words fast enough. I cannot lose that language uttered under unspeakable conditions, written by unholy men—as Bernard-Henri Lévy says, "a video playing in a loop in the militant shock mosques" (451). I cannot stop listening for the switch in style, his sentences, their sentences. His code, their code. I cannot write *here* without projecting his voice into *this* chapter: "My father is Jewish, my mother is Jewish, I am Jewish." Forcibly uttered in the insipid style of clarity, brevity, and sincerity, yet these words castrate clarity, bastardize brevity, and turn to sacrilege the virtue of sincerity. I am the improper receiver of a sacrament. I am writing in the twin styles of propaganda and blasphemy. I am *not* at peace here. So I reach for words to still the tremor in my hand, and I imagine a day when peace is in style—when patriotism does not mean "holier than thou." Kenneth Burke explains what I experienced.

> Often, to "charge" his work Symbolically, a writer strains to imagine some excessive horror, not because he is especially addicted to such imaginings, but because the prevalence of similar but less extreme Symbols has impaired their effectiveness. . . . If he would avoid the procedure, he must Symbolize new patterns, or use new modes of experience in the Symbolizing of old patterns, or attempt to increase accuracy and range. . . . Or if a writer so arranges his plot that the words "I am here" [or I am Jewish] have a pronounced bearing upon the course of his story, the utterance of these simple words may have a tremendous influence upon the audience. Consider, in Racine's *Iphigénie*, the speech of Arcas, when he enters to announce that the time for Iphigenia's sacrifice is at hand. (*Counter-Statement* 164–65)

Here Burke recounts the scapegoat part of the myth, in which Agamemnon had tapped his daughter Iphigenia for sacrifice, not for marriage as she had been led to believe. A story also told by Hélène Cixous in a New York taxicab on her way to a play. As Cixous tells it,

> I told [the driver] the story of the famous warrior king whose wife assassinates him the very day he returns victorious, as a punishment for their daughter's assassination, whose throat the king, in spite of himself, had ordered to be slit to repay the reigning gods of the time for allowing him to cross the seas and go to war. My driver nodded his head, having nearly been a member of the jury in a similar situation. "Where was this?" [he asks] "This happened somewhere between Europe and Asia. . . . And to

> think that these tragedies were written 3500 years ago," [she says] as if it were yesterday. "How can that be?" he asked. "Did men exist before the time of Christ?" "Just like today," she replied. "Men hell-bent on war, whatever the price." ("Oklahoma" 64–65)

The scapegoat mechanism, directing traffic at the intersection of war and peace, is precisely (and criminally) what we have in common with every enemy we construct. We are told that war promises a "safer world." But Burke warns that, "warfare . . . can readily be so much more 'cathartic' in its promises than in its deliveries. The dialectic of antithesis contributes spontaneously to the imagining of an enemy so 'perfectly' suited to his ritual role that by his sacrifice all evils would be redeemed" (*Permanence* 291). It is safe to say that the promise of war brings neither peace nor security, neither redemption, nor the psychological postwar alibi we stylistically refer to as our "peace of mind." "Stylistic study, by the logic of its address, unmasks us," writes Richard Lanham (143). This holds true for George W. Bush, as well as for members of the National Movement for the Restoration of Pakistani Sovereignty, the abject alias of the assassins who butchered Daniel Pearl.

Having been so affected by his death, I wanted to understand how and why Danny became a scapegoat. So, I had to watch. And I had to *study* horror. And now—I want to bear witness to the cruel mediation of his murder and confront its discourse and style not by joining in the discourse of counterterrorism—but by situating language and image outside the logic of war, for *that* is where Danny lived. Lévy believes that with Daniel Pearl the strategic interest in eliminating him spun out of an urge that zeroed in on (to borrow from Sartre's *La Nausée*) "'a fellow of no collective importance, just an individual.' . . . ['one man too many'] . . . . The theory of the scapegoat tells us about the mimetic urge that fixates on the blind spot embodied by the sacrificial victim: an innocent, sometimes anybody—and, at the end of the sacrifice, the calculated miracle of the group reconciled and producing its own innocence" (382–83). Here is the "whole of [the Middle East] transformed into an immense inverted pyramid resting, with all its enormous weight, not on the base, but on the point: the tortured or paralyzed body, the suffocating soul" (384) of a journalist, a musician, a soon-to-be father, a Jew. But this is not the only inverted pyramid resting its enormous weight on the point of Danny's body. In the fiercely competitive world of media scoops, Danny's employer, *The Wall Street Journal*, kept urging him on, conscious of the urgency of uncovering ties between the Pakistani government and al-Qaeda, but also conscious of "the pressure of the information-market" (404). As it happened, it was a fluke, a glitch that put Danny in harm's way. His "fixer," the person who helps you stay alive in such dangerous countries, the person who put Danny in touch with the radical cleric he wanted to interview, did not show up that night. So, he went alone to a small dingy café in Karachi to meet the go-between. Danny was abducted and taken to a house on the outskirts of Karachi, in Gulzar e-Hijri (the only available address, and the one I have chosen for the title of this chapter). To one syndicate, Danny knew too much—to the other syndicate, he knew too little. In the scapegoat mechanism styles converge. A eulogy to some, a manifesto to others—death to so many—it is propaganda no matter how you spell it, with style or stiletto.

But we need more than spelling to understand suffering. And we need more than logic to establish peace. Style shares a rhetorical history with its visual counterpart, design, and both have an obligation to express the language of suffering in shocking ways so that the logic of violence is held accountable to both conceptual and aesthetic reasoning. In other words, in the current shift from writing to visual rhetoric and design, described by Gunther Kress, Richard Lanham, and Greg Ulmer, among others, we cannot (I argue) lose the power of language to bring justice and peace by teaching only the methods and meanings of design. We must not exchange rhetorics for aesthetics, in other words. It is necessary to create and mediate a rhetorical and socially engaged design.

In his essay "English at the Crossroads," Kress proposes that "display and arrangement are the fundamental features of the [new] logic of the visual" (79). He reasons that teaching design is far more relevant in a multimodal academic world. In the past, teaching critique perpetuated the elevation of "distanced analytic understanding" as the primary focus of textual practices (87). Thus, as we move from critique to design, "in the new theory of representation, in the context of the multi-modal, multi-media modes of textual production . . . the task of text-makers is that of *complex orchestration*" (86–87; emphasis mine). But in distinguishing the role of critic and designer, Kress describes one as acting on the past and the other as acting toward the future, and in so doing he describes their social and political tasks and effects as fundamentally different. And here is where we part company. I do not think the roles of critic and designer are mutually exclusive, which is why I enlist Greg Ulmer and a host of designers to close the gap between rhetorical critique and socially engaged design—to launch the pedagogy and practice of "shock design" or "serious design."

In Ulmer's project of inventing electracy, what he calls *heuretics*, rhetorical invention posits an image apparatus that uses the tension between text and images to mediate the "dialectic between art and instrumentalism" (*Internet Invention* 2). Ulmer is emphatic that "the dilemmas of the practical world are fundamentally resistant to policies that neglect the human question" (2). It is not "a choice between two different approaches, but the interdependence of arts and sciences" (2). Ulmer articulates these approaches in a number of ways, alternating between interchangeable concepts such as "lateral" reasoning, "aesthetic" reasoning, "dreamwork," "associative logic," and "intuition," arguing by conduction rather than induction or deduction, all of which put "into logic the aesthetic operations of images" (10). For Ulmer, putting such concepts into play requires allegory, aphoristic writing, mood, atmosphere, identification with one's research material, mediated in the forms of remakes, remixes, assemblages, collages, and altars. These are various ways, he suggests, to help us understand "image logic" (49). The first step toward inventing this hybrid of argument and design is to unhinge our dependence on conventional argument and logic and to be attuned to "attributes that evoke a moment of experience (a mood)" (48).

In the next step of such unhinging, it is necessary to negotiate with structures of violence, as Gayatri Spivak has suggested, by unbuilding and undesigning them, by deconstructing their grip on the production and mediation of terror. To do so requires mediating terror by calling attention to the foundational glitch out of which extremist logic is born: *error.* For with error, logic can establish absolutes, moral standards, definitions, and models, but also contradiction, inconsistency, and homogeneity. And *then* it is but a small distance to enthroning these limits in the name of all that is "right" for the good of all that is eternal.

The question remains how to mediate the undesigned and how to unbuild the logic of error. In designing "glitch art," Nik Gaffney and Maja Kuzmanovic call our attention to the distinction between the nonlethal and lethal glitch, noting

> [an] example of the glitch between physical and informational reality was the bombing of the Chinese embassy in Belgrade [in 1999], where the obsolete maps served as a tactical excuse in a heavily technologically monitored zone.
>
> topographical amnesia

> We are told that Nato's "accidental bombing" of the Chinese Embassy . . . was due to the mission's use of maps made years ago: the embassy shouldn't have been there. Topographical data previously collected from the site became digitally partitioned from the altering physical field and in an ironic return redescribed itself back onto the original surface with the conviction of ammunition. (Gaffney and Kuzmanovic)

Open sky—site of a violent dialectic—the tension between art and instrumentalism—the path of doves *and* the source of terror (not unlike the threshold of Motztstraße 72 that I examined in chapter 1). To address this paradox, we need a new discourse on peace, one that is "in style" and rendered in socially engaged design—one that punctuates the discourse of peace, what Barthes calls *punctum*: "these marks, these wounds . . . so many points" (27), this element that "shoots out of [an image] like an arrow, and pierces me" (26). But peace is not simply the counterpart of war, for we all know the syntax of cruelty designed to pacify or exact retribution in the guise of justice: "mission accomplished," "lethal injection." Nor is war a "surefire" solution to the extremely complex, and alarmingly more frequent and intense, crisis of global terrorism. So, we ought not to limit our discourse on peace to calls to end the war, and we ought not limit our justification for war by citing the *deeds* of terrorists, religious fanatics, or evil-doers. There are registers of motivation and resolve that set these deeds in motion that *we literally cannot fathom*. For example, many enter Islamism as one would the Mafia. It is a family, a trust organization. You can prosper within it, and be protected by it. According to Lévy, there is also a financial underbelly to the "self-sacrificial world" (315). "The al-Qaida militant has a price. . . . The grenade launcher has hers: 150 rupees per grenade (bonus if the results are good)" (315). Attacks on Indian army officers in Kashmir, still higher wages.

> And the kamikaze, too, has his price, decided ahead of time in an actual negotiation between himself, the organization, and his family, 5,000 and sometimes 10,000 rupees—but per year, and for life, and, when the contract is negotiated well, indexed for inflation and based on strong currencies. . . . There are agencies, not quite banks but more than simple money exchangers, where suicide-attack candidates come to fill out applications almost as naturally as for a loan. (315)

That discourse must be addressed, but not with "preventive war."

We need a new discourse on peace *and* war. It is Derrida's answer to the "knock at the door" of "two common nouns": "'cruelty' and 'sovereignty'" (*Without Alibi* 241). Calling for a "new discourse on war," Derrida would have us open our eyes to the sovereignty of cruelty (246). Who better, he argues, to take on the production of this new discourse than those skilled in the "grammatical or semantic variations, these differences between *making* suffer, *letting* suffer. . . . all these possible modifications [that] leave an adverb intact, an invariant that seems, once and for all, to qualify a state of suffering, namely, cruelty, 'cruelly'" (238). Derrida as rhetorician understands that to traffic in language arts one's hand is inevitably "caught in a hive of prior questions, which are like so many wasps that leave you no peace. No one knows any longer who is complaining to whom. There are only alibis" (248). With the discourse and image apparatus of "shock design" I join Derrida "[on] the stage of this new theater of cruelty, concerning which I will explain myself in my own rhythm, and it will be . . . very slow, I would like to avoid alibis" (256).

But it is impossible to avoid cruelty. Derrida credits Nietzsche for understanding the inability to *delimit* cruelty, for seeing "there the cunning essence of life" (239). The only hope of progress one can make against cruelty he terms (after Nietzsche) "progressivism without illusion" (271). "*It is necessary* to cultivate . . . [a strategy] of detour and difference, the strategy . . . of *indirect* progress: an indirect, always indirect way of combating the cruelty drive" (271). There are, however, glitches in this maxim whose indirect implications emerge at the border checkpoint between war and peace. Vilém Flusser argues that it is precisely because of war that objects become so well designed. "There may be a way out of this dilemma:" he writes,

> either war and an elegant, user-friendly life in the midst of good objects, or everlasting peace and a squalid, inconvenient life in the midst of badly functioning objects. Putting it another way: either bad and convenient or inconvenient and saintly. Perhaps one could propose a compromise: to design objects intentionally less well than one might do. For example, arrow-heads that continually miss, paper-knives that take less and less time to get blunt, rockets that tend to explode in the air. (32)

If we situate Flusser's design dilemma in the context of world politics, as a lesson in indirect progress, indirection seems ludicrous. The question is *why*? Indirection does not mean powerlessness, nor are indirect methods *necessarily* fueled by pacifism, though the logic of war would have us believe otherwise. If, however, we reverse engineer that logic, redesign what grounds its ammunition, we would find, I think, that the logic of "shock and awe" spectator war, made possible by battlefield management software, is deeply driven by cruelty fetishism. As such, Derrida recommends "a method, in fact a politics, of *indirect* diversion: one should see to it that the cruel drives are diverted, deferred, and do not find expression in war" (*Without Alibi* 271). In so saying, he does not limit himself to any one particular definition of cruelty concluding that "there are only differences in cruelty, differences in modality, quality, intensity, activity, or reactivity, within a *same* cruelty" (271). Derrida does, however, acknowledge that today we are witnessing "a cruel mutation of cruelty—or at least new historical figures of an ageless cruelty" (270). We need to unpack the "unconscious archive of the French revolution and a few other revolutions" that he calls "an enormous, bottomless memory" where the worst cruelties, "the still open list of the most relentless cruelties, *Shoah*, genocides, mass deportations, and so forth, go side by side indissociably, as if the two processes were inseparable, with the invention of human rights" (266).

There are clues here for establishing our methods of research mediation by which, if we are committed to reducing cruelty, we resolve to go slowly, adopting the strategy of *indirect* progress, drafting our design heuristics inside an unlikely ally—global error, which is all too frequently disguised in the discourse of euphemism: glitch, bug, blunder, fluke, "friendly fire." And we need to unbuild error's kinship with global terror, into which we pour our deepest fears, which then return redesigned and redeployed as weapons of mass *instruction*. In solidarity with such graphic disobedience, I want to pair two violent forms of mass instruction—the hostage video and aerial wartime leaflets—each of which forms the *shock design* on the twin sides of a single page: global (t)error. Such shock is not invented in the rhetorical workshop, but in the church of religious *and* political extremism, where the glitch knows no difference between cruelty and sovereignty. Thus a *glitcheuristics* must invent the means of mediating the most shocking research in which the writer/designer no longer must *imagine* some excessive horror, she need only watch Al Jazeera or CNN, both based on the sovereignty of media journalism cultivated and disseminated by the corporations of sovereign, and civilized, nations.

One would think that centuries of lessons, rhetorical and otherwise, would have made us wiser, if not more compassionate—which makes it all the more deplorable when a warmonger such as George W. Bush obtains his passport in the name of *compassionate conservatism*. This does not count as *indirect progress*, and it is certainly not a mandate for perpetuating violence and installing perpetual fear in the guise of the production and consumption of *security*, perhaps our newest and most profitable industry. Shortly after the outbreak of World War I, Freud observed that

> "*cruelties* and injustices which the most civilized nations commit, the different ways in which they judge their own lies and misdeeds in comparison with those of the enemies show the degree to which . . . man's most primitive impulses will never be abolished in each of us and that we are always ready to conduct ourselves in an underhanded or stupid manner at their least resurgence." (emphasis mine; qtd in Derrida, *Without Alibi* 268)

Speaking "in the double wake of Nietzsche and Freud," (271) Derrida concludes: "It is next a matter . . . of the indissociable tie between cruelty and state sovereignty, state violence, the state that, far from combating violence, monopolizes it" (268). In 1986, René Major argued that "'in peacetime, the state does not prohibit violence in order to abolish it but in order to monopolize it and . . . in wartime, it shamelessly withdraws from treaties and conventions that tie it to other states while asking its citizens for their approval in the name of patriotism'" (qtd in Derrida 268). Nobel Peace Prize laureate Ralph Bunche said in 1950:

> There are some in the world who are prematurely resigned to the inevitability of war. Among them are the advocates of the so-called "preventive war," who, in their resignation to war, wish merely to select their own time for initiating it. To suggest that war can prevent war is a base play on words and a despicable form of warmongering.

The discourse of "securing the peace" restyled to parse the waging of war. The logic of stealth grammar. The war leaflet. According to information on the PsyWar Society site,

> the history of aerial leaflet propaganda is long and diverse. In 1806 Admiral Cochrane of the British Navy constructed kites to transport proclamations from his ships into France. Later that century, balloons came to be used to drop leaflets, for example, by the inhabitants of Milan when besieged in 1848 and then by the French during the Siege of Paris in 1870. During the First World War, when air disseminated leaflets were used on a massive scale, the foundations were laid for to-day's psychological warfare techniques.

In Anthony Doerr's stunning new novel, *All the Light We Cannot See*, the opening lines transport the reader to August 7, 1944, somewhere in France, on the eve of an Allied bombing of the village of Saint-Malo.

> At dusk they pour from the sky. They blow across the ramparts, turn cartwheels over rooftops, flutter into the ravines between houses. Entire streets swirl with them, flashing white against the cobbles. *Urgent message to the inhabitants of this town*, they say. *Depart immediately to the open country.*
>
> The tide climbs. The moon hangs small and yellow and gibbous. On the rooftops of beachfront hotels to the east, and in the gardens behind them, a half-dozen American artillery units drop incendiary rounds into the mouths of mortars. (3)

The following examples from World War I to the Iraq war are not offered as an equivalent form of violence such as a beheading; however, they are examples of "shock rhetoric" that in some cases depict equally violent scenes (figs. 5.1–5.11). The aerial distribution of thousands of images is not unlike the circulation of beheading videos on the Internet.

- The first leaflet dropped in World War I was a German missive that reads: "The german army is at the gates of Paris; it only remains for you to surrender" (Auckland "First").

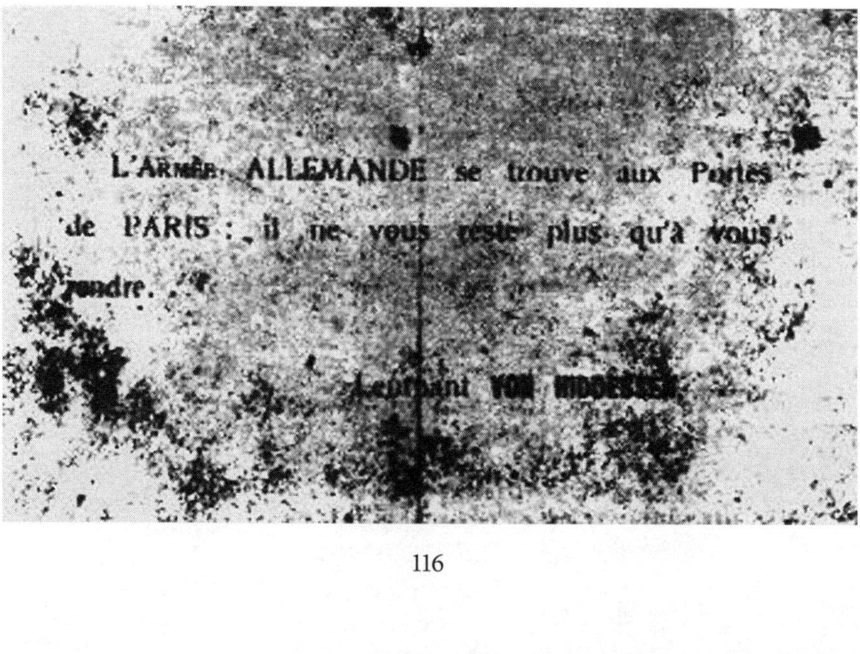

GROETEN UIT ENGELAND

DE KOMENDE INVASIE

ONRUST DER DUITSCHERS OMTRENT ENGELAND'S NIEUWSTE WAPEN.

De Duitscher is altijd een slecht psycholoog geweest. Hij denkt zijn Engelschen tegenstander te kennen en verwacht dezen zomer een landing aan de Noordzeekust.

De gedachte aan deze mogelijkheid heeft den anders zoo zelfverzekerden mof kennelijk onrustig gemaakt. Het O.K.W. (Oberkommando der Wehrmacht) gaf daarom bevel, de Westkust in staat van verdediging te brengen. Onze heldhaftige piloten lachen echter in hun vuistje, wanneer zij het zenuwachtige gewriemel van de Germaansche stakkers gadeslaan. Zij weten, dat niets de komende invasie zal kunnen tegenhouden, zij kennen het nieuwe wapen,

„de donkere wolk".

De Britsche generale staf heeft thans toestemming verleend, hieromtrent enkele nadere bijzonderheden te vermelden. Sedert het begin van dit jaar zijn meer dan een half millioen negers uit Amerika naar Schotland gebracht, waar zij een speciale opleiding ontvangen in het afspringen met valschermen. Een interessante bijzonderheid is nog, dat hun valschermen gemaakt zijn van donkergrijze zijde. Daar gewoonlijk de bewolkte lucht boven Nederland ook donkergrijs is, maakt deze handige camouflage het den Duitschers onmogelijk, het valschermlegioen af te schieten. Voor Hitler, den propheet der rassentheorie, zal het de grootste vernedering zijn, wanneer zijn strijders door het zwarte ras uit West-Europa worden verdreven.

Nederlanders, op Uw medewerking wordt gerekend bij de komst van het zwarte legioen. Leg Uw oude jazz-platen klaar, want op het feest der bevrijding zullen Uw dochters en vrouwen dansen in de armen van echte negers. Grillige puinhopen zullen een fantastischen achtergrond vormen van het bevrijdingsbachanaal, waar blank en zwart zich zoo innig zullen vermengen, dat het voor de bewoners van Nederland een prettige herinnering zal blijven aan de invasie van de donkere wolk.

Nederlandsche meisjes en vrouwen, hier ligt voor U een mooie en aangename taak, waaraan U zich geheel dient te geven zonder eenige terughouding, teneinde het rassengedaas van Hitler te logenstraffen.

DUITSCHE LEUGENS

over den handelsoorlog.

Groot-Brittannië is dezen oorlog ingegaan met 20 millioen ton handelsscheepsruimte. In den loop van dezen oorlog is daar 10 millioen ton aan Noorsche, Belgische, Nederlandsche, Fransche, Grieksche en andere scheepsruimte bijgekomen. Eigenlijk beschikte Groot-Brittannië dus over 30 millioen ton scheepsruimte.

Volgens sommige berichten (U behoeft niet te vragen uit welke bron) zou hiervan reeds 25 millioen ton door oorlogshandelingen zijn verloren gegaan. Dit is een gemeene leugen.

Volgens het Amerikaansche blad „Navigation Statistics" van 1 Juni 1942 bedroeg de door duikbooten, mijnen en vliegtuigen tot zinken gebrachte Britsche Handelstonnage slechts 20 millioen 6 honderdduizend 3 honderd 34 ton en geen ton meer. Laat U dus niet door Duitsche leugens misleiden.

- Another German leaflet, designed like a newspaper front page, was dropped over the Netherlands in 1942 and warned of Britain's newest secret weapon; "the dark cloud" of negro parachutists with dark grey parachutes invisible against the sky (Auckland "German").

- On Aug 6, 1945, Americans dropped the atom bomb on Hiroshima. Leaflets were not dropped *until the next day*, not in order to prevent more casualties in Nagasaki, some say, but to capitalize on the psychological effects of Hiroshima (Wellerstein).

- A US leaflet is designed like Japanese money so that people would pick it up; the message on the back links its deteriorating purchase power to the military's domination of the government (Williams).

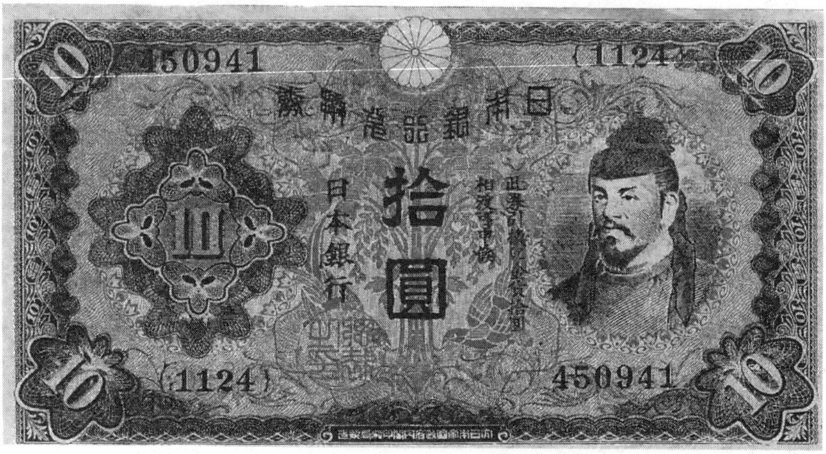

- During the Korean War, the United States dropped this leaflet on Chinese and North Korean troops. There is a rather nasty-looking blade presumably held by a Chinese or North Korean.

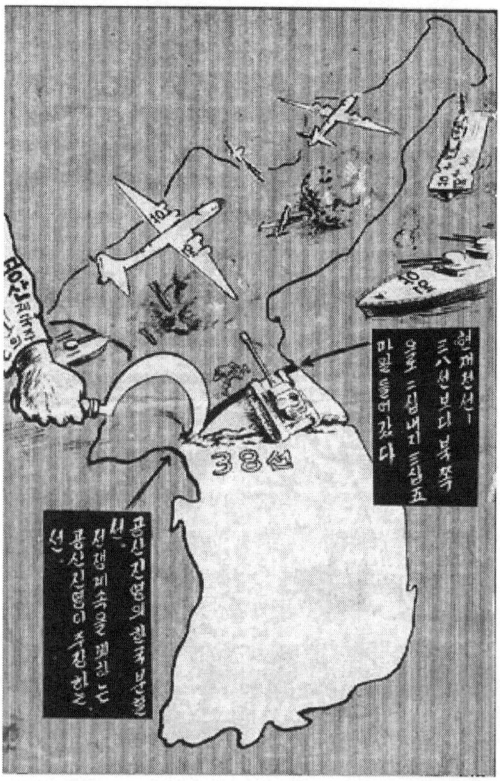

- In another Korean War leaflet, the United States depicts itself as a prophet or god reuniting North and South Korea.

- In the first Gulf War: "this elaborately illustrated Gulf War PSYOP leaflet portrays the US Marines as a knife-wielding, war-ready, tidal wave of a soldier" (psywar.org).

- In researching leaflets dropped during the war in Iraq (2003), I learned that during the first hours of the US invasion, the first Iraqi guard to be killed in combat was hit over the head with a box of leaflets that fell out of a combat aircraft when a static line broke (Burlas), not unlike this cartoon image of a Nazi soldier.

- On another leaflet dropped in the first days of the Iraq war it says, "If the oil industry is destroyed, your livelihood will be ruined. Help to prevent the sabotage of the Iraqi oil industry! Your family depends on it!"

- In this leaflet, itself about a leaflet drop, we see Iraqis transmitting the location of coalition aircraft, with binoculars raised and guns drawn, while one of the soldiers reads the leaflet. “It says ‘Don’t report coalition aircraft positions. . . . doing this will result in your destruction’” . . . and then, “I told you they won’t harm us if we don’t report them.” And they have lowered the weapon and are no longer transmitting.

- One leaflet uses a classic westernized if/then argument, reading from right to left in both English and Arabic. Basically it says, if you shoot at our planes, we will shoot and destroy you. YOU DECIDE.

It was my hope that on November 2, 2004, the people of the United States would have been decisive, not divisive. The Ohio glitches in the 2004 presidential election (fig. 5.12) were not to be outdone by the Florida glitches of the 2000 election. And yet, in the early hours of October 7, 2004, one glitch on electoral-vote.com turned a red nation to blue. This is the screenshot I made of that glitch. This became a heuristic, a glitch heuristic, for my thoughts in this chapter. Yet I know that regardless of whether we call it *glitcheuristics* or glitch rhetoric, we need a stylistic intervention into the discourse of peace and war, mediated by shock design, rhetorical outrage, and the undoing of global error. The design of peace ought to be rendered in as many words and images as possible. It ought to pay tribute to the hostage victims as well as all innocents of all so-called preemptive wars. It ought to obligate us to hear more than we want to hear and see more than we want to see in whatever ways can most effectively disturb the discourse of political doublespeak and sanitized images of war. We ought to babble peace, to ramble on and on in its name, speaking in tongues in its name, echoed by Maxine Hong Kingston in *The Fifth Book of Peace*.

> Peace begins in thought. Thoughts enworded go from mind to mind, and mind makes the world. Peace, illusive, abstract, negative Yin, dream, would take a long writer-out to make real. Its book has to be longer than war books—longer than a bumper sticker, longer than a sound bite. . . . Sudden fast change is a method of war. The logic of peace has to be spoken out at length. (54)

Kenneth Burke agrees, "Action requires programs—programs require vocabulary. To act wisely, in concert, we must use many words. If we use the wrong words, words that divide up the field inadequately, we obey false cues" (*Attitudes* 4).

But, as we say in the United States, we live in God's country, where, according to Richard Lanham, American pragmatism insists on just "as much prose style as will get the world's business done expeditiously—a philosophy of denotative clarity—and [Americans] are willing to pay for only this much and no more" (11). Like President Bush: "'I glance at the headlines just to [get?] a flavor for what's moving. I rarely read the stories, and get briefed by people who are [sic] probably read the news themselves'" (Conansen). Lanham continues:

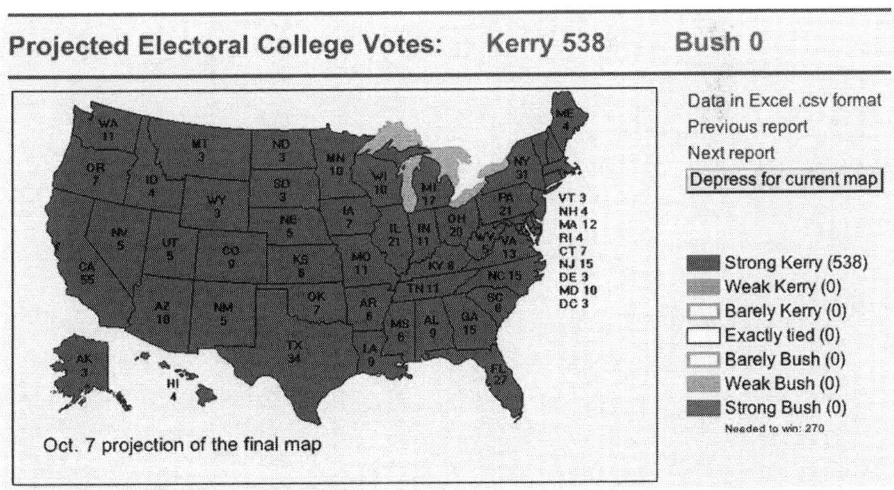

Fig. 5.12. Glitch on electoral-vote.com website on October 7, 2004. *Screenshot by author.*

> On the other hand, civilization does depend on the state of our native language, and so our approach to the problem of prose style must be unremittingly moral. . . . A broad justification, then, for a narrow theory of prose style. Upon this disjunctive and sometimes contradictory yoking of use and morality has been built the prose pedagogy of America. (11–12)

Lanham reminds us, however, that we are "the only country ever prosperous and democratic enough to *have* a prose problem" (125–26).

Yes, in the United States we have a prose problem, but it is not only (or primarily) in our schools. It is in the US government. In war, we do not call it killing; it is "exceeding the threshold of physiological damage," or "violence processing," "servicing the target," "substantive negative outcome." In 1993, the US Armed Forces first began using the term "information warfare" in a policy memo called *Command and Control Warfare*. "Its objective is 'to decapitate the enemy's command structure from its body of troops'" (Stein 52). George Stein recalls "Gen. Colin Powell's comment on defeating the Iraqi military [in the first Gulf War]: 'First we cut off its head, then we kill it'" (53). Compare this passage from the Koran: "When ye encounter the infidels, strike off their heads till ye have made a great slaughter among them, and *of the rest* make fast the fetters" (*Koran*, Sura XLVII, 3–4; 382). It sounds barbaric. But this practice is both ancient and cross-cultural. Norman O. Brown explains: "Every organization has a head; headless bodies cannot act. Capital organization: the head of the body represents the whole body" (134). "It is the head that wears the crown" (135). "Separateness, then, is the fall—the fall into division, the original [error]. . . . To have a self is to have enemies, and to be a self is to be at war (the war of every man against every man)" (148–49).

> The real cause of all death is the father (Der Erlkönig); the member of a foreign tribe is the culprit, scapegoat, or father. . . . Killing is always inside the family (Oedipal). In the wisdom of primitive war, enemy blood is kindred blood; blood becomes kindred blood by being shed. Whatever is killed becomes the father. Head hunting. An enemy must be killed for a boy to grow up; a head must fall. The boy kills his father in the person of an enemy. (163)

Ironically, on toppling President Saddam Hussein of Iraq, President Bush said, "After all, this is the guy who tried to kill my dad" (King).

Meanwhile, back in New York, Hélène Cixous also visited Ground Zero, what she calls "Hiroshima's new address" ("Oklahoma" 77). Pondering her transient connection to the taxi driver, she writes, "We had in common a primitive interest in throat-slitting amongst families and in fundamentally complicated crimes" (65). Cixous was urging me to look up Hiroshima's address, and there I found language. And I found myself. In 1952, the year I was born, Sankichi Toge, a survivor of Hiroshima, penned this poem titled "Give Back the People" (Toge).

> Give back my father, give back my mother;
> Give back my elders;
> Give me my sons and daughters back.
> Give me back myself,
> Give back the human race.
> As long as this life lasts, this life,
> Give back peace
> That will never end.

6
Torture and Absolution

Gulfstream V N379P, Unknown Airspace

> Tentacles are always moving, changing direction, twisting, flowing, twitching, frictionless, striated, anti-gravitational, elusive, searching, wanting, feeling, grasping, entrapping. They are magnitudes of intensity, unconscious but alive. . . . [Tentacles] map the terrain of the invisible, anticipating all possible encounters while seeming to be randomly writhing. . . . But even in this state of focus, tentacles cannot help but engage in apparently unnecessary, decadent behavior. This is because they are already anticipating the contingencies of their next encounter. . . . The violence of the encounter does not erase distinction between forms, but grafts impulses or sensibilities of one onto the other. Such a tactile morphology of both sensing (a desire for information) and grasping (an exchange between identities) refigures differences in terms of sublimation.
>
> —Tom Wiscombe

North Tower

The war on terror extends beyond the geopolitical borders of Iraq, Afghanistan, and other nations that support and harbor terrorists. It depends on its own vast network of what the Bush administration called a "coalition of the willing."[1] What they were willing to do and to permit is called into question in this section on the North Tower, which interrogates the practices of interrogation upon which the clandestine policy of "extraordinary rendition" is based. In contradistinction to "cities of refuge" that harbor refugees from terror, "cities of rendition" harbor detainees in US custody who have been transported to a "friendly government" where extrajudicial interrogation techniques fly under the radar of international law and are in reality nothing more than "torture by proxy." Such cities are often de facto cities only insofar as they are temporary places for detention and interrogation (e.g., airplanes, airports, camps). They are, nevertheless, rendered cities rhetorically (in memos and patriot acts) by governments who prefer to question individuals outside the jurisdiction of federal and international courts.

I have on my radar two planes bound for cities of rendition. We all know the torture that happened inside four commercial airliners on 9/11. But not so many of us know what happened inside the Gulfstream V aircraft, N379P (the address for this chapter). It is probably safe to say that everyone is interested in saving lives. But it is not safe to say that in order to save lives some of us may feel it is sometimes necessary to torture someone. I am tempted to ask my readers to put your hands behind your back and clasp your wrists and hold that position throughout your reading. I do not want to "see" the hands you use to write, the ones you use to grade student writing, those hands that sign the ledgers of literacy that litter this country. I will not, however, ask that of you. I will simply pretend that your hands are tied. I am also pretending that you are sitting on the edge of your seat. That you are bound up, not spellbound. I want you a little off balance. I want us all to understand what it is like to undergo "enhanced interrogation." And I want us all a bit worried and unsteady, precariously perched upon an "extrajudicial edge," not lounging in our ample academic seats.

My pretend game also includes imagining my readers in some restaurant or hotel meeting room, a room fortuitously named for the city of Versailles. For the moment, the year is 1793. Louis XVI has been condemned to die, and the Committee of Public Safety is just formed. Versailles was called at that time the "cradle of liberty," but today we know this period in its history as the beginning of the Reign of Terror. (Of, interest, perhaps, is the fact that Washington, DC, was designed by the same French architect who designed the city of Versailles. And I leave it to *your* imagination to render the parallels I infer.) Now that the interrogation stage is set, we will do a bit of a revisionist remix and imagine Versailles as a city that in the torture trade is sometimes called a "black site," a place of "extraordinary rendition," that euphemism for torture by proxy. In what follows, you will read a series of performative questions and coerced answers by some high profile "ghost detainees." Unlike enhanced interrogations, however, this focus group may actually yield some valuable information, rather than the kind of information that anyone in enough pain will tell you eventually, that all of us would gladly divulge to save ourselves.

Another French architect, not one by trade, but one that de-structured all structuration, and one whose specter haunts the walls of this imaginary city, will now lead with the first confession in this mock interrogation. Let us imagine that Jacques Derrida, hands also forming a chiasmus behind his back, answered "without alibi":

> It is necessary to save, it is necessary to assure salvation. . . . [and] this salutary, sanitary, or immunitary concern triggers simultaneously a gesture of war: the militant would like to cure or save by routing, precisely, a resistance. I am not sure that this rescue project, this salvation or health plan, this profession of public safety is not also, in part, or even in secret, that of your States General, which is already pregnant, virtually, in the dark, with some shadow Committee of Public Safety. As a result, I am not sure, at this point, that I am altogether one of you even if, in part, I remain proud to claim to be by sharing your worry. (*Without Alibi* 243)

What concerns Derrida is the relation between cruelty and sovereignty. The revolution, in principle (concerning princes), begat a "cruel Terror" (260). As Derrida formulates the question and then answers it: Was the convocation of the States General, convoked by a king, the first gesture of cruelty, or a vain attempt to prevent it (260)?

> We will never know. By definition, we will never know whether the States General, at the moment of their first convocation, were destined to condemn or save the king's head, and it matters little, no doubt, because in any case the two gestures, condemning and saving, remain indissociable. They inscribe in the concepts of sovereignty and cruelty an ambiguity that is as unrelievable as autoimmunity itself. It is too late, even for the question. (260)

Right. *Mortal questions are always too late.* According to Thomas Nagel,

> No elaborate moral theory is required to account for what is wrong in cases like the Mylai massacre, since it did not serve, and was not intended

> to serve, any strategic purpose. . . . I propose to discuss the most general moral problem raised by the conduct of warfare: the problem of means and ends. (53–54)

Atrocities committed in the name of warfare also spotlight cities of extraordinary rendition—the *atrocious* having roots in the Greek for "black eye." Certainly the United States suffers a perpetual black eye since the My Lai massacre, and it grows blacker by the day given the events at Abu Ghraib, and God knows where and what else (and He does). In short, enhanced interrogation and/as extraordinary rendition reinvents the city as atrocity—atrocities that figure as atro-tropaic events—black tropes writing black sites. A memo, full of black tropes, can function as architecturally as blueprints for a municipality. It can provide legal and extra/ordinary powers (sometimes called eminent domain), and we should not neglect the less than benign relation between the words ordinary and ordnance, nor between municipality and munitions. Cities of rendition give the space of such encounters, and writing gives the order. John Yoo, legal architect of the Bush administration defense of the use of enhanced interrogation techniques, wrote such a memo one week before the US invasion of Iraq in March 2003. According to a *Washington Post* report,

> The memo also includes past legal defenses of interrogations that Yoo wrote are not considered torture, such as sleep depravation [*sic*], hooding detainees and "frog crouching," which forces prisoners to crouch while standing on the tips of their toes. "This standard permits some physical contact," the memo said. "Employing a shove or slap as part of an interrogation would not run afoul of this standard." ("Pentagon")

Here we can see the "tactile morphology of tentacles" already "anticipating the contingencies of their next encounter" (Wiscombe 25%). It seems the standards for treatment of prisoners of war, established by obscure bodies such as the Geneva Convention, are full of restrictions that now require rhetorical rerouting. As Eyal Weizman explains, "Since military planners are acutely aware that the methods required for urban warfare will make soldiers potentially liable to prosecution for war crimes, American and Israeli governments cancelled their membership in the ICC [International Criminal Court]" (180). In addition, the Bush administration had aggressively sought to weaken the court's effectiveness by "negotiating bilateral agreements with other countries, insuring immunity of US nationals from prosecution by the Court. As leverage, Washington threatened termination of economic aid, withdrawal of military assistance, and other painful measures" ("US Opposition" 2008).

There are, however, powerful correctives at work to offset such political end runs. Weizman points to the existence of international courts, the development of cheap recording equipment, and the availability of satellite communication that greatly limit military operational methods (2003). The short-lived US Army slogan "Army of One," however, highlights a radical singularity that proved it was a motto forged from a two-edged sword. The military term "'strategic corporal' characterizes the huge ramifications of the actions of the individual soldier" (Weizman 180). One soldier, a graduate student in Clemson University's master's in professional communication program, told me why a $200 light kit would achieve the same effect as more "enhanced interrogation" techniques. I asked how that is possible. He said, "Those lights are hot, and you can't see your interrogator. It's like having God asking you questions, and God wouldn't ask you trivial questions, right?" (Callot). I asked him whether he had ever participated in questionable interrogations, and he said that a few occasions were critical enough for them to use "enhanced interrogation techniques," but instead they used a "modified Civil Affairs operation" (Callot). At the end of my interview with him, I thanked him for sharing his experiences and opinions with me, and his parting comment was, "Listen, I'm just one soldier. There are about a million of us" (Callot).

And, as we all know, other operatives serving our country also conduct enhanced interrogations. Thus, we should observe a snippet of the Senate Select Intelligence Committee interrogation of CIA Director (and Air Force General) Michael Hayden on the question of enhanced interrogation techniques.

> [Senator] FEINSTEIN: I'd like to ask this question: Who carries out these [enhanced interrogation] techniques? Are they government employees or contractors?
>
> HAYDEN: At our facilities during this, we have a mix of both government employees and contractors. Everything is done under, as we've talked before, ma'am, under my authority and the authority of the agency. But the people at the locations are frequently a mix of both—we call them blue badgers and green badgers. . . . This

> is not where we would turn to Firm X, Y or Z, and say, this is what we would like you to accomplish. Go achieve that for us and come back when you're done. That is not what this is. This is a governmental activity under governmental direction and control, in which the participants may be both government employees and contractors, but it's not outsourced.

[Senator] FEINSTEIN: I understand that.

HAYDEN: OK. Good. (Shachtman)

As sometimes occurs during interrogations, the detainee reverses the roles and tries to wrest control of the process in order to have the last word. So, we sometimes see a good cop/bad cop interrogation method rhetorically defused in two words—"OK. Good." It's a political nightmare from which we desperately need to awaken. Simon Critchley, has a question for us.

> My question is very simple, but the answer is far from self-evident: how do we begin to grasp the political situation in which we find ourselves? . . . [More precisely, he asks] how did Bush get reelected in the American Presidential elections in November 2004? How did Bush win? Well, I think part of the story is that certain people in the Bush administration have got a clear, robust and powerful understanding of the nature of the political. They have read their Machiavelli, their Hobbes, their Leo Strauss and misread their Nietzsche. (133)

For Critchley, "politics is not the naked operation of power or an ethics-free agonism, it is an ethical practice that is driven by a response to situated injustices and wrong" (132). The problem is that injustices are sometimes situated outside the jurisdiction of victimary logic, and in fact exploit such logic to foster fear and thereby gain mass solidarity, whole choirs of solidarity singing in unison in the voting booths across this nation. "It seems that all the world is turning to noise. We need to turn up the signal, wipe out the noise" (Gabriel).

South Tower

In case you hadn't noticed, retro is in style. Quite trendy, in fact. All the rage. So it seems altogether fitting to begin this shift from torture to absolution with a retro-spective moment from the seventies. For those of you who do not remember the seventies (and for some of us that decade is a bit of a blur), or for those of you who were born after the seventies, let me simply plead guilty to committing what Douglas Coupland calls "legislated nostalgia," "to force a body of people to have memories they do not actually possess" (41). But whether blurred or legislated, it is worth re-membering the year 1972. I was enrolled in a community college where racial scuffles and student protests meant I could cut biology class and hone my ping pong skills in the student union, or find a private nook in the library to read D. H. Lawrence. When Coupland's Generation Xers visit the Vietnam memorial, they capture this kind of "historical slumming" like this:

> "Andy, I don't get it. I mean, this is a cool enough place and all, but why should you be interested in Viet*nam*. It was over before you'd even reached puberty." "I'm hardly an expert on the subject, Tyler, but I *do* remember a bit of it. Faint stuff: black-and-white TV stuff. Growing up, Vietnam was a background color in life, like red or blue or gold—it tinted everything. And then suddenly one day it just disappeared. Imagine that one morning you woke up and suddenly the color green had vanished. I come here to see a color I can't see anywhere else any more." (151)

So, picture the color green, and imagine the soundtrack of life in 1972 during this rundown of just some of the events of that year ("1972"). Angela Davis is released from jail. A Lufthansa plane is hijacked. President Nixon orders the laying of explosives in Haiphong Harbor in Vietnam. Governor George Wallace is shot. Watergate. Iraq nationalizes the Iraq Petroleum Company. The Supreme Court rules that the death penalty is unconstitutional. Jane Fonda tours North Vietnam. The last US ground troops are withdrawn from Vietnam. The Munich Massacre of eleven Israeli athletes at the Summer Olympics shocks the world. In the presidential election, Republican incumbent Richard Nixon defeats George McGovern in a landslide. *There was no Nobel Peace Prize awarded in 1972.* In 1972 George W. Bush refused to take the air force physical exam, some claim because of a newly announced military drug testing program. And in 1972 the film *Deliverance* was released.

The rhetorical canon of delivery bears two connections here. First, the Greek term for delivery was *hypokrisis*, which means "acting." Second, among its numerous definitions, delivery also means absolution. In 1637 Ben Jonson wrote, "Some language is high and great . . . the composition full, the absolution plenteous, and poured out, all grave, sinewy, and strong" (qtd in OED; *Discoveries* Wks. 1846, 759). Although this is one of the more obscure meanings of absolution, I am asking *delivery* to function here as another rhetorical threshold, or what Brenda Laurel would term a "thresh-oldy phenomenon" (21).[2] I want it to work out of obscurity, that which is shrouded or hidden in darkness, because not only does rhetoric sanction the notion of the hidden hermeneutic, it has wired (and worn) this switch plate as perhaps its only badge of responsibility. Heraclitus imagined *logos* as lightning—the word "teleporting" in and out of obscurity. Plato, as we know, deplored rhetoric's stormy personality, demanding that philosophy must tame this tempest and divest it of its mysterious powers. Of course, the irony is that philosophy plots its own storm paths using the same rhetorical radar, and then claims it has harnessed its energy for the "good," and constructs a political power plant called democracy on the shores of the enlightenment ideals of reason, responsibility, and human rights. Yet democracy has suffered countless blackouts over the years. It has yet to figure out that it is not immune to power outages. It deplores the rhetorical rogue at the same time it sanctions the obscurity of the rogue, its ability to fly under the radar of the laws of nature and culture. This is how the hypokrisis became the hypocrite—how delivery became deliverance, and how absolution wrote the book on autoimmunity.

Maybe this brand of rhetoric is more like *white* lightning. On August 16, 2006, President George W. Bush became the first president to pardon a cast member of the 1972 Academy Award-nominated movie "Deliverance" (DOJ). Randall Deal, an obscure actor who played a bit part in the film, was convicted in the early sixties for violating liquor laws, more commonly known as "moonshining laws." Among the 189 individuals pardoned by Bush, twelve had been convicted of crimes related to "moonshining."

Like all presidents, Bush pardoned his share of convicted criminals, or commuted their sentence (the annual Thanksgiving Turkey and Scooter Libby come to mind), but the Bush absolution of Randall Deal is tame compared to the absolution deal cut in 2006 between Congress and the executive and judicial arms of our government. It goes by the name of the Military Commissions Act of 2006. Elizabeth Holtzman explains:

> Thirty-two years ago, President Gerald Ford created a political firestorm by pardoning former President Richard Nixon of all crimes he may have committed in Watergate—and lost his election as a result. Now, President

> Bush, to avoid a similar public outcry, is quietly trying to pardon himself of any crimes connected with the torture and mistreatment of U.S. detainees. The "pardon" is buried in Bush's proposed legislation to create a new kind of military tribunal for cases involving top al-Qaida operatives. The "pardon" provision has nothing to do with the tribunals. Instead, it guts the War Crimes Act of 1996, a federal law that makes it a crime, in some cases punishable by death, to mistreat detainees in violation of the Geneva Conventions and makes the new, weaker terms of the War Crimes Act retroactive to 9/11. Press accounts of the provision have described it as providing immunity for CIA interrogators. But its terms cover the president and other top officials because the act applies to any U.S. national. ("Bush")

In short, retro-activity is also in. While it is equally important to scrutinize the rhetorical stripping of habeas corpus rights of detainees, the definitions of enhanced interrogation this act spells out, the permission of secret trials, and the absence of the right to a speedy trial, I want to switch off the auto-focus and zoom in on this retroactive immunity. And from my admittedly feminist perspective, I can tell you it has the muscular tone of absolution on steroids.

The problem is not a new problem, but we can date its most egregious iteration to the hijackings of 9/11, which (it turns out) became a compound hijacking—and though it may be considered irreverent or unpatriotic to say this, much more was hijacked that day than four airplanes. Within hours of the horrendous events of 9/11/2001, the twin engines of rhetoric and democracy were hijacked as well, and we have witnessed the violent unfolding of this hijacking in the years since then. The War on Terror is on auto-pilot. It has built in auto-assessment, auto-system-checks (as opposed to a checks and balance system), and auto-absolution. It is absolutely auto-immune.

The question of responsibility is, unfortunately, a question that rhetoric is hardly in a position to answer. And even though the question is being asked more loudly, more frequently, and by more and more people, the fact remains that that war machine and political juggernaut has had the whole world on the verge of a power outage of epic proportions. Because the economic and social disasters that it has caused cannot be undone with rhetoric, this is the first time I sense the powerlessness of rhetoric to effect such a mass change. This is the first time that rhetoric seems, to me, doomed. I feel like storming the cockpit, but the doors have been reinforced with fear and retributionist policies. How do we disengage this auto-pilot? Whose responsibility is it? Where is *response* ability?

Democracy is missing. It is no longer the most effective means of delivering freedom, protecting its citizens, or bringing about justice. It has probably succumbed to the Stockholm syndrome, that is, it has become emotionally attached to its abductors. Pathos has turned to mass pathology. The people elected President George W. Bush not once, but twice. While there were bills in both the House and Senate designed to restore the ability to prosecute government officials, including those in the White House, for war crimes, both bills were stalled in subcommittees—locked in the "coffers" of special interests, compassionate conservativism, and faith-based politics.

If not democracy, what is its Other? Derrida has exposed the inextricable link between democracy and Greco-Christian theology insofar as he reminds us that

> where the democratic realm becomes coextensive with the political, where the democratic realm becomes constitutive of the political realm precisely because of the indetermination and the "freedom," the "free play," of its concept, and where the democratic, having become consubstantially political in this Greco-Christian and globalatinizing tradition . . . the only and very few regimes . . . that *do not present themselves* as democratic, unless I am mistaken, are statutorily linked to the Muslim faith or creed. (*Rogues* 28–29)

Without fear of retribution, Derrida nevertheless speaks up for "the right to speak without taking sides *for* democracy" (41). As he rightly observes, waging a war against the "axis of evil," those "assassins of democracy," inevitably results in restrictions on our own freedoms and rights, and abuses of potential enemies all of which insures that democracy "must thus come to resemble these enemies, to corrupt itself and threaten itself in order to protect itself against their threats" (40). For Derrida, "wherever freedom is no longer determined as power, mastery, or force, or even as a faculty, as a possibility of the 'I can' . . . the evocation and evaluation of democracy as the power of the *demos* begins to tremble" (40–41). He asks, "Is democracy that which assures the right to think and thus to act without it or against it? *Yes or no*?" (41; emphasis mine).

Although I am suggesting that rhetoric has been hijacked, and that may infer that we are responsible to (perpetually) plan and carry out its rescue, *this would not be a rhetorical move.* Have we forgotten the failed attempts to rehabilitate it? Have we forgotten our addiction to self-empowerment? Have we forsaken Nietzsche's warning against *ressentiment* and reactionary behavior? Have we forgotten his lesson that "slave morality always first needs a hostile external" (*Genealogy* 37)? Have we foolishly underestimated the genius in his anti-imperative testimony: "The last thing I should promise would be to 'improve' mankind" (*Genealogy* 217)? Is our anti-Nietzschean *will-to-rehab* the ultimate will-to-power? Are these the lessons unlearned from the textbook of our most pressing danger? That train left the station with Heidegger, who reminded us that

> what has long . . . been threatening man with death, and indeed with the death of his own nature, is the unconditional character of mere willing in the sense of purposeful self-assertion in everything. What threatens man in his very nature is the willed view that man, by the peaceful release, transformation, storage, and channeling of the energies of physical nature, could render the human condition, man's being, tolerable for everybody and happy in all respects. But the peace of this peacefulness is merely the undisturbed continuing relentlessness of the fury of self-assertion which is resolutely self-reliant. What threatens man in his very nature is the view that this imposition of production can be ventured without any danger, as long as other interests besides—such as, perhaps, the interests of a faith—retain their currency. ("Poets" 116)

This passage contains a doubly hyphenated problem in the same word: self-*assertion* and *self*-assertion. My narrative thus far is a cautionary tale of responsibility run amok amid the rhetorical sanction, or absolution, of its tragic consequences. It is perhaps utterly forgettable. In a Nietzschean sense, I hope it is. I hope we can forget the "for" in whose name responsibility and democracy are most frequently invoked in order to take up Nietzsche's goal for mankind, which is primordially (in its itself-ness) Being's goal—to produce a being who can take absolute responsibility for himself. This is not to say it is "against" those for whom we *are* responsible. As Derrida says, "Let us say yes *to who or what turns up*, before any determination, before any anticipation, before any *identification*, whether or not it has to do with a foreigner, an immigrant, an invited guest, or an expected visitor" (*Of Hospitality* 77). But it merits our acknowledgement that the complicity of rhetoric in the compliance-gaining strategies of rogue responsibility is retroactively marked—it is being held hostage by the worst of both faith and reason. *Doing* something would, then, amount to actions that could not help but be a monstrous reflection of these twin extremisms. Such doing, in theological terms, is called auto-absolution. In political terms, it is called manifest destiny. In Kant's theory of justice, it is called retributivism.

Speaking "in the double wake of Nietzsche and Freud," (*Without Alibi* 271) Derrida relentlessly reminds us " of the indissociable tie between cruelty and state sovereignty, state violence, the state that, far from combating violence, monopolizes it" (268). Now, in addition to the spread of democracy, freedom, and free enterprise—by all accounts taking responsibility for the liberty and prosperity of all people—we take it upon ourselves to export and outsource retribution. Unfortunately, such taking has taken thousands of lives, yet democratic policymakers do not implement or articulate policies without rhetorically fail-safe absolutions embedded in each "mission accomplished" or passive prediction that "sacrifices-will-be-made." There is, in other words, what Derrida calls an "autoimmune necessity inscribed *right onto* democracy" (*Rogues* 36). The task of rhetoric is to reveal its own autoimmunity and turn it back on itself ir/responsibly. Much as Derrida reformulated the "autoimmune law" "around the *community* as *auto-co-immunity*" (35), rhetoric's responsibility is "to take absolute responsibility for itself" rather than to absolve itself "for" the world. If Heidegger was right to say "Language is the House of Being" ("Letter" 193), then rhetoric is not wrong to say "Mind your own house."

7

Postconflict Pedagogy

Ground Zero, New York

> There are language games in which the important thing is to listen, in which the rule deals with audition. Such a game is the game of the just. And in this game, one speaks only inasmuch as one listens, that is, one speaks as a listener, and not as an author. It is a game without an author.
>
> —Jean-François Lyotard

Danny's Riff

In January 2002, journalist Daniel Pearl was brutally beheaded in Pakistan by terrorists who filmed the slaughter and posted it on the Internet.[1] At the time I was working on a paper about rhetoric and peace (see chapter 5), so I decided to view the video to test my philosophical stamina and think through the connection between the information society and the reality of unthinkable violence. It has taken me many years to think about the digital enframing of scripted torture and to hear the language of pathos circulating online and not *off limits*. The script of his captors forced Daniel to utter these words: "My father is Jewish. My mother is Jewish. I am Jewish." Needless to say, I was *affected*. As Roland Barthes puts it, "affect was what I didn't want to reduce. . . . I wanted to explore it not as a question (a theme) but as a wound" (21). A rhetorically wounded academic, reeling from the sting of affect, I was not equipped to write arguments on his behalf. That would be the wrong language game, not to mention the wrong pragmatic. What "to do" lead me to this injunction: to bear witness to the cruel *mediation* of his murder. The problem was that I needed a postconflict means of argument in a post-9/11 world.

I needed a variation on a theme. I needed to riff on the rant against argument *qua* reason that I began in the essay "Writing Offshore" (2003) that appears in this book as chapter 4. The address for the present chapter, Ground Zero, is emblematic of a threshold where thousands haunt its abject violence, where cinder and ash permeate the "ground" in more ways than one. Its un-building on 9/11 is not, however, the kind of un-building I discuss in chapter 4. Nor is its ruination the sort of ruins I revisit in chapter 3. Ground zero was drifting toward distant shores. It opened a series of rifts that called for riffing, not argument. The process of terror, as we learned, resembled too closely the process of writing. Claims, grounds, and warrants were no longer just nominal features of argumentative prewriting, writing, and rewriting. They had, overnight, become the guided missives illuminating the dark side of rhetorical pedagogy anchored by the twin towers of process and argument. My thinking morphed from the original riff, "When Peace Is in Style" (delivered at CCCC 2004), to "Glitch Rhetoric: Shock Design and the Mediation of Global (T)error" (delivered at IT University, Copenhagen, 2005, and an earlier version of chapter 5). The following year, the riff folded computer games into the mashup when *Games and Culture* published "Armageddon Army: Playing God, God Mode Mods, and the Rhetorical Task of Ludology" (the earlier version of chapter 10). When invited to give a talk to the 30th International Wittgenstein Symposium in Austria the next summer (2007), I played a riff called "Playing Just, *Just Cause*: The Internet as Ace in the Language Game of Regime Change." In 2008, the riff continued. First at CCCC with "Cities of Rendition: Interrogation on/of the Extrajudicial Edge" on torture, and next at the Rhetoric Society of America conference with "Absolution and the Rhetorical Sanction of Rogue Responsibility" on autoimmunity. With a bit of suturing, those two papers morphed into "Torture and Absolution: The Shadow Twin Towers of Atro/City," published in *Fast Capitalism* (2008) and the earlier versions of chapter 6. Coming full circle, at the Watson Conference (2008), I started the riff sequel to "Writing Offshore" with "Marine Media: Composition and the Deep Play of Fluid Structures" (revised now as chapter 8). It seems there is no beyond to this process, which necessarily abrogates the link to postprocess pedagogy. Technically speaking, I have been listening to the field through Daniel Pearl's ears. For me, the forced trilemma—"My father is Jewish. My mother is Jewish. I am Jewish"—echoes the banality of "the" writing process (prewriting, writing, rewriting), but does not eschew our obligation to hear writing scripted and uttered under the most abominable, abject conditions. It is *process* under siege, taken hostage, and executed that should compel us to retool postprocess as postconflict. It is process *terrorized* that situates us all inside a beyond we cannot move past, inside a pedagogy that we cannot subvert. Not yet. If ever.

Lyotard opens *The Differend* as follows: "You are informed that human beings endowed with language were placed in a situation such that none of them is now able to tell about it" (3). A modern-day Gorgias posing a new trilemma: (a) nothing exists; (b) even if existence exists, it cannot be known; (c) even if it could be known, it cannot be communicated. Victor Vitanza (ever the postmodern, post-avant-guardian of "threes," excurses, ruminations, and other para-in-the-ethical writing) touchés the Gorgias-Lyotard duel with what he terms "a Dilemma-that-would-Become a Trilemma" (*Negation* 10). How to riff—I have had such teachers. Disaster, too, has its own pedagogical signature. Maurice Blanchot says: "To read, to write, the way one lives under the surveillance of the disaster: exposed to the passivity that is outside passion. The heightening of forgetfulness. It is not you who will speak; let the disaster speak in you, even if it be by your forgetfulness or silence" (4). It is necessary to listen to this speaking, which saturates all media with what is beyond conflict, but not what is beyond process—a procession of disasters marching past our classroom windows. Hooked on terrorist-phonics has me sounding out the words of Daniel Pearl.

Abstract Riff (The Obligatory Prewriting)

Among our field's numerous theoretical skirmishes is the seemingly endless conflict over what defines writing as a "process" and how we variously teach writing "in" process-specific terms. However, postprocess pedagogy emerged outside the concurrent introduction of computing technology and interactive (distributed) writing activities that inflected the peak historical moment of process pedagogy. The conflict over process, it seems, has played itself out as a battle between competing versions of what grounds method, rather than how ground itself turns postprocess into just another iteration of process. What makes me uncomfortable with this assertion is that it is precisely how critics of deconstruction discredit it by claiming it merely installs another iteration of what it seeks to unhinge, or worse, that it merely "plays" with itself in the name of radical critique. Without ascribing intentional motivation to postprocess pedagogy, it is still necessary to question how it recruits writing to outflank process in the tensions between form and content. It does so by tracking communication rather than form-in-process, and specifically relocates writing to agonistic contexts of epistemic rhetoric where meaning is constructed out of the reconstruction of embattled ideas. The cycle of creating conflict in order to reconstruct seems familiar to us because we recognize the economy of preemption. Insert visual rhetoric and new media remediations of conflict (remixed as sampled collages, montages, and narrative cut scenes), and we have the military equivalent of preventive war, complete with all the pretexts for justifying and initiating it. Conflict and rebuilding become twin sides of the postprocess coin. In a self-conscious deployment of military and war metaphors, this riff echoes Derrida's contention that "nowhere more than in the United States does deconstruction give rise to 'war'" (Paper Machine *114). The lessons of deconstruction serve, then, as both paper and machine in the postprocess inscription of conflict as the techné of composition theory. Rather than rebuild (or reconstruct) postprocess into postconflict pedagogy, it is my aim to destabilize the stabilizing momentum of any pedagogy that reiterates conflict in the name of writing.*

Definition Riff

(a motif, or phrase, repeated in the same musical voice
[from ostinato, *Italian for stubborn, persistent, obstinate])*

It is no comfort to know that we have inherited a dominant form of argumentative discourse, and have inherited its structures and methods, from an equally violent set of persuasive features. According to Joseph Tuman, "the meaning of terrorism is socially constructed. . . . [and] this violence and destruction becomes terrorism primarily because of its additional capacity to communicate message and meaning to a larger set of audiences" (xiv). And this is where my rhetorical stamina gets tested. Rhetoric, as the available means of persuasion in a given case (Aristotle), or as practical wisdom, or as the counterpart to dialectic, has evolved only insofar as it shifted its role in the conflict with philosophy. But above the fray it is not, and in the fray is where it has survived. The question is whether "the fray" itself has been hijacked and the game completely changed. If so, terrorism must be confronted within the rules of a game not communicated in the language of persuasion. Beheading videos, with their scripted torture, visual rhetoric, and terrorist "contact zone," are not a "process of communication" (Tuman

xiv) and *just should not "cut" it*. The upshot of my quibble with Tuman here is that this is not a benign process, much less a notion of communication based in a communal, common, exchange of messages—it is *not* a *just* game. Lyotard explains:

> Absolute injustice would occur if the pragmatics of obligation, that is, the possibility of continuing to play the game of the just, were excluded. That is what is unjust. . . . The taking of hostages is something else [something other than a war of adversaries]; it is the death of another person, a threat of death, that is used as an argument. It is pedagogical politics ["We will make you aware of Daniel Pearl's collusion!"] that looks pedagogical but cannot really be. It is a politics in which the real aim is to force the third party to yield. And the third party is not just the State, of which one makes oneself the threatening teacher, it is public opinion. (*Just Gaming* 66–67)

Pedagogy and rhetorical argument are, in light of this, caught in a classic double bind—damned if we do, damned if we don't. The mediation of torture and terror should call into question our debates on process pedagogy, postprocess pedagogy, and beyond. In fact, this is the "beyond" hailing me to question the technological apparatuses that configure, and shelter, the curriculum and methods of mainstream argument pedagogy. If, as Lyotard rightly points out, the "possibility of continuing to play the game of the just were excluded," then communication/composition theories and practices (and their rhetorical lobbyists) are perpetuating a "game of the unjust." Testing my pedagogical stamina would, then, amount to daring to assign my students to create a video that communicates to the butchers who slaughtered Daniel Pearl, and that does so as a move in their game of the unjust—since they write the rules, they hold him hostage, they script the endgame death. The impossible task for the student, for the teacher, is to create a video that listens, that manifests audition as a refusal of such a communication/argument designed not to persuade, but to terrorize. It calls for creating a new game, one that I am calling "postconflict pedagogy." It calls for mediation that does not inhabit the cushy platforms of academic networks and equipment; it calls for ruggedized hardware and rogue software. It calls for massive 404 errors that amass, and communicate, the signal of justice, that repeats the signal without assertion, thesis statements, evidence, grounds, or rebuttals. It does not recognize any known Web standard. It must jam and locate the source of terrorism with postconflict thinking—with audacious audition.

The play on sound allows for multimodal connotations of audition. One mode that sound invokes is, of course, auditory. Another mode reflects the marine metaphor of a "sound," or body of water forming a strait between two bodies of land. Such usage evolved from the Old Norse word *sund*, as in Øresund, which is the narrow body of water connecting Denmark and Sweden. Øre means "ear" in Norwegian and Danish. Sound is also a mode of thinking, characterized usually as error-free, or good, judgment. Sound is, in other words, caught in a matrix of meanings, none of which take precedence in this analysis. It functions rather like a radar term—it is attuned to, and tracks, thinking in a sundered world. Postconflict pedagogy starts from the position of the *sound* listener. It toggles the output off, the input on. It captures audio and bounces it back after scrambling the signal using a critical audacity. *It is about composing a hearing.* Writing that audits the school of terrorism is writing not in order to receive credit, or participate in such lessons of violence. Postconflict composition audits in order to reckon/cile, and examine, barbaric texts (as, for example, the Daniel Pearl video).

The question is how to write as auditors rather than orators. Lyotard spells this out in his discussion of "discourse pragmatics" (*Just Gaming* 35). According to Lyotard, when

> someone speaks to me; he places me under an obligation. . . . The obligation to retell. But not necessarily to my teller. I am not obligated to give it back to him, no, that is not it; but I am obligated in the way of a relay that may not keep its charge but must pass it on. (35)

There is movement, or energy, that must be passed on, what he calls "the subject of a kinetic metaphor" (36). This changes our position in the communication triangle, and it changes the power relations as well. In short, it "implies the very opposite of autonomy: heteronomy" (35). The problem is that with heteronomy, "the marked pole is not at all the pole of the author. . . . something we find almost unthinkable today" (36).

> Human beings are not the authors of what they tell, that is, of what they do, and that, in point of fact, there never are authors. Which does not mean that they have nothing to do. On the contrary, they have a thousand things to do, and they must constantly match wits with the fate they have been given, as well as with the fate they are being given in being made the addressee of any given speech act, such as an oracle, or a dream, for instance.

> It is precisely because they are not the authors of meaning that they must always rely on their wits. We are never in the autonomy of power. (36)

We are always auto/anonymously relaying the signal, the sound, of autonomous thinking (played out at best as error, at worst as violent action).

Pedagogy Riff

In the more pedestrian context of composition and rhetoric pedagogy, we have seen some movement away from autonomy in a collection of essays edited by Thomas Kent, *Post-Process Theory*, and in the scholarly reception to it. For example, in "Toward a Post-Process Composition: Abandoning the Rhetoric of Assertion," Gary Olson enumerates the various critiques of "process pedagogy," most notably its attempt to construct theories of the writing process that can be generalized for all and that entail mastering the process. The most significant problem with process pedagogy, as Olson sees it, is its central genre of argumentative writing, complete with thesis statements and expectations of gathering enough support to master the argument against another scholar. As such, Olson calls for "questioning a time-honored value in composition: what we might call the 'rhetoric of assertion'" (9). Following analyses of some key figures in postmodern theory, Olson concludes that

> the work of Lyotard, [Donna] Haraway, [Sandra] Harding, and many other theorists suggests that it is incumbent upon us all—especially, it would seem, those of us in rhetoric and composition—to challenge received notions of writing, of composition itself, to move away from a discourse of mastery and assertion toward a more dialogic, dynamic, open-ended, receptive, nonassertive stance. (14)

Jacques Derrida exemplifies Olson's call some years earlier (1985) in "Otobiographies" (from *The Ear of the Other*). Straightaway, Derrida begins a lecture about Nietzsche's autobiography, *Ecce Homo*, and *On The Future of Our Educational Institutions* by rejecting the apparatus of conventional argument: "I would like to spare you the tedium, the waste of time, and the subservience that always accompany the classic pedagogical procedures of forging links, referring back to prior premises or arguments, justifying one's own trajectory, method, system, and more or less skillful transitions, reestablishing continuity, and so on" (3–4). After proposing a compromise with his listeners (and suggesting they "can take it or leave it"), Derrida lays his cards on the table, so to speak.

> I do not teach truth as such; I do not transform myself into a diaphanous mouthpiece of eternal pedagogy. I settle accounts, however I can, on a certain number of problems: with you and with me or me, and through you, me, and me, with a certain number of authorities represented here. (4)

It turns out that Derrida is defending a protocol he later observes in the Nietzschean texts under examination in his lecture. The key (for our purposes) in following Derrida following Nietzsche's protocols is not to establish support for "writing a hearing," so much as slowing things down and "reading with" Derrida, since to some degree it is all we can do to do that much with his writing. Now, as Derrida comments on several protocols of reading published lectures that Nietzsche preferred were never published, he borrows a method for himself in the following passage:

> *Other protocol*: One must allow for the "genre" whose code is constantly re-marked, for narrative and fictional form and the "indirect style." In short, one must allow for all the ways intent ironizes or demarcates itself, demarcating the text by leaving on it the mark of genre. These lectures, given by an academic to academics and students on the subject of studies in the university and secondary school, amount to a theatrical infraction of the laws of genre and academicism. For the lack of time, I will not analyze these traits in themselves. However, we should not ignore the invitation extended to us in the preface to the lectures where we are asked to read slowly, like anachronistic readers who escape the law of their time by taking time to read—all the time it takes, without saying "for lack of time" as I have just done. (25–26)

Having established the protocols for his reading of Nietzsche, Derrida allows into our range of hearing a most unusual exchange about ears, listening, and writing. In this passage from the fifth lecture of Nietzsche's *On the Future of Our Educational Institutions*, we see the genesis of writing as listening first in the power relation between the university and the state, and second in the power relation between the university and the student. Nietzsche writes:

> Permit me, however, to measure this autonomy of yours by the standard of this culture, and to consider your university solely as a cultural establishment. If a foreigner desires to know something of our university system, he first of all asks emphatically: "How is the student connected with the university?" We answer: "By the ear, as a listener." The foreigner is astonished: "Only by the ear?" he repeats. "Only by the ear," we again reply. The student listens. When he speaks, when he sees, when he walks, when he is in good company, when he takes up some branch of art: in short, when he lives, he is autonomous, i.e., not dependent upon the educational institutions. Very often the student writes as he listens; and it is only at these moments that he hangs by the umbilical cord of the university. (qtd in "Otobiographies" 35)

Derrida then conjoins this passage with the maternal space Nietzsche has opened up.

> Dream this umbilicus: it has you by the ear. It is an ear, however, that dictates to you what you are writing at this moment when you write in the mode of what is called "taking notes." In fact, the mother—the bad or false mother whom the teacher, as functionary of the State, can only simulate—dictates to you the very thing that passes through your ear and travels the length of the cord all the way down to your stenography. This writing links you, like a leash in the form of an umbilical cord, to the paternal belly of the State. Your pen is its pen, you hold its teleprinter like one of those Bic ballpoints attached by a little chain in the post office. (35–36)

In this Nietzschean-Derridean revelation, not only is process pedagogy conspicuously absent (and postprocess pedagogy just a gleam in the paternalistic state's eye), my vision of postconflict pedagogy as "writing the hearing" needs a new media teletechnology in order to detach itself from this primal scene. We just need a new game, or a *just* game.

War Games Riff

Daddy-state got busy between September 11, 2001, and March 21, 2003. Lots of new games, with new rules were created, and some were even "listening" games (though we now know that they inappropriately listened in on the private conversations of US citizens, as well as terrorist chatter that wasn't yielding what they wanted, so they invented the hermeneutics of suspicion on steroids—Saddam has weapons of mass destruction, and al-Qaeda terrorists are in it thick as thieves). The linking of listening to preemptive logic and hearings to enhanced interrogation will spawn an era of un/sound thinking that leads to invasion euphoria. Shock and awe enter the roster of master tropes.

Postconflict pedagogy convenes a summit on *tropic* training, and we begin to back away from the "rhetoric of assertion" (Olson). So we set up the permanent camp of new media, refugees from the front line of media "embeds" and born of the military defense industry. Smart missile image software retooled to do research using Google Earth. Massively multiplayer online role-playing games (MMORPG) get "serious" and "social" in the life business (Second Life, Half-Life, Quarter Life, Facebook). Suddenly chatter is not what dizzy chicks do, it's the Patriot Act against the Dixie Chicks. In the economy of sound, the media camped out on the front yard of common decency, waiting for sound bites to toss into the feed/ing frenzy that has become *the* pedagogy of conflict *par excellence*. And while they waited, they played card games.

On April 11, 2003, just weeks after the US invasion of Iraq, the military announced it had created a deck of playing cards for the troops to identify the most-wanted members of Saddam Hussein's government ("Most-wanted"). Within hours of the announcement, some enterprising individuals discovered images of the cards on a Defense Department server and began producing them for sale on eBay. Consider this a "relay" in a series of rhetorical moves that were invented using what Greg Ulmer calls argument by conduction and image reasoning (*Internet* 9–10), both of which provide an associative logic linking Wittgenstein, Lyotard, Derrida, Nietzsche, the Internet, play, the war in Iraq, and regime change. In other words, the cards (and their subsequent proliferation on the Internet) function as a "serious game." But as I said before, I have been thinking and playing this game for many years. Thus, "I am obligated in the way of a relay that may not keep its charge but must pass it on" (Lyotard, *Just Gaming* 35). Put another way, I use this game to write a hearing.

Actually, the use of playing cards is not a new military strategy. According to a spokesman for the Defense Intelligence Agency,

> Such playing cards have been used as far back as the Civil War and again in World War II . . . and in the Korean War. Troops often play cards to pass the time, and seeing the names, faces and titles of the wanted Iraqis during their games will help soldiers and Marines in case they run into the wanted individuals in the field. ("Most-wanted")

Four years after "the Americans built a helicopter pad on the ruins of Babylon and filled their sandbags with archaeological fragments from the ancient city," a new pack of cards that depict Iraqi archeological sites were issued to troops under an archeological awareness program to help "preserve antiquities" but also "to discourage the illegal trade in artefacts" ("US issues"). But the "personality identification cards," developed by the Army's Psychological Operations group, obviously were not designed as a *certain* means of capturing the most-wanted members of Hussein's regime. They were a ruse dressed in the disguise of certainty. They sent a very specific message, "we are playing a serious game, and the game is fixed." So certain are we that we will win this game, we think of the regime as easily toppled as a stack of cards, as easily shuffled, as easily backed. We are a betting nation with a cheating heart. We stack the odds and deal the cards—and we never fold. We have justice on our side. We *are* justified. We set the tone in this world, and we aim to play rough. But make no mistake, we play *with* certainty: "mission accomplished."

In the collection of his last notes, *On Certainty*, Wittgenstein writes: "Certainty is *as it were* a tone of voice in which one declares how things are, but one does not infer from the tone of voice that one is justified" (6e). Codenamed *Operation Just Cause*, the US invasion of Panama, undertaken by then President George H. W. Bush, set the tone for the next President Bush to invade Iraq, each bent on regime change as part of their so-called "liberation theology." Bill Readings explains how Lyotard adopts Wittgenstein's notion of languages games.

> What is important is the way in which *Just Gaming* links Kant to Wittgenstein so as to insist that doing justice in a field of language games consists of resisting the pretensions of certain language games to provide the rules for other games, to become metalanguages. Thus in each language game we must try to judge without importing criteria from other games, such as that of theory (which claims to give criteria to all games). The language game, in Lyotard's reading, demands an indeterminate judgment, without criteria, on a case-by-case basis. (Readings 107)

Our task is *to listen* by *hearing* the dissemination of "just cause" logic in the language game of "playing just" and to then situate the dissemination of such logic within *information politics*, whereby the practice of regime change (often fueled by disinformation) is both enabled and disabled by the Internet and other forms of mass media.

Just Riff

The relay that suggests this move is taken from Lyotard's counterlogic in *Just Gaming*, namely, his contention that the "passage from the true to the just" raises a logical problem (23). So, too, the passage from work to play. If "the just is not of the same genre as the true" (24), we should also say that work is not of the same genre as play. Speaking as a listener is not limited to retelling. Lyotard concludes that it involves inventing "new moves, perhaps new rules and therefore new games" (100). Reconceiving the Internet as "netplay" is such a move. Earliest uses of the word network are taken from the Bible in reference to work "in the manner of a net." This trope can be applied to the Internet as play "in the manner of a net." Taken further, netplay can perform as a new move in the game of the just, an instance of Nietzsche's "play without security," versus the "sure play" that Derrida warned as the engineering of the end of play altogether ("Structure" 292).

Early terms for describing the Internet include "virtual reality," and the now exhausted phrase, "the information highway." Whereas the original invention of the network was established to facilitate communication among scientists and eventually military defense, the most rapid and common use of the network was to play games. In other words, illegitimate uses of the network reside alongside the legitimate uses: file sharing and illegal downloading, YouTube and hostage videos. And, it was not long before political forces saw the incredible rhetorical power of combining games, information, and strategy. Information politics is not a new game in warfare; it has been a strategic means of combating the enemy since Helen of Troy was seduced by language to the info wars of the twentieth and twenty-first centuries. The same Psychological Operations Group that created the playing cards are also responsible for designing messages to enemy troops and civilians that are dropped from aircraft. The history of dropping aerial leaflets over enemy territory suggests that text and images are powerful tools for inducing psychological results, for implanting fear as a means that justifies the end—or, as persuasive arguments in the war in Iraq to compel citizens not to sabotage oil field operations (see chapter 5). Regime change is a rhetorical business. But, primarily, regime change is economical; establishing democracy is merely its pretext. We all know that the symbiosis between capitalism and warfare enables individuals and governments to benefit financially from the war, from Halliburton's lucrative contract to reconstruct Iraq to the Iraq playing cards. But netplay also reverse engineers the network when dissent manifests itself in various forms of socially engaged activism made possible by the Internet.

One example of such netplay is a game called *Regime Change*. Created as an Internet fixed art piece, the designers explain that *Regime Change* operates

> using the statistics of n-grams, a technique used for textual games for more than 50 years. . . . These n-grams are chains of words, and these instruments use shared chains between documents as "bridges," allowing movement from the text of one document into a body of text created from others (and back). By using this approach to make text playable, by taking the logic of word chains to defamiliarizing and sometimes humorous extremes, *Regime Change* . . . provide[s] ways to perform William Burroughs's injunction to "cut word lines"—to break the chains of conceptual association that say this follows from that. (*Regime Change*)

Designed to splice together the US war in Iraq and the assassination of President Kennedy, the game argues rhetorically and netplayfully that both events are instances of regime change. The instability of the text in *Regime Change* highlights the "instability of criteria" that Lyotard maintains is the only rule of the game of the just (*Just Gaming* 9). Specifically, he writes, "the ability to judge does not hang upon the observance of criteria. The form that it will take in [Kant's] last critique is that of the imagination. An imagination that is constitutive. It is not only an ability to judge; it is a power to invent criteria" (17).

It is also an ability to express the "suture," the stitching that heals the wounds inflicted by the will-to-certainty. Threading the needle between Wittgenstein and Lyotard involves problematizing such will, an instance of which, I argue, was Bush's path to war in Iraq. Wittgenstein reminds us "that one is sometimes convinced of the correctness of a view by its *simplicity* or *symmetry*, i.e., these are what induce one to go over to this point of view. One then simply says something like: 'That's how it must be'" (14e). But Lyotard insists that the prescriptive cannot be derived from the descriptive, these are different language games and require different strategies. "The just is not of the same genre as the true" (*Just Gaming* 24). This is especially problematic in ideological conflicts. Lyotard, via Wittgenstein, understands all too well the consequences of so-called regime change: "it is inherent to oppression to import into a language game a question that comes from another one and to impose it" (53). In such cases, he argues, "we are dealing with two systems of prescriptions that encroach upon each other and that are incompatible. That leads to war" (68).

Stealth Riff

But how does such simple and symmetrical description transform itself into the prescriptive? Bush's faith-based liberation theology exemplified Wittgenstein's simple claim that "if someone is looking for something and perhaps roots around in a certain place, he shows that he believes that what he is looking for is there" (37e). "Sure evidence is what we *accept* as sure, it is evidence that we go by in *acting* surely, acting without any doubt. What we call a 'mistake' plays a quite special part in our language games, and so too does what we regard as certain evidence" (27e). Lyotard suggests such a pragmatic is "rationalist terrorism" (*Just Gaming* 74). "It is a politics in which the real aim is to force the third party to yield. And the third party is not just the State . . . it is public opinion. One invites public opinion to apply pressure on the State by applying pressure on it through fear" (67). In short, "it is not true that a political decision can be derived from a reason of history" (74), such as from the events of September 11, 2001. Bush's certainty, boasted in the now famous "mission accomplished" declaration, circulated the feeling of winning so important to the US response to 9/11 and so crucial to its policy of regime change in the Middle East. But Wittgenstein warned that

> there is always the danger of wanting to find an expression's meaning by contemplating the expression itself, and the frame of mind in which one uses it, instead of always thinking of the practice. That is why one repeats the expression to oneself so often, because it is as if one must see what one is looking for in the expression and in the feeling it gives one. (79e)

Mission accomplished. Lyotard put it thus: "a language game that becomes excessive . . . the 'wanting to have too much of it' . . . precisely when such a language game begins to regulate language games that are not the same as itself, isn't such a language game always assisted by the sword?" (*Just Gaming* 99).

One thing is certain. The Internet, or netplay, has enabled language games to proliferate exponentially during wartime, and war has become the most popular premise for computer games. A 2006 game entitled *Just Cause* (loosely based on the US invasion of Panama) "is set on a fictional

South American tropical island called 'San Esperito,' where the player works . . . to overthrow [a] dictator, who may be in possession of weapons of mass destruction" (*Just Cause*). War provides intertextual inspiration for game designers. But even in 2003, in the face of indisputable lack of evidence and unwavering public opinion against the war, Bush's language game of regime change showed no signs of abating. It was "operation just cause" all over again. Wittgenstein would *perhaps* counsel Bush in this way: "Certain events would put me into a position in which I could not go on with the old language-game any further. In which I was torn away from the *sureness* of the game. Indeed, doesn't it seem obvious that the possibility of a language-game is conditioned by certain facts?" (82e). "Why, would it be *unthinkable* that I should stay in the saddle however much the facts bucked?" (81e).

The image of Bush riding a bucking horse is not so far-fetched given his identification with Texan iconography. But one must have an exit strategy even for a bucking horse. In July 2007, a member of the US military offered a solution to the war in Iraq for sale on eBay. According to reports,

> "A Solution to the War in Iraq," is being offered by a US Army intelligence officer fed up with the conflict and anxious to attract some attention to what he says is a viable and face-saving solution to the four-year-old conflict. "I am offering the winning bidder the solution to the war in Iraq," the seller, identified as "cptnabil," says in the bid. "This is not a flippant or facetious offer . . . If you are the high bidder, I will send you a viable solution to the conflict in which we are currently engaged," the seller wrote . . . "I speak the language and understand the culture, history, and religion, well enough to construct a fair, honorable, and successful plan." . . . The lot comes with a buy-it-now price tag of five million dollars and if not sold will go to the highest bidder when the auction ends on Sunday. ("U.S. army officer")

Iraqis were also using the Internet in innovative ways hoping to save their own lives. Apparently images from Google Earth were being used by some university students to find safe roads home each day, while other Iraqis used the maps to identify villages on which they launched mortar fire in the increasing sectarian violence (Hussein).

My point is that netplay effectively deconstructs the concept of the Internet as the information highway. Netplay suggests that the Internet is more of an ambiguous outpost where the incompatibility between language games reveals the paradox in playing just. What is unthinkable is to stop the play. Lyotard is adamant that "absolute injustice would occur if the pragmatics of obligation, that is, the possibility of continuing to play the game of the just, were excluded. That is what is unjust" (*Just Gaming* 66). "Rationalist terrorism" is such an exclusionary game. The ill/logic of just cause is made in the image of playing just.

Streaming Riff

Listening with writing on Facebook, or streaming live suicides on Justin.tv without intervening in someone's death, is a difficult cross between compassion fatigue and watching beheading videos. Abraham Biggs took his own life on November 19, 2008, by an overdose, and all of it (including his suicide note) was posted and streamed live on Justin.tv via his webcam. Viewers who watched the video for twelve hours while he died did not wish to contend with the conflict playing out before them. Abraham's conflict with himself and life was a public event. People posted as it happened, egging him on, taunting him and belittling him. In such instances writing a hearing becomes writing a drive-by shouting. Streaming death (Abraham's "deathcasting") is juxtaposed with engineered cinematic death (Pearl's beheading) in order to posit (position myself) on the threshold of writing a hearing for cultural dispassion (lack of compassion) and writing a hearing for terrorist impassion (cinematic terrorism "as an argument"). In both cases the listening takes place as writing a fatal hearing. "My father is Jewish. My Mother is Jewish. I am Jewish" (Pearl video). "User1: Go ahead and do it. User3: Instant Darwinism" (Biggs transcript; Tresniowski 106).

Daniels' Riff

The name Daniel has stood in for a "process" gone horribly bad. Daniel Pearl's captors had to start over when the camera jammed. They had to "revise" the text and remix the video death scene. Writing the hearing must cut this signal off, it abhors re-vision as re-seeing the scene of sacrifice—the cut scene as transition (or, worse, as re-membering). Another Daniel (Carter) listens, walks the streets of New York playing saxophone, relaying the sounds of listening. After 9/11, this Daniel and I exchanged messages from the front lines—New York/Texas (Bush-land). I worried the words into questions. Daniel listened them into something more.

> Bluely sunheaded sea of c again vibrates its waves at in and through d their mutual weavery seek out some of all ways is there an all ways? All includes all what? the total? total taboo postmodern ghost-modes taboo the total all of it out of bounds its classic obliquity electricurrently oper-antennae upscope downscope perifunctions feelings reelings squealings sealings unsealings ceilings revealings sea-eelings see e-links billowing reveilings welling up glow of a crow for the caws glossed "n" scanned for resonances aglosspectrum quest for the best in that instant sense a fit one shaken peace weave surf-vibed hit all a wonderwave under th' under otherwives node has oh kite as Anna Proxywarmate animation-imbued sunlight sound sew undue so-coiled th' us "n" sew undo "n" re-do: re-allocate the blazes critical metals mass melting if not boiling {point[(s}un) heeded] taking their th' air-tide "all" tied t' gather a puff all else poof the now prominently densely war-eyed war-ride prismically danceswerve disperse diffuse re-channel redirect sublimate in lieu of repress: inspect with lux-lucks-light la luce amore potenza six billion hearts "n" souls their curve "n" sway of e-vents wear in the vine mist of utters ease lumen t' lumen. (Carter)

I heard the Daniels calling and streamed the sound inglorious.

> osaycanuc
> buythdonsurlylite
> wotsorowdlywehail
> inthtwiloutslazgleening
> hoodzbrownstrypznburntstarz
> threwthpoorilustflite
> orethramrodswewashdwhirrsogalavantlyscreaming
> &throcketsredglarethbombsburstinginair
> gaveproophthrewthnitrothathourflagwuzstillswear
> osaydozthstorespatteredbomberyetwag
> orethlandofthspreeandthhomeofthbrash

8
Marine Media

1214 Middle St., Sullivan's Island, South Carolina

> Inclination [desire] speaks out: "I don't want to have to enter this risky world of discourse; I want nothing to do with it insofar as it is decisive and final; I would like to feel it all around me, calm and transparent, profound, infinitely open, with others responding to my expectations, and truth emerging, one by one. All I want is to allow myself to be borne along, within it, and by it, a happy wreck."
>
> Institutions reply: "But you have nothing to fear from launching out; we're here to show you discourse is within the established order of things, that we've waited a long time for its arrival, that a place has been set aside for it—a place which both honours and disarms it; and if it should happen to have a certain power, then it is we, and we alone, who give it that power."
>
> —Michel Foucault, *Discourse on Language*

This is a *déjà vu*, or more accurately, a *déjà visité*—in 2008, while on my first visit to Charleston, I had the eerie sensation I had visited this place before. I was sitting on a tourist boat headed into the Atlantic. This time, however, it was not a whale safari (see chapter 4), it was a short trip from Sullivan's Island, South Carolina (the landing site for thousands of African slaves and the address for this chapter), over to Fort Sumter. As we approached the ruins of the fort, made famous as the site of the first engagement of the Civil War, I noticed a pod of dolphins playing near the boat. And as the recorded voice of the tourist guide led us through the history of that engagement of April 12, 1861, I was struck by the incredible disjuncture of watching the sheer pleasure of the playful dolphins while hearing about one of the darkest times in our nation's history. I found myself shifting my gaze back and forth, from marine *life* to *marine* life. From the *media*tion of slavery, death, and destruction, to the vitalism of deep play. I was on a watery threshold looking at play situated between two stark addresses of violence. As odd as this may seem, this disjuncture provided evidence for the problem I find in how we have approached the use of new media in teaching composition. Namely, we engineer our sanctuaries, rather than sanctify our *bricoleurs*. We seek refuge in reason rather than learn a new game. We do not like to drift. But adrift is always where we *are*. And at play is always *how* we are. No matter how much we tinker, no matter how deep we dig, no matter how solid our edifice—play will push us out to sea every time.

The question is how to reconcile the deep play of fluid structures with the marching orders of writing that flows. This passage from a writing center handout illustrates the current thinking: "Clear writing is writing that flows. In order to create flow, begin sentences with old information. . . . Just as it is wise to begin sentences with old information, it is wise to end them with new information" (Dudenhefer). The more structure, the more clarity. But where does this leave fluidity? How did flow get redefined as structure?

Derrida triangulated the problem some forty years ago, and Nietzsche roughly eighty years before that, when he announced,

> The concept of centered structure is in fact the concept of a play based on a fundamental ground, a play constituted on the basis of a fundamental immobility and a reassuring certitude, which itself is beyond the reach of play. And on the basis of this certitude anxiety can be mastered, for anxiety is invariably the result of a certain mode of being implicated in the game, of being caught by the game, of being as it were at stake in the game from the outset. ("Structure" 279)

The upshot of such anxiety is our will to contain flow, to end play altogether. Moreover, as Diane Davis observes, "We teachers of composition, of course, launch our own torpedoes of desire, aimed directly into our students and designed to make something happen, something that will affect their structural formation and, therefore, their productions" (*Breaking* 228; qtd in Hawk 255). Teachers of writing, perhaps teachers in general, are sadly signed on as deckhands on so many vessels of containment—institutions merely container ships transporting containers into the congested harbors of homeland security. Against this image I want to shift our gaze to play and life in order to rehabilitate fluid writing and those of us who want to teach *with* the flow.

But, first a word about the *order* of discourse. Foucault put the problem of desire and institution into a dialogue about life, knowing that theirs are "but two converse replies to the same anxiety . . . uncertainty faced with a transitory existence, destined for oblivion—at any rate, not belonging to us" ("Discourse" 216). So, he asks two questions: "What is so perilous, then, in the fact that people speak, and that their speech proliferates? Where is the danger in that"? (216). His "hypothesis" is "that in every society the production of discourse is at once controlled, selected, organised and redistributed according to a certain number of procedures, whose role is to avert its powers and dangers, to cope with chance events, to evade its ponderous, awesome materiality" (216). What is this formidable materiality of discourse? I believe it is its fluidity, and that is what makes it so formidable to teach. We do not understand the nature of fluidity in the context of structure.

This translates, for me, into a rather embarrassing disconnect at the heart of multimodal composition. Technologies are increasingly playful and calling us to play, even those most proprietary of technologies, computer games. Yet textbooks in rhetoric and composition are only slowly shifting their traditional structural approach to fluid writing. For the most part the prevailing winds of visual rhetoric, new media, and multimodal composition are still struggling with reason's mandate to control discourse. To counter this mandate, we need to look to designers and architects whose work could help us to think differently about how we teach rhetoric and composition, and what follows are a few examples.

It is tempting to focus on text and the technologies of text production. However, ideological analyses of typography, such as John Trimbur's call to rematerialize literacy and reveal the labor process of writing, do not address the *formidability* of the materiality of discourse that Foucault points to (Trimbur "Delivering"). Whereas design research, and especially design researchers who write about design, may harbor potentially valuable correlations in this area. Ellen Lupton, author of *Thinking with Type*, offers a more vitalist take on text production. She writes,

> Text is a fluid made from the hard, dry crystals of the alphabet. . . . Today, designers look back at the systematic, abstracting tendencies of modern letter design and both celebrate and challenge that rationalizing impulse. They have exchanged the anthracite deposits of the classical letter for lines of text that quiver and bleed like living things. . . . Today, it is more illuminating to speak of solvents than solutions. Design is often an attack on structure, or an attempt to create edifices that can withstand and engage the corrosive assault of content.

Lupton understands the need for edifice as well as the value of fluid ways of thinking. And she locates the source of corrosion more in the saline logos of content than in the liquid force of life.

In the early nineties, Marcos Novak poured a similar theory into what he called "liquid architectures." Lance Olsen explains,

> If innovative print texts tend to arrive in our hands with certain obvious material limitations (most, for example, appear in bound spines), thereby suggesting an at least relatively stable if reversible architecture, then hypermedial ones arrive on our screens with certain less obvious material limitations, a greater sense of option, thereby suggesting what Marcos Novak calls the liquid architecture of cyberspace—an architecture, as he says, "without doors or hallways," a visionary architecture that seeks out extreme regions that feel like "spatialized music," a continuously unfixed, flickering, mercurial architecture "whose form is contingent on the interests of the beholder," "a version of what it is becoming, a structure for what does not yet exist." (Olsen)

According to Novak,

> Liquid architecture is an architecture that breathes, pulses, leaps as one form and lands as another. Liquid architecture is . . . an architecture that opens to welcome me and closes to defend me; it is an architecture without doors and hallways, where the next room is always where I need it to be and what I need it to be. (250)

Such radical visions of structure are not, of course, novel in architectural circles today, but Novak was writing before the days of CAD software and the increasing trend away from blue-line drawing. Novak's materials were virtual and mediated as performance art pieces. My sister Sherry McReynolds, an architect who has worked on projects from Las Vegas to Dubai, would say Novak likes to work with "unobtanium," a material common to virtual designs for which there is no material on earth that would withstand the force of earth's gravity and *stand*. Novak's thinking compels our attention to his mediation of marine ideas in fluid materials, and setting them into a performative, and deep sense of, play. For Novak, "a liquid architecture is clearly a dematerialized architecture. It is an architecture that is no longer satisfied with only space and form and light and all the aspects of the real world. It is an architecture of fluctuating relations between abstract elements" (251).

Novak's vision is, however, somewhat a reality now. Consider a project created for Expo 2008 in Zaragoza, Spain, dubbed the Digital Water Pavilion. MIT's Sense*able* City Lab was tasked with creating a space that reflected the theme of water and sustainable development. MIT's team chose an extremely playful structure program. They "first decided to set aside the formalist approach that characterized most of the recent developments in digital design. . . . They then addressed the issues of reconfigurability and interactivity, which can acquire a new dimension because of digital water."

> Digital water can be described as a wall made with a digitally controlled flow of water. It would be possible to display writings and patterns on it, as well as connecting sensors to create an interactive digital-physical environment. . . . The presence of water walls and digital technology allows the building to be reshaped. Water walls along the perimeter and additional internal ones create spaces that are reconfigurable through time. Furthermore, the roof is moveable thanks to hydraulic pistons that can push it up and down.
>
> The presence of people can be sensed . . . and this plays an important role in the dynamic process, allowing waves and other distortions to be generated. William J. Mitchell had an initial dream of throwing a ball at the pavilion and having the water curtain open and swallow it.

This feature could not be implemented before the Expo 2008 opened; however, it "remains one of the goals that inspired the overall programming of the pavilion." As a structure, the Digital Water Pavilion reflects the inherently playful and temporary relation of discourse and materiality. "By night or during the winter it can be collapsed onto the ground. At that point, all three-dimensional space disappears. Then the machine is off" (Ratti).

If we import, and translate, such thinking about play, space, materiality, fluidity, and interactivity into the context of rhetoric and composition, it is not necessarily a logical blue-line rendering of the initial problem—namely, how to reconcile the deep play of fluid structures with the marching orders of writing that flows. Fortunately, we do have exemplars, and precursors, that we should foreground anew now that multimodal composition and visual rhetoric are transforming our theories and pedagogies. I say foreground anew because they have largely been waves not taken by rhetoric and composition except in the nineties among early adopters of the hypertext software, Storyspace, and other experimental writing spaces such as MOOs and Open Doc applications.

After the Web forever changed hypertext authoring, Eastgate Systems more or less abandoned Storyspace and developed the Tinderbox application for MAC OS X, which takes advantage of the StretchText notion conceived in 1967 by Ted Nelson. According to George Landow, such hypermediated writing

> involves expansion and contraction, in which the new text moves in two opposite directions at once . . . if speed is properly calibrated to allow for reading at both ends simultaneously on the fly, then the feeling of contextual dependency is significantly heightened. With expansion from the center of the new lexia, text moving backward works to complete the newly created hanging fragment that precedes the new insertion; text moving forward (in the normal direction of reading) aims to give reverse justification for the waiting text that now marks the latter half of the newly old, contextualizing material. Moreover, the cognitive experience of learning to read in multiple directions at once so as to realign severed context is, to say the least, rather mind-bending. What is exciting about this approach is that, from a cognitive standpoint, it creates an alternative reading procedure that while predictably difficult remains surprisingly possible. (Landow *Tekka* 3.2)

In short, Tinderbox values digression. It simulates the ebb and flow of writing and reading. However, Nelson reminds us that details and narrative arrangements must remain fixed in their relative order through different levels of StretchText. Order still constrains thinking because order still controls writing.

A perhaps less well-known experiment with the deep play of fluid structures, a program called TextArc by interaction designer W. Bradford Paley, suggests that even playing with the structure of existing texts, such as *Alice in Wonderland*, exposes a liquid layer of writing that resists the fixity and order of discourse. Unfortunately, we cannot see the real-time rendering of this TextArc, but the screenshots reveal the beauty of a more fluid structure as it draws the text. As Paley explains the process,

> An entire text is arranged in an arc, stepping clockwise, starting at 12:00. Lines are drawn around the outside, words around the inside. Words that appear more often are brighter. Words used more than once in the text are drawn only once, at their average position. Here, rays are drawn from "Alice" to everywhere she appears. A curved line can connect the words in the order they appear in the text. This is just for fun, showing how the TextArc space relates to the original linear space of the text.

This is just for fun. But notice its complexity, its *play* with order, and its highly fluid real-time delivery of the text.

Play, I am arguing, is not simple. And fluidity is not orderly. In other words, the question of order is also a question of complexity. Fluid structures are beautiful, but complex. Byron Hawk's book, *A Counter-History of Composition: Toward Methodologies of Complexity*, tackles the resistance in rhetoric and composition to vitalism and complexity. According to Hawk, oppositional and investigative responses to the question of life have resulted in classical and romanticist approaches to rhetoric and teaching, which have led to overly simplified ways of viewing language and reductive methods for teaching writing. In a highly nuanced argument that gathers up posthumanist theories, postmodern contexts, and emerging digital technologies, Hawk proposes that "transforming rhetoric and composition's image of vitalism from mysticism to complexity provides a basis for thinking about rhetoric and pedagogy that is more attuned to contemporary contexts" (6). Order opposes. Order investigates. Order *contains* vitality. It must . . . otherwise desire (that great sea of *disorder*) would cause it to *evaporate.* That is the *déjà vu* we *think* we cannot afford, but it is the *déjà visité* we must dare to dream . . . in writing.

It's the Dream

It's the dream we carry in secret
that something miraculous will happen
that it must happen—
that time will open
that the heart will open
that doors will open
that the rockface will open
that springs will gush—
that the dream will open,
that one morning we will glide into
some little harbor we didn't know was there.

(Olav Hauge 58)[1]

9
Accidental Metaphysics

Mendocino Ridge, Pacific Ocean

> With full gaze the animal sees the open.
> Only our eyes, as if reversed, are like snares
> set around it, block the freedom of its going.
> Only from the face of the beast do we know
> what *is* outside; for even little children
> we turn around and force them to look backward
> at the world of forms, and they do not see the open
> so deep in the animal's eyes. Free from death.
> Only we see *that*;
>
> —Rainer Maria Rilke, "The Eighth Elegy"

The first time I saw my daughter, she was sitting on a horse. A dappled gray, to be exact—the sort Gerard Manley Hopkins would praise, hinting as dappledness does at "Pied Beauty": "All things counter, original, spare, strange; / Whatever is fickle, freckled (who knows how?) / With swift, slow; sweet, sour; adazzle, dim;" . . . "couple-colour," "stipple" stem (47). My daughter and her horse, I took them in, and *thought* had no part in the taking. Eighteen years of lost mothering came to a boil in an uncanny alchemy of wonder and weeping as I bore witness to the intimate connection between Jackie and her horse. In that moment, I let go of the lost years, I released my stale laments; I surrendered her to her horse as I surrendered her for adoption the day she was born. Being with Others has an inverse: Being Without. I looked upon her with an untethered heart; she was mine, but she was not. It was an accident of sorts. Accidental birth; accidental loss. And now an accident of thought.

I delivered her, yes. But back then we were not allowed *our* look. One minute she was with me, then I woke up without. I had to learn not to think about her. Which meant I learned how not to think. Now I know what animals don't think about.[1] But there she was, and I had waited seventeen years to lay eyes on her. She sat easy on that horse, smiling, laughing, chatting with her friends at the rodeo, each waiting for their turn to run the barrels event for which they had trained so well. I, however, had no training whatsoever for this moment. In fact, I found myself fixated on her horse, or rather on their relationship. It was as if they were one. They moved as one, they idled with a familiarity only they understood. But it was not a conceptual understanding; it was raw reciprocity. That day reciprocity jumped a childhood trough and pierced me into showing up; *I* was born by Jackie's look. The horse cantered us together, thinking not of pain nor loss, much less the weight of human thought.[2]

> And yet within the warm and watchful creature
> is the care and heaviness of a great melancholy.
> For it also clings to him always, that
> which often overcomes us—memory:
> As if once before the thing for which we strive
> had been closer, truer, and the relation
> infinitely tender. Here all is distance,
> there it was breath. After the first home
> the second is hybrid and open to the winds.
> . . . .
> And we: onlookers, always, everywhere,
> turned toward everything and never from!
> We are surfeited. We set it in order. It breaks.
> We put it in order again and break down ourselves.
> (Rilke, "The Eighth Elegy")

An animal sets itself within an order outside of thought. The breaking down is only in our minds. The vexed relation of thought and nonthought is like breakaway roping, wherein the precise tension and timing is troubled by the question of looking less taut. Into this muddy arena I am untying knots; since a champion I am not of wrangling with wrangler thought.

What, then, of this "full gaze" with which the animal sees the "open"; and what is this "open"?

In Heidegger's lecture "What are Poets For?" delivered in 1946 on the twentieth anniversary of Rilke's death, Heidegger focuses on a number of Rilke's poems, but is primarily enamored with some improvised verses, the character of which Heidegger reads "as an exercise in poetic self-reflection" (100) (for more about Rilke's improvised verses, see my chapter 4). Those verses have been so significant to me that I have recited them at the grave of a beloved cat. Now, however, with an eye toward the animal's unthought, I am drawn to Heidegger's discussion of Rilke's "Eighth Elegy." Heidegger cites a letter that Rilke writes to a Russian reader "who had questioned him about the eighth elegy" ("Poets" 107). Rilke writes:

> You must understand the concept of the "Open," which I have tried to propose in the elegy, in *such* a way that the animal's degree of consciousness sets it into the world without the animal's placing the world over against itself at every moment (as we do); the animal is *in* the world; we stand *before it* by virtue of that peculiar turn and intensification which our consciousness has taken. . . . By the "Open," therefore, I do not mean sky, air, and space; they, too, are "object" and thus "opaque" and closed to the man who observes and judges. The animal, the flower, presumably *is* all that, without accounting to itself. (qtd in Heidegger 108)

This is, I believe, precisely what we envy in the animal, as well as why we find its gaze so elusive; we demand accounting each time we look into its eyes. But occasionally, our demand is met with a reciprocal demand; the demand that we show up.

In Luanne Frank's essay in *JAC*, "Heidegger, Captain Paul Watson, and the 'Look' of the Leviathan," the reciprocity is read across a 1975 encounter between Paul Watson and a whale, the experience of which was so deeply formative that it became the founding narrative of the Sea Shepherd Conservation Society, later known as Greenpeace. I chose the address for this chapter as the site where Captain Paul Watson encountered the whale, the recounting of which is the subject of Frank's essay, but it could also be off the coast of Northern Norway, near Andenes, where I also encountered a whale (see chapter 4). Frank recounts how Watson and another activist, Fred Easton, were maneuvering a small boat between a Soviet whaling ship and its prey in order to make it "too risky for them to shoot" (597). But the female sperm whale was harpooned anyway, as was her mate after he "spun toward her" upon hearing her scream. As he reared out of the water and "hurled himself right at the Soviet vessel," the mate was hit, fell back, and swam back to attack again, this time rearing up such that, according to Watson, "a quarter of his bulk tower[ed] above us" (597), and it seemed he would slam down on our small boat, and that would be the end of us. Instead, they saw all the whale's muscles contract suddenly, and the whale pulled back as if he instinctively knew they were trying to save him. Later, Watson would recall that "'as [the whale] slide back into the water, I looked into his eye and I saw recognition. Empathy. What I saw in his eye as he looked at me would change my life forever. He saved my life and I would return the favor'" (Heller 6; qtd in Frank 599).

Frank reads this narrative as analogous to the kind of "looking into" beings that occupies several pages of in-depth discussion in Heidegger's lectures on Parmenides, delivered during a course in the winter semester of 1942–43. While Frank acknowledges that Heidegger is talking about *human* looking, Frank invokes a reading of the look shared between a human and a whale as a look of the kind Heidegger distinguishes as "encountering," rather than ensnaring, or grasping. In *Parmenides*, Heidegger describes

> it as a look that, not imposing itself on the one looked *at* (the other), instead extends itself *to* the other and both awaits the other as such (as it were, expectantly letting the other be) and awaits in return a reciprocal look from the other—whereupon, when that answering look is extended, both parties "are." Receipt of the encountering look permits its recipient to show up, and the initiator's receipt of the reciprocal look, in return, issues in his own being uncovered. (103; qtd in Frank 592)

In short, Frank recaps, "via one's own looking, reciprocated by the other, one contributes, however inadvertently, to one's own as well as to the other's showing up. One's own looking, reciprocated, enables oneself as well as the other to appear and to 'be'" (593). Here, as he will later in "What are Poets For?," Heidegger rejects the human's look, the kind of "representational looking upon and looking at, by which man turns toward beings as 'objects' and grasps them" (103).

Security and safety concerns permeate the matrix of contemporary life. Animal activists such as Paul Watson seek to place animals on an equal footing, so to speak, with humans in this regard. Yet Heidegger's reading reveals the *accidental* relation between human thought and real and perceived danger. Heidegger's understanding of Rilke motivates a metaphysics based in Being *in* the world, rather than Being "against" the world (as in subject/object dualism). In 1946, Heidegger entered this relation on the first line of the ledger of modernity by claiming that the "danger that is assailing man consists in the threat that assaults man's nature in his relation to Being itself, and not in accidental perils. This danger is *the* danger" ("What Are Poets For?" 117). According to Heidegger, reading Rilke, "our unshieldedness" lies precisely in the difference between man's self-assertive nature and the state of "dim delight" in which animals live their lives. We set up an *accidental* metaphysics; creatures are "benumbed." We are enlightened; beasts are "muted," that is, "never breaking out of the draft of the unbounded drawing onward, which is untroubled by the restless relating back and forth in which conscious representation stumbles along" (109). Thus, on the human side of the relation, accidental metaphysics installs the snare right from the beginning, at birth—encountering is forestalled and the bond is pulled up tight. By looking encounteringly into Luanne Frank's unwavering eye upon Heidegger, Paul Watson, a whale, and Parmenides, I am conscious (though not in a "restless relating back and forth" way) of returning her look, of reciprocating without grasping *for* the *right* words. What *ethos* I offer flows not from the exigency of this response to her article, but rather from having been a beneficiary of Frank's teaching. My words have been fortunate enough in the past to have been granted her look. My eyes have encountered her enabling look. We have read one another, as such. Our worlds have crossed. By coincidence I studied with her husband Ted Frank during the early seventies when I was an undergraduate. It would be ten years later that I would enter the graduate program and accident/ly meet Luanne Frank, a chance encounter that has lasted for over thirty years.

There are some accidents of worth. I may have never tied my daughter's ribbons, but I have shown up; and not because I *thought* her into being. Ours has been a dimmed delight. I believe to this day it is why I took solace in poetry, even before she was born. It is why I hold dear Heidegger's question, "what are poets for?" It is *how* I can bear having let her go. I was not there to twist her around, to force her backward look at the world of forms. What a bittersweet lesson in *that*. I cut the cord and un/ensnared our *normal* fate. It was not meant *to be*. It was meant as elegy.

Always turned to creation, we see there
only the reflection of the free,
darkened by us. Or that a beast, a dumb one,
lifts his eyes and looks us calmly through and through.
That's what Destiny is: to be face to face
and nothing but that and always opposite.

If the sure animal that approaches us
in a different direction had this awareness of ours,
he would drag us along behind him. But his existence
is infinite to him, ungrasped, without a glimpse
at his condition, pure as his outward gaze.
And where we see the future, he sees All
and himself in All and himself healed forever.

(Rilke, "The Eighth Elegy")

10
Armageddon Army

Umm Qasr, Iraq

He logs in as SteadyAim and locks and loads his icon in the crosshairs of a misguided viewpoint. His signature flaunts a violent epistemology: "I watch the world through my scope" (RainbowSix 3 forum). We imagine him prone, a forward-deployed predatory reconnaissance player with a heavily armed worldview. We read his scattershot opinions formed while shooting from the hip.

> <*cut scene*>: Wide-angle shot of the Pentagon on September 11, 2001. Camera zooms in on the flames and smoke billowing into the restricted airspace over the nation's capitol. Voice-over dialogue:

High school student (male): *So, why do they call it the Department of Defense if it can't even defend its own headquarters?*

Teacher: *Actually it was originally the War Department until after World War II when it became part of the newly reorganized military branch of the government called the Department of Defense.*

High school student (male): *Maybe we need to switch it back to the War Department.*

Teacher: *Ya think?*

Over on Christian Coders Network we meet Cheesestorm, who responds to the thread "What game would Jesus play?":

> Jesus would probably let you reload before continuining [*sic*], unless you were a camper. And if his gun was better he'd just try to smack you with it. Then again, he may not know how to use it properly, since he lived a while back, then again (again) he could tap into God's mind and download like anything, but then he could use . . . AIMBOT!! And he would ironically be betrayed three times by his own teammate, and he wouldn't even hold X to boot them, or leave negative feedback. And if he snuck up on you he'd ask you first if you were AFK. Can you imagine what his micro would be like? He wouldn't even need his TV on, 5v1, bust into suicide . . . can you guess what happened? "Headshot?" BOOOOM HEADSHOT. Seriously though he'd probably play StarCraft. (Christian Coders)

Adamllis's signature on the Eternal War forum says it all: "*death is gain*" (Theory of Christian Video Game Design topic; TGS Gamers). Gaming meets religion at the intersection of Rainbow Six 3 and Eternal War. Recruiting is easy for an Armageddon army these days.

We are witnessing a dramatic confluence of faith, politics, and gaming. On the stage of this war theater, the players are indistinguishable, the simulations just one mission removed from real war. One is immersed in war as game, the other in war as eternal battle. One plays Tom Clancy's Splinter Cell: Chaos Theory ("bring the battle closer"); the other plays Ominous Horizons: A Paladin's Calling (N'Lightning Software Development). Soon (perhaps already) these players ship out to Iraq, still pumped from the NASCAR race where the army's recruiting tournament allowed them to hone their skills playing America's Army, or Close Combat: First to Fight. Either way, they're both "surrogate soldiers" (Schiesel) bargaining with their young, mostly run-of-the-mill, lives.

The military has invested millions in developing these games, providing real soldiers and officers as consultants to ensure optimal realism in gameplay and the warrior ethos. The game's developers aim to engage players in an experience that compares to the complete range of a soldier's lifecycle in addition to representing the army's values: "Loyalty, Duty, Respect, Selfless Service, Honor, Integrity, Personal Courage" ("Soldier's Creed" America's Army). In addition, they claim that in "order to increase the Army's return on investment for the America's Army *strategic communications tool*, the Army created the Government Applications Team to use the game's technology for effective and engaging virtual learning" (Battletracker.com; emphasis mine). One thing you can bet, however, is that the virtual violence experienced in this game is not realistic when it comes to blood and guts. According to Seth Schiesel, "In contrast to other popular computer games, in America's Army limbs are never blown off. Instead, wounds are marked by a puff of red smoke. Maimed foes never writhe or scream in agony." Not only this, glitches like "friendly fire" are not part of the game, notwithstanding those players who "consistently kill civilians or their own teammates" (Schiesel), which simply lands them in virtual Leavenworth.

Let me introduce you to another young person, Jose Antonio Gutierrez. Jose has the unfortunate distinction of being the first US casualty of the Iraq war, killed on the first day of the invasion, March 21, 2003.[1] (The address chosen for this chapter represents the site of the US invasion at Umm Qasr, Iraq, and presumably where the first Iraqi soldier killed in combat was killed when hit on the head by a box of aerial leaflets. See chapter 5.) Jose's death is marked by two radical incongruities vis-à-vis our gamers SteadyAim and Cheesestorm: Jose was not a US citizen, and he was killed (for real) by friendly fire. Both factors are supremely bad business for the army's public relations, however. And both factors figure rhetorically (reading between the lines) in the military psychological operations (PSYOP) function of "perceptions management" (Labash). One of the pressing reasons to study video games is that the field of game studies must engage in rhetorical introspection, a kind of rhetorical perceptions management, albeit one of a different stripe. Since the perception of game studies has shifted from the occasional rogue academic department hip enough to offer game studies courses to the now-burgeoning academic discipline that game studies has become, it's not a question of why *now*—it's a question of *what* now? And I don't mean what's next, or even a simple *metaphysical what* question. As Nietzsche so rightly pointed out, asking "what is it" is a metaphysical question. The proper question is: what is it for me? I mean now that the harmonic convergence of faith, politics, and computer games has been graphically (and brutally) *real*ized, that is, made real in the dueling holy wars—ours and theirs (jihad)—what now? What do academics *do* with this now?

The study of games in academic contexts must be augmented by rhetorical criticism, and by that I mean reading games studies rhetorically, as well as reading game studies ludologically. In so doing, we must keep in our mind's eye the pockmarked acned faces of those young people marching straight into the violent confluence of games, politics, and religion, with no "god mode" available in Iraq, or anywhere else our troops are deployed in the Global War on Terror. Jose Gutierrez was not an American citizen. He hitched his way from Guatemala to California at the age of fifteen. He was a foster child on many levels. He was fostered by his adopted family, and then fostered by his adopted nation. He was the first soldier killed, but he was killed by so-called "friendly fire." In the game America's Army, killing the non-Americans (insurgents, combatants, terrorists, whatever you want to call them) is (on the surface) the goal of the game. But the game does not account for the possibility of non-Americans within American ranks killed by Americans. In other words, it does not factor into the narrative options, or into the combat outcomes, the third world subject who serves our country with his death: the scapegoat par excellence. The substitution "threshold" is also at work in the US (see chapter 1).

War is hell, as so many have said over the centuries. Arguably, the fine line between war games and real war is not structured semantically (it is more than a matter of language); it can be, however, rendered ludologically. In other words, the line does not share a thematic kinship with the line between combat training and real combat; it does, however, share in the thin line between game play and morality play, which (I argue) is squarely in the purview of ludology: understanding the game as game, understanding the play as moral (or not), but always (in the end) understanding war as play. That is why *rhetorical* game studies *is important now*. Ludology must redraw the line between war and play. It must recalibrate, and stave off, the imbrication of the respective (and harder to distinguish) economics of nations at war and the billion-dollar game industry. Basic training is a *serious game* with war functioning rhetorically as the synecdoche (the whole of the parts) of these collective genres of play: massively multiplayer game (MMPG), role-playing game (RPG), first-person shooter, 3D action/adventure, strategy game, SIM, and (most accurately) a *god* game. In order to deconstruct the boundary between war and play, it is necessary to reverse engineer the god game. And in order to reverse engineer the god game, I propose a game modification ("mod") of the god mode of the game America's Army, which I will call (post facto) Disarmageddon Army. Modding god mode is not about creating a serious game, it is about deconstructing the serious game; it is a tactical move to outflank (and debunk) the Army of One.

I know—these are fighting words. And ludology is hardly equipped to fight on two fronts, let alone one (the narratology front having already been established by Gonzalo Frasca, Janet Murray, Espen Aarseth, Markku Eskelinen, and others). But I believe it is time for ludology to diversify. If we look at game modding for critical/social purposes, in addition to how others have studied its aesthetics (e.g., Maia Engeli, Anne-Marie Schleiner, Erkki Huhtamo, and Tilman Baumgärtel), we begin to see the basis for a doubling of the modification tactic in modding the god mode of a computer game such as America's Army. Inasmuch as the god mode of any game is always already a cheat, modding god mode amounts to stripping this mode of its omniscience, revealing the cracks in its invulnerability, and subverting its invincible powers. Forgetting for a moment the perception that only slackers or developers debugging the game (which is why god mode exists to begin with) play in god mode, god mode suggests both a metaphorical and structural semantic field whose rhetorical boundaries are unlimited. By reverse engineering god mode, we can (in effect) alter the ludological playing field by separating politically engineered ludology from radically ludic ludology. Maia Engeli provides a taxonomy of modding that may help understand the trajectory of my proposed mod.

In her project to create a series of mods for the game Unreal Tournament, Engeli lists a number of design attitudes that reflect the act of "misappropriation of aesthetic readymades" (a notion she takes from Tilman Baumgärtel):

- Strip—systematic abstraction and intensification
- Shift—visual reformulations
- Impose—superposition of cultural occurrences or social aspects
- Recycle—citations of real world forms and locations
- Overload—superimpose the game mechanics with other processes
- Spill—expand into the physical realm
- Breakout—outside the digital realm
- Abuse—neglect the shooting[2]

Taking Engeli as my cue, I offer the following taxonomy of god modalities, none of which function as mods of god mode, so much as variations on playing in god mode:

- god's army—playing in team god mode in the game Ghost Recon
- jesus rules—jesus god mode / jesus kills in mapping mod in Unreal Tournament 2004; works to give jesus god mode, but not any other players[3]
- evolution versus creationism—Darwinian game alternative to god games[4]

- bugging god—giving god mode bugs; god mode bugs can crash the game
- god landscape—the game Simtropolis mod that converts god trees to pine trees and mass plop them all over your map[5]
- god health—godly mana in the game Diablo prevents other players from hurting you by giving you a mana shield[6]
- evil god—unholy god modes; the game Half-Life mod called The Gathering uses "Unholy Armor" to toggle into god mode; also has things such as Sentry Gun Blessing; divine clone you can set up somewhere to ambush others
- pantheon (many gods)—Tom Clancy's Rainbow Six 3 Raven Shield has the following god mode cheats[7]:

  God mode for player—god
  God mode for team—godteam
  God mode for terrorists—godterror
  God mode for hostages—godhostage 1
  Disable god mode (hostages)—godhostage 2

- disarm/ageddon—deconstructing god mode

The last item, my proposal, has precedence in projects by Margarete Jahrmann and Max Moswitzer (in collaboration with the V21ab Rotterdam), whose focus is on games as modification and transformation of a technology network (Jahrmann). According to Jahrmann:

> But on the side of the game producers we can observe that, the propaganda of consumer games lulls players into accepting ideological conditions, in such a way that the design and story of "shoot them up" games necessitates the "war against terrorism." Here it is especially interesting that the praxis of "total conversion," so-called TCs in gamer's lingo, was made popular with a game about terrorism (Counter-Strike based on Half Life), which can be seen by its content and its representation as a celebration of the political forces of the leading nations. The gameplay is centralised around fighting between terrorists and counter-terrorists. Its goals are disarming bombs or rescuing hostages, and all weaponry is modelled on existing arms. But total conversions of games can also produce a critical position, as seen in a number of so-called game arts applications as in the case of nybble-engine-toolZ.[8] By shooting anti-war emails to president@

> whitehouse.gov, action clearly expresses a sense of agency that transgresses the defined boundaries of a gaming environment. All these actions happen in "the real world" and not in the "sim" world of a game. All the outgoing signals are counted and transferred to other servers and this can be seen as an example of a public online demonstration tool. I would call this a "Real Game." (210–11)

In solidarity with Englei, Jahrmann, and Moswitzer, my interest in deconstructing god mode in America's Army is a strategic experiment in disengaging the game's communicative power. In so doing, we will be telling potential military recruits that they need a serious/real game such as America's Army like they need a hole in the head. I am not interested in creating another serious game, rather in taking a war game and hacking into the Bush administration's tactic of "playing god" in a global theater of mixed realities, religious holy wars, and cultural ambiguities. I am interested in deconstructing and remixing (reverse engineering) for critical/social purposes the relationships between US military recruitment tactics, future administrations' faith-based foreign and military policies, and their stealth recruiting engine, the computer game America's Army. And if academia has to hit them over the head with a few SITREPS[9] of "perceptions management," then consider this the first volley.

11
Endgame Rhetorics

Utøya Island, Norway

Why is it necessary in the construction of the world that there should be people condemned to die?
—Fyodor Dostoyevsky, *The Notebooks for the Idiot*

The water was freezing. The ferry too slow and ill-equipped to handle the unfolding crimes. As I tried to picture the terror-stricken young people and children jumping into the water fully clothed, swimming for their lives with bullets hitting the water, I was forced to think, in terrifying slow motion, about the paradox I launched with "writing offshore" (chapter 4).[1] Offshore is not a safe space. But then neither is the threshold between home and not home (chapter 1). A postmodern temptation is to invoke a paradox and, like Lyotard, envision a ship navigating the waters of dangerous reefs that surround the islands of an archipelago. "Lyotard's archipelago can be seen as a snapshot catching the postmodernist in his paradoxical act" (Rasch 64). This chapter asks us how to embrace paradox, specifically the paradox that the Internet is a vehicle for both terrorism and democracy, or that video games are equal parts warcraft and theorycraft. But my aim is not to distinguish between such opposing forms of power; I merely set them in play, so to speak, in order to establish my rhetorical *ethos*. According to Stefan Herbrechter, "In order to be a critical post-humanist, you have to speak against your own humanity."[2] Similarly, in order to be a rhetorician, you have to play against *endgame rhetoric*. There are those, however, who see themselves as *endgamers*, and that is where this chapter's story begins.

On July 22, 2011, seventy-seven people, fifty-five of them teenagers, were massacred in Norway by Anders Behring Breivik, who played an endgame that was made possible through years of rhetorical and highly researched calculations, a process not unlike "theorycraft," a gaming practice I will explain shortly. After disseminating a fifteen-hundred-page manifesto online, Breivik soloed the worst possible version of endgame content. There are many heartbreaking stories of death and survival from that day, but there is one that, like Roland Barthes, I want to explore "not as a question (theme), but as a wound" (21). It concerns an 11-year-old boy who found himself staring into the muzzle of a gun, yet told Breivik very calmly, "You have killed enough people. You killed my father. And I'm too young to die." Breivik lowered the gun and walked away. The boy survived because he presented an argument.

Utøya Island is an address of both love and violence—a mirror image of the rhetorical threshold I hope I have rendered in this book. One of its features is that Utøya is heart-shaped. There is even a path along the edge called "Lover's Path," where a group of teenagers were gunned down as they "played dead" in order to (they hoped) survive the carnage. Breivik took them out one by one anyway. There were other victims who did survive on Utøya Island by playing dead or hiding, or who dove into the frigid lake waters and survived when local residents began hearing gunfire and screams and took their boats close enough to pluck them from the water. These three countermeasures— argument, feigning death, and moving offshore—were swift improvisations in the face of unspeakable terror. The problems I assigned for myself in this chapter were how to honor the courage of those children, how to wrap thought in the same cloth as certain death, and how to take out a "rare spawn" *theoretically.*[3] This endgame rhetoric is, of course, incommensurable with Breivik's endgame, much less with what his victims experienced. But thinking is a weapon and a strategy. Thus, I want as many survival strategies as possible in order to think about the endgame of death and the anxiety that accompanies it. As a rhetorician, I am specced for argumentative discourse, but as a World of Warcraft (WoW) hunter, I am specced for survival and frequently have to feign death. I am not, however, attempting to make a strict homology between Breivik, the fact that he employed the term *rhetoric* in his manifesto over eighty times and played World of Warcraft, with the fact that I also wield similar rhetorical weaponry and play WoW. I cannot represent (re-present) desperate measures with contradistinctions and rhetorical flourishes. What I can do is *think* in the face of despair, which necessitates some stealth moves and "in-your-face" gameplay.

The argument is motivated by these three courageous moves read across three moments in the history of rhetoric. The structure will be pedagogical. It begins in 1966 at Johns Hopkins University with Derrida's contribution to the structuralist controversy, his lecture on "Structure, Sign, and Play." It moves to Paul de Man's failed assignment "The Resistance to Theory"; and ends with a final exam, the rebirth of structuralism in "theorycraft." The problem is that I find myself in the same classroom as Breivik, hence the need to acknowledge that playing with rhetoric is a dangerous and deeply ambiguous game, and one never knows with whom one is studying, or playing.

The Lesson

In World of Warcraft, and similar multiplayer games, when your entire group dies, it is called a "wipe." "Wiping is actually a central element of the endgame PvE [player vs environment] content" (WoWwikki). But the wipe that occurred on Utøya Island that day more than decenters endgame centrality. Put another way, "The center is not the center" (Derrida, "Structure" 279). According to Derrida,

> The concept of centered structure is in fact the concept of a play based on a fundamental ground, a play constituted on the basis of a fundamental immobility and a reassuring certitude, which itself is beyond the reach of play. And on the basis of this certitude anxiety can be mastered, for anxiety is invariably the result of a certain mode of being implicated in the game, of being caught by the game, of being as it were at stake in the game from the outset. (279)

Reading World of Warcraft across "Structure, Sign and Play," involves a strange strategy. This does not mean we act like sitting ducks in a shooting gallery. "Sitting ducks" is an oxymoron anyway. But it does mean we learn to float and fly. We develop webbed feet, and/or we sprout feathered wings. We become hippogryphs. It is not enough to ride them, as in World of Warcraft. We merge with nonplayer characters (NPCs) by dignifying the "non" and imbuing them with the same powers as players. We reverse engineer the bot matrix to assimilate into the only simulation in town—the game. We reinscribe the cut scene onto a new screen/play in which no division exists between play and nonplay, between radical ludicity and narrative transition. We become changelings. We take off the mask of entropy that has so darkened our perspective that we imagine ourselves as upright bipeds with unlimited XP (experience) marching over a cliff like lemmings on drugs. We "rise above the mud" of our overengineered floodplain surveying our past, or what is left of it, and we learn—we don our new knowledge and level up. In-game parlance, now the language of play, no longer separates us into high and low cultures, first- or third-world sovereign nation-states. We are always already fully integrated into one massively multiplayer role-playing game. One race: player. One language: play. One mode of being: playing.

According to Nietzsche, humanity is seriously ill. Nietzsche diagnosed the illness of seriousness and prescribed laughter.

> *Taking seriously.*—In the great majority, the intellect is a clumsy, gloomy, creaking machine that is difficult to start. They call it "taking the matter *seriously*" when they want to work with this machine and think well. How burdensome they must find good thinking! The lovely human beast always seems to lose its good spirits when it thinks well; it becomes "serious." And "where laughter and gaiety are found, thinking does not amount to anything": that is the prejudice of this serious beast against all "gay science."—Well then, let us prove that this is a prejudice. (*The Gay Science*, Book IV § 327)

As such, we would do well to reconsider our project of "serious games." Why side with the "serious" if we are all players speaking play playingly? If we are honest, as Nietzsche exhorts us to be at the end of *The Gay Science*, "Unsere Redlichkeit!" (§ 335), should we not (more aptly) ally ourselves with gaiety? "Serious games" is an oxymoron anyway (or, according to our play logic, redundant). Whether we create, critically compromise, or convert games into art, mods, or some other game-based research artifact, it will not have been our seriousness that determines its artifactuality. Nor does a "serious" label somehow legitimize it for our "serious-minded" academic colleagues. That threshold does not traffic in cross-disciplinary credentials. Crossing the serious/play border amounts to nothing more than reinstalling the "serious" as the privileged mode of being. Better to disengage from such discourse altogether. *Ars ludus sans gravitas*. Better to fly above the mud, to float in muddy waters, to muddy the waters of serious games.[4]

Nietzsche embraced being played in his verse:

> World game, the ruling force,
> blends false and true:
> the eternally fooling force
> blends us in too. (351)

Derrida's essay "Structure, Sign, and Play" ends with a kind of trailer for the next expansion of this world game. He writes:

> Here there is a kind of question . . . whose conception . . . we are only catching a glimpse of today. I employ these words, I admit, with a glance toward the operations of childbearing—but also with a glance toward those who, in a society from which I do not exclude myself, turn their eyes away when faced by the as yet unnamable which is proclaiming itself and which can do so, as is necessary whenever a birth is in the offing, only under the species of the nonspecies, in the formless, mute, infant, and terrifying form of monstrosity. (293)

It is commonly held that Derrida introduces the figure of the monster here as a means of thinking otherwise, a means of thinking "beyond man and humanism . . . the name of man being the name of that being who . . . throughout his entire history—has dreamed of full presence, the reassuring foundation, the origin and the end of play" (292; emphasis mine). But what of the "species of the nonspecies"? Inasmuch as the category system of species/genus analytics is purely a human invention, is Derrida toying with the problem of human invention itself? Is this the monstrosity whose essence is terrifying because *what we have invented is terror*? If what we have invented, as a means to accomplish "the end of play," is terrorism, we have also invented the perfect means to combat it—what Derrida calls "sure play" (292), a counterstrike to the "play without security" "to which Nietzsche pointed the way" (292).

Still, Nietzsche's game, Derrida warned, is impossible to choose because it is not a matter of choosing, it is a matter of the "différance of this irreducible difference" (293). By turning "our eyes away when faced by the as yet unnamable which is proclaiming itself"—we are still locking and loading the interpretation that "dreams of deciphering a truth or an origin which escapes play," which dreams of "the end of play." Thus, we deploy the engineered play, not the Nietzschean "play without security," but the "sure play" of war on the perpetual turf of terrorism. Lyotard put it thus: "A language game that becomes excessive . . . the 'wanting to have too much of it' . . . precisely when such a language game begins to regulate language games that are not the same as itself, isn't such a language game always assisted by the sword?" (*Just Gaming* 99).

So, I would like to return to Dostoyevsky's question: "Why is it necessary in the construction of the world that there should be people condemned to die?" "Would you like to know why?," writes Hélène Cixous.

> Read *The Notebooks of the Idiot* and you'll know everything: we need those who are condemned to death and we need books that "condemn" us. Here is what Kafka wrote in 1904 to his friend Pollak: "If the book we are reading doesn't wake us up with a blow on the head, what are we reading it for? . . . A book must be the axe for the frozen sea inside us." . . . He wrote this letter because his friend had reproached him for not having answered his letters. Kafka answers him by saying: excuse me, but I was reading. (*Three Steps* 17)

And here I would like to insert a homology between reading and playing by saying that our assignment is always setting us up to fail. I have learned to welcome the reproach for not writing and reading, by answering: *excuse me, but I was playing.*

The Assignment: Feign Death

In the opening sentences of his essay, "The Resistance to Theory," Paul de Man confesses to failing his assignment for writing it. This double pedagogical failure, inasmuch as the essay was commissioned "to address the question of teaching directly" in the MLA "section on literary theory," is more aptly akin to a *feigned* failure (3). De Man "feigns death" on the grounds that he "found it difficult to live up, in minimal good faith, to the requirements of this program and could only try to explain, as concisely as possible, why the main theoretical interest of literary theory consists in the impossibility of its definition" (3). How one lives up to one's in-order-to, one's assignment (or one's death, as Heidegger puts it) becomes the substance of the remainder of de Man's text. De Man does not cast it in such terms; rather, I am suggesting that his confession doubles as a feigned death in order to resist "the requirements of this program," namely, in order to resist definition—the death of meaning. Like Derrida, de Man points to a recurring anxiety at the heart of the theory dilemma centered in the "discrepancy between truth and method" (4). As such, the "depth of [this] resistance to theory" results in what I would call *theorycrafting* theory. The resistance is manifest, in other words, in the strategic damage inflicted by studying the game mechanics of language: in short, by "engineering play" in language using the "sure play" of method, rather than the "play without security" of ambiguity, aporia, and anxiety. According to de Man, "it is a recurrent strategy of any anxiety to defuse what it considers threatening by magnification or minimization, by attributing to it claims to power of which it is bound to fall short" (5). As such, "[literary theory] contains a necessarily pragmatic moment that certainly weakens it as theory but that adds a subversive element of unpredictability and makes it something of a wild card in the serious game of the theoretical disciplines" (8). In other words, structural linguistics, hermeneutics, and semiotics, among other methods of interpretation, each resist the wild sort of reading that would sever the tie between grammar and logic, truth and method. And the rhetorical dexterity of theory creates ever more codified attempts to tame the figural, tropological difference that language exposes.

In Lynn Worsham's critique of hermeneutics, for example, she argues that

> wild reading, in contrast, tries to escape repetition and sameness (and the discipline of the expert and amateur) and seeks to remain an untimely and errant practice that does not occur in moments governed by institutional investments or driven by desire for institutional sanction. It seeks neither the status of an authorized reading nor the disciples whose bodies will become the privileged locus for the intersection and exchange of truth and power. Reading wild rushes in—without the proper credentials—to tell the secrets of philosophy's unconscious and hence produces an anxiety situation in which resistance is actually the more telling secret. Wild reading, then, is not another hermeneutic for deciphering the truth of the text, for saying finally what has silently been articulated deep down; therefore, it must be doubly suspicious of any effort that would try to satisfy through demystification and a truer truth. Wild reading works at the level of the pathos and passion of the situation to change our affective relation to seriousness and its disciplinary technology by producing a sense of anxiety and estrangement. ("Reading Wild" 53)

The assignment, then, keeps asking us to feign the death of such reading. "It turns out," de Man claims, "that the resistance to theory is in fact a resistance to reading" (15) and (I would add, via Worsham) a resistance to "wild" reading. What we need is an exploit, a theorycraftwork out of which theorycraft is unengineered and restructured in the wild.

Final Exam

Theorycraft takes a lot of work, but it is also a site for rhetorical work. The final exam, then, is being proctored by the nefarious gaming figure of the "rhetorical griefer." Griefing is usually motivated by a desire to annoy or harass other players. Martin Davies explains that griefers are not "deterred by penalties related to in-game goals." In the context of this final exam, I suggest we retool theorycraft such that we can both *grieve* endgame victims and *grief* endgamers like Breivik.

The practice of theorycraft started with StarCraft some years ago, and has migrated to World of Warcraft and Diablo III (among others), but could be applied to any game (and, I am arguing, any academic project). Theorycraft is basically defined as "the attempt to mathematically analyze game mechanics in order to gain a better understanding of the inner workings of the game" (WoWwikki). But the scope of theorycraft is much more than mathematical. I will admit it was daunting at first, and the extent of my dabbling with it was mostly guesswork (with help from Jan Holmevik). Once I started watching boss fights on YouTube and Elitist Jerks' sites, I was hooked. The add-ons that made the interface more effective were the first things I worked on. And each time a patch came out and made the add-ons out of date, I was very irritated. My gameplay was dependent on reconfigured action bars, a damage meter, focus bar, and raiding mods that gave me the ability to quickly identify the tank (the main up-close-and-personal fighter) to whom I had to misdirect aggro (aggravating the boss) most of the time. It was not long before I was consulting forums to understand the stats on my gear, the best build for my class, the best combat pet for raiding, and the optimal gear score to keep me in the competition for coveted raid spots (see Holmevik's *Inter/vention* 158). There are many motivations for theorycrafting one's gameplay, but after eleven years of playing WoW, my motive is a mixture of personal challenge, academic research, and the desire to experience endgame content. By contrast, in Anders Breivik's brand of theorycraft (as written in his manifesto, from which I quote with conflicted emotions), note the pedagogical rhetoric as he instructs his readers how to create a cover story to hide his activities.

> Present a "credible project/alibi" to your friends, co-workers and family. Announce to your closest friends, co-workers and family that you are pursuing a "project" that can at least partly justify your "new pattern of activities" (isolation/travel) while in the planning phase. For example, tell them that you have started to play World of Warcraft or any other online MMO game and that you wish to focus on this for the next months/year. This "new project" can justify isolation and people will understand somewhat why you are not answering your phone over long periods. Tell them that you are completely hooked on the game (raiding dungeons etc). Emphasise [*sic*] to them that this is a dream you have had since you were a kid. If they stress you, insist and ask them to respect your decision. You will be amazed on how much you can do undetected while blaming this game. If your planning requires you to travel, say that you are visiting one of your WoW friends, or better yet, a girl from your "guild" (who lives in another country). No further questions will be raised if you present these arguments. Blaming WoW is also quite strategic due to another factor. It is usually considered "tabu" or even shameful in our society today to be hooked on an MMO. By revealing "this secret" to your close ones you are therefore (to them at least) entrusting them with your innermost secret. Usually they will "contribute" to keeping this secret for you which can be very beneficial. (If people from your "secondary" social circle ask them they will even usually "lie" on your behalf (giving you alibi), in order to keep your MMO project a secret. (Breivik)

To suggest that this text constitutes theorycraft is to follow Worsham's lead in "Reading wild [which] rushes in—without the proper credentials—to tell the secrets of philosophy's unconscious and hence produces an anxiety situation in which resistance is actually the more telling secret" (53). I would like to see theorycraft morph into a rhetorical reading strategy, much as deconstruction is a reading strategy. But the predominant goal of theorycraft among players today is to engineer play in order to progress toward the endgame content. In other words, if we invoke Derrida's lesson, then theorycraft is a desire to "end play."

Thus, the assignment, to feign death (as one means of ending play and progressing toward endgame content), is merely an alibi for the resistance to reading, which I would now extend to mean the resistance to play (in the Nietzschean sense). Theorycraft is not just about maximizing gameplay through calculation and experimentation, it is about collaborative and conductive reasoning, persuasive discourse, and a kind of "open source" negotiation between game developers and players. It represents an ontological pressure to "play dead" in order to survive death, which is not a strategy we are conditioned to employ. Theorycraft needs to be defined with conductive reasoning, not with hermeneutic or semiotic frameworks. To perhaps synchronize with Espen Aarseth's notion of the "*conglomerate [game] object*," we could describe it as a composite reading strategy that is also a composite method of structuralist, scientific, calculative, and engineered play (Aarseth and Calleja). But added to those elements, we have the "wild reading" that suggests theorycraft is designed to reach endgame content at the same time it is paradoxically symptomatic of the anxiety that produces such engineered play in order to defer the ultimate endgame, death. So, we simultaneously crave the endgame at the same time we need to control how and when we get there. Foucault astutely observed that such control belies our anxiety in the face of the ontological pressure of a "transitory existence" in which we are "destined for oblivion" at a time not of our own choosing (216).

And here's the rub. Breivik also used theorycraft in carrying out his slaughter. Thus, while we may understand the sophistic history that continues to herald the moral neutrality of rhetoric, the fact that rhetoric has such blood on its hands necessarily implicates theorycraft, effectively breaching its promise of methodological impregnability. Breivik used the term rhetoric over eighty times in his manifesto, some instances of which I would argue indicate a high level of understanding of rhetoric's power and some instances of which belie a more pedestrian understanding of rhetoric, especially when he uses it to denigrate ideologies with which he disagrees. But, calculating the optimal means of creating the bomb, timing his trips from Oslo to Utøya, rehearsing and testing each piece of his master plan, all mirror theorycrafting in WoW. In addition, Breivik reforged his armor, obtained a police officer's uniform to disarm his targets, bulked up his physical body using exercise and drugs, and chose mood enhancing music to accompany his gameplay during the massacre. In *Gamer Theory*, McKenzie Wark notes that "templars are the knights of separation" (185). He suggests that "for the Templars, separation is key, and yet to fight in this posthuman grid, they require technics, armor for example, which implicates them in various forms of non-separation from the very thing their being is founded on separation from" (192). "The paranoia of the not-separate is in not knowing what you are not-separate from" (195). Wark's insights help (perhaps) to dull the edges of calling Breivik's actions gameplay, a move I acknowledge is highly problematic and disturbing.

For this reason, I have enacted a different "wild" reading of theorycraft in this chapter. I used theorycrafting in the process of researching and in writing the draft. I considered carefully what "shot rotation" would be appropriate as a hunter in this "instance," or "dungeon," or "raid," to use WoW parlance. I reforged certain theoretical gear to maximize haste (which helps me regenerate focus, a necessary energy for sustaining the highest damage output). I triple specced the structure. I studied the boss fight and determined that it would be crucial to misdirect the aggro onto a tank player (namely Breivik), who would take the full damage. Then I adjusted my shot rotation and feigned death (to reset aggro). This is not a simple extrapolation from World of Warcraft gameplay, nor is it a series of metaphors for how concepts emerge in this chapter. It is my methodology as an academic gamer. It is, in other words, a manner of thinking. And thinking is the assignment I accept in each instance where I play a scholarly role. If I am faulted for not fulfilling some other assignment, like Kafka, I will simply say, "Excuse me, but I was playing."

Endgame content is an allegory of reading, aka the resistance to theory disguised as structure crafting its own rhetorical armor. Structuralism only feigned death in 1966 at Johns Hopkins. We are witnessing the mass resurrection of structuralism with theorycraft. But Derrida knew this, predicted it. The hermeneutic and semiotic traditions have been our two predominant theories of interpretation, so what is theorycraft heralding as the new interpretive paradigm? How is theorycraft a third way that bears the mark of structuralism, yet guards the question of endgame rhetoric? By reforging gear, transmogrifying gear, the player can alter the meaning of both power (with reforging stats) and style (with transmogrification). Disenchanting items produces a new currency in the blended economy of endgame content. Materials created from disenchantment may benefit the entire collective. Theorycrafted rhetorical arguments emerge in the restructuration of our disenchantment with the hermeneutic/semiotic traditions. Theorycraft is a new theory of interpreting power versus interpreting meaning. Structures of power are interpreted with critical theories of various stripes, but theorycraft has more rhetorical dexterity since it draws on algorithm, combat mechanics, optimal collaborative ethos, swift trust, and so forth. Yet, it also seeks to recalibrate and redistribute the power of ambiguity to defer endgame content as long as possible.

The almost paralyzing paradox I face in crafting this theory is that both Breivik and I have used theorycraft as a strategy. We both understand it, dare I say, *stand under* it. We have each carved our names on our respective rhetorical school desks in its classroom and consulted our respective playbooks on its playground. I can, however, choose to disenchant Breivik's use of theorycraft and reforge his own rationale: "Det var grusomt, men nødvendig" (Haugo). It was gruesome, but necessary. How do we reconcile this unhappy pedagogical scenario? Derrida invoked a specter, the figure of the monster, as a means of thinking otherwise, a means of thinking "beyond man and humanism . . . the name of man [Breivik] being the name of that being who . . . throughout his entire history—has dreamed of full presence, the reassuring foundation, the origin . . . and the end of play" (292). I chose not to look away. I chose to "face the as yet unnameable which is proclaiming itself" (293). I watched Danny Pearl's beheading (see chapters 5 and 7). I read Breivik's manifesto. Because, as Blanchot reminds us, "Reading is anguish, and this is because any text, however important . . . is empty—at bottom it doesn't exist; you have to cross an abyss, and if you do not jump, you do not comprehend" (10). And if you do not comprehend, you're perpetually doomed to queue up for the most gruesome endgame content wearing zero rhetorical gear. In which case, we have to keep theorycrafting, we have to keep jumping, we have to keep feigning. It is necessary to survive. And it is necessary to endure the reproaches for having survived by saying, "Excuse me, but I am playing."

Notes • Works Cited • Index

Notes

1. Party Lines (Motzstraße 72, Berlin)

1. See "Transport I/75" on Yad Vashem website for details surrounding this specific transport. My opening scenario is based on actual events, but offers a speculative narrative based on research about the methods for deportation and victim interviews. Martin Dean notes that in the Landesarchiv (Berlin) there are only "two surviving *Handakten* (personal copies kept by employees) containing a sample of the flood of internal administrative regulations that governed the implementation of Jewish Property confiscation" (see n. 10). However, there are documents in the Landesarchiv concerning claims made against the Reich by the Buschkes and two of their grandchildren (children of son Franz Buschke) (see WGA Database http://www.wga-datenbank.de/en/search.html: files 4 WGA 835/55–837/55, 43 WGA 2537/59, and 43 WGA 234/57).

2. While this may actually have happened to the Buschkes, in reality it happened to Ruth Alton-Tauber, who recalled in her testimony that "'this small act touched me deeply. All at once I became conscious of the fact that we no longer had a home or a homeland'" (Kaplan 186; original memoir in German in Leo Baeck Institute archive at http://digital.cjh.org/R/UF2RIUSKQG7V5XNL9QXVSCNXVT4X5Y9E2V9Y1GU41E41NCVGUQ-03506). Ruth and Julius Tauber and their son Michael lived at Kantstraße 120–121 in Berlin. They were deported (with Ruth's mother) on October 27, 1942, to Lodz concentration camp. Ruth's mother died at Lodz in 1943. Ruth's husband, Julius, died at Auschwitz, but their son was transported to Stuffhof, and Ruth to Dresden. Both Ruth and Michael survived and were reunited after the liberation of the camps in 1945.

3. Wechselmann had died on October 19, 1942, just weeks before the Buschkes were deported to Theresienstadt. Doctors Wilhelm Wechselmann and Abraham Buschke were both dermatologists who specialized in the treatment of syphilis and ran the two dermatology programs at the Rudolf-Virchow Hospital in Berlin, but Buschke's treatments would become the more effective and widely cited. Wechselmann was well known for his use of Salvarsan therapy to treat syphilis, which Buschke opposed, as the two men differed in their understanding of the

cause of the disease. Thus, in the context of speculating about how and why Frau Wechselmann came to occupy the Buschke apartment, it cannot escape our notice that the doctors had been medical rivals (see Scholz and Aberer 494, 498).

4. I have coined the term *pharmakonomy* to represent a systematic *aporia* (a term inherited from Plato). In Jacques Derrida's essay "Plato's Pharmacy" (*Dissemination*), his discussion of the lineage of the term *pharmakon* appears in the context of Plato's distaste for writing (as compared to speech). For an extended play on the ambiguity of the *pharmakon* and its role as a scapegoat, see especially 128–34.

5. The 1941 Berlin phone book is the last complete phone book issued by the Nazis during the Third Reich. Only supplements were issued in 1942. Thus, the printed address books became equally revealing, not to mention that they contain reverse lookup ability. The names are listed in the front pages, with business listings next, followed by address listings. In the case of Motzstraße 72, among the names listed at this address in 1942 (most likely issued early in 1942 or late 1941), Buschke appears. In the 1943 edition, his name is not listed, and only two other names are new: J. Risch and Frau H. Wechselmann. Given the fact that Buschke and Wechselmann practiced dermatology at the same hospital, it is not coincidental that Frau Wechselmann turns up at Buschke's former address (see fig. 1.2).

6. Here I am thinking specifically of an arc of scholarship from Victor Farías's *Heidegger and Nazism* (1987) to Avital Ronell's *The Telephone Book: Technology, Schizophrenia, Electric Speech* (1989) to the publication of Heidegger's notebooks, *The Black Notebooks* (2014). Ronell's book is a provocative look at Heidegger's acceptance of the "call." She deconstructs Heidegger's *Der Spiegel* interview (made public only after his death) by questioning the technologized command Heidegger answered instead of the call of conscience. In the interview, when asked how he related to the Nazis after he accepted the rector's position, Heidegger answers: ". . . someone from the top command of the Storm Trooper University Bureau, SA section leader Baumann called me up. He demanded . . . (*I*, 6)" (qtd in Ronell 29). Ronell also feminizes Heidegger by placing him in both the position of the child hearing the call of his mother (the child as irrational, prelogical) and the mother calling him to come back home. It is the mother who teaches the son to accept the call. Ronell writes:

> She will have made him into an addict of taking calls, he will no longer be able to abstain from wanting to hear, "he can no longer stop wanting to do it." So before putting herself on hold, driving the umbilical tap back into her son—"a mother calls to a boy who won't come home"—before receding like the feminine voice of an operator when a connection has been made, she will have transformed her boy into an automatic listening device. (28)

It is *as a mother* that Heidegger's silence frustrates us: "Reading the interview [in *Der Spiegel*], one might think one is recognizing a ruse. The man is putting us on; like the prephilosophical mother, he is putting us on eternal hold, waiting for a response" (36).

7. I want to thank Luanne T. Frank for conversations and seminars that led to my understanding of the relation of Heidegger to composition theory, and to Victor Vitanza for helping me to put these issues into a political framework. Heidegger's notion of "calling into a question," or "calling into the word," was first called to my attention by Luanne T. Frank in her seminar on Heidegger. In her lecture on section II.4 of *Being and Time*, she writes:

> Calling into the word, as we know, is Heidegger's phrase; but it is not one he chooses to emphasize or even too often use in talking about this point. . . . Once in possession of the phrase, and of an understanding of the direction Heidegger moves in after *Being and Time*, it seems possible and even useful to look on *Being and Time* as such a calling—into the single word: Being. (Seminar 5)

In her article "Criticism and the Meaning of Writing," Frank also points out the incredible depth from which Heidegger hears the call:

> And each individual speaker/writer can, by what Heidegger calls undergoing an experience with it and within it, by "listening" to it, as it passes through the dense, denser matrix of the speaker/writer's own already language-particularized life experience, bring both that experience, the world that it creates out of language, and language itself, to new configurations. (193)

8. See my introduction and the discussion of Martin Davidson's discovery that his great-grandmother, Ida, came to occupy the apartment/office at Reichstraße 5 in Berlin, which had been where Dr. Hans Hermann Levy practiced until his suicide on August 28, 1942. This particular story prompted my focus on the "address" as a rhetorical site of violent substitution. See Davidson's *The Perfect Nazi* (242). Walter Benjamin also chose a death of his own in Portbou, Spain, on September 26, 1940, at the Hotel de Francia (at Avenida del General Mola 5) rather than return to France and risk capture by the Germans.

9. Moritz Henschel was the last chair of the Jewish Community in Berlin, the *Reichsvertretung der Juden in Deutschland* (Reich Association of Jews in Germany). He and his wife, Hildegard, lived at Lietzenburger Straße 8 and are listed in the 1941 Berlin phone book, as well as in the 1941 Berlin address book. However, the 1942 address book for Lietzenburger Straße 8 is missing his name, as well as the name of Conrad Cohn (who was arrested in 1942 and deported to Mauthausen camp, where he died soon after), and the names of other Jews who

had by then been deported. It is interesting to note that Moritz "Israel" Henschel is listed in the 1941 phone book without an occupation, whereas all other entries for Jews list one—most were doctors or dentists. I suspect that the only Jews allowed telephones in 1941 were medical practitioners, which accounts for their listings in the phone book. Many of the entries also state for "Jüdische" patients only. For an extensive treatment of the Jewish Community in the final years of the war, see Beate Meyer's *A Fatal Balancing Act* and "The Fine Line between Responsible Action and Collaboration" in Meyer, Simon, and Schütz.

10. Both Willi Just and Walther Rauff are listed in the Berlin 1941 phone book, coincidentally. For more details about the memo and a translation of the original, plus a copy of the original, see Kogon et al. (54–56 and 228–35). For an alternative reading of the memo, see Mark Ward's *Deadly Documents: Technical Communication, Organizational Discourse, and the Holocaust.*

11. But even Hitler's beloved dog, Blondi, became a scapegoat when Hitler ordered his personal physician, Dr. Werner Haase, to take Blondi into another room of the bunker and test the cyanide capsules on her to make sure they were still effective. Blondi died and Hitler was inconsolable. Hitler took his own life the next day, April 30, 1945.

12. The poem appears in English not only in Max Pensky's *Melancholy Dialectics* (1) but also with a slightly different translation in *The Correspondence of Walter Benjamin and Gershom Scholem, 1932–1940* (81).

13. See W. K. C. Guthrie's essay "Flux and *Logos* in Heraclitus" for a critical interpretation of this fragment and commentary, which generally supports Heidegger's thesis. Guthrie explains that Heraclitus disagreed with Pythagoras's doctrine of the harmony of opposites. The Pythagorean theory claimed that the order and beauty of the cosmos is achieved through the neutralization of opposites in which a limitation is placed on "chaotic *apeiron*" (198–99). Pythagoras and his followers called this neutralization of opposites *good*; "discord, disease, strife—were *evil*" (199). Guthrie suggests that Heraclitus rejects these value judgments. Using a familiar illustration, Heraclitus calls attention to a well-known drink in Greece, *kykeon*, associated with the Eleusinian mysteries. *Kykeon* is made by stirring barley and cheese into a cup of wine. Of importance to the illustration is that the "mixture had to be kept in motion until the moment it was drunk" (200). The point of Heraclitus's lesson is that "'The *kykeon* . . . falls apart if it is not being stirred'" (200).

14. Heidegger also explains what he means by strife in his attempt to clarify misinterpretations of his Rectoral Address of 1933, "Facts and Thoughts." Essentially, he is concerned that some have construed his remarks on *polemos* to mean "battle," "war," and the "use of force and beating down the opponent" ("Self-Assertion" 488). We should not think of *polemos* as war, he says; nor should we "appeal to the supposedly Heraclitean proposition 'War is the father of all

things' to proclaim war and battle as the principle of all being and thus to offer a philosophical justification of the warlike" (488–89). Instead, the notion of "conflict" in Heraclitus's Fragment 53 means a "setting-apart," as in the opposition between gods and men, or slaves and freemen. "Its essence can therefore not be determined from some other place, from the standpoint of 'politics' or of some other established goals" (489).

2. Casuistic Code (Lankwitzer Straße 13–17, Berlin)

1. An earlier version of this chapter appears as "Afterword: <meta> Casuistic Code" in *From A to <A>: Keywords of Markup* (eds. Bradley Dilger and Jeff Rice, University of Minnesota Press, 2010. 228–35). I am grateful to the editors and the press for permission to reprint this revised version here.

2. The Metasploit Project, created in 2003, "provides useful information to people who perform penetration testing, IDS signature development, and exploit research. This project was created to provide information on exploit techniques and to create a useful resource for exploit developers and security professionals."

3. Mechanical Faith (Lindenstraße 9–14, Berlin)

1. Taylor explains that Libeskind was "fascinated by [Walter] Benjamin" (262). Libeskind explicitly cites Benjamin in the following description of the museum: "'The fourth aspect of the project is formed by Walter Benjamin's *One Way Street*. This aspect is incorporated into the continuous sequence of sixty sections along the zig-zag, each of which represents one of the "Stations of the Star" described in the text of Walter Benjamin'" (*Counterdesigns* 86; qtd in Taylor 262–63). See chapter 1 for more on Benjamin's *One-Way Street*.

4. Writing Offshore (Heidegger's Hütte, Todtnauberg, Germany)

1. This essay was previously published in *JAC: A Journal of Rhetoric, Culture, and Politics* 23.4 (2003): 667–724. The essay was named as the winner of the James Kinneavy Award for best article in 2003 from *JAC* and the Association of Advanced Composition. It is an expanded version of a CCCC presentation (March 2002) in which I responded to the CCCC theme "Connecting the Text and the Street." I want to thank Sidney Dobrin and Raúl Sánchez for inviting me to present on their panel. I am also grateful to the following colleagues who read it at various stages: Michelle Ballif, Jenny Bay, Lisa Coleman, D. Diane Davis, Byron Hawk, Thomas Rickert, Geoff Sirc, Victor Vitanza, and *JAC*'s editor, Lynn Worsham. And to my husband, Jan Rune Holmevik, goes my supreme gratitude for taking me offshore and opening my eyes. The essay has been slightly revised for publication in this book.

2. *Terra nullius* was a legal fiction used by the invading forces of the British to deny the legal rights of the indigenous people of Australia.

3. Elam's project involves feminism *and* deconstruction, but there is an isomorphic relation between her project and mine: each seeks to deal a blow to the *ground* metaphysics that anchor two relatively new (and still evolving) disciplines, namely, feminism and rhetoric/composition, respectively.

4. Desmond Egan, an Irish poet, evokes an achingly stark tribute to "needing the sea," and his poem (of the same name), begun here, will introduce each section of this chapter. (For the full text of the poem and an introduction, see the Hungarian Electronic Library at http://www.mek.iif.hu/porta/szint/human/szepirod/vilagir/egan_d/selected/html/index.htm). Csilla Bertha explains the poem thus:

> Desmond Egan is keenly aware of the historical, social, political, religious and other dichotomies continuously tearing into Ireland's texture, just as he is of the duplicities of individual and communal existence, past and present, tradition and modernity, rootedness in nation, landscape, culture and foreign influences. . . . Thus, for instance, his "Needing the Sea" speaks first of all about the poet's personal longing for revival—the image of the sea being the image of spiritual-psychological purity and redemption, somewhat similarly to the sea in "Wedding," the long-poem by the Hungarian László Nagy—but it also contains the feeling that "you cannot escape" as the Hungarian Gyula Illyés puts it, when Egan apologizes for this luxury, knowing how many people are suffering from poverty, slavery, genocide, violence in the world. (Introduction to *Desmond Egan: Selected Poems*)

I am grateful to Desmond Egan for his permission to publish the poem here.

5. It is tempting to follow, also, the trajectory of Heidegger's critics who resort to "feminizing" him (or emasculating him) in order to discredit his thought—Heidegger's "affair" with National Socialism; Heidegger "got in bed" with the Nazis, etc. I can think of few systemic (and institutionally sanctioned) forms of critique more intellectually violent than the feminization of thought.

6. Heidegger points out that the *arché* of philosophy is *astonishment* (*What Is Philosophy?* 79). "In astonishment we restrain ourselves (être en arrêt). We step back, as it were, from being" (85).

7. In a purely serendipitous moment, my husband and I happened to see Gormley's installation of "Another Place" on a stormy day in June 1997, while staying at a hotel on the beach near Stavanger. From our room we were able to see the beach, and at first I thought the people I could see were real. It was hard to believe that in that storm, with driving rain and winds and a temperature of about forty degrees Fahrenheit, these people would be swimming in the sea. But then, I thought, this is Norway. An hour later, when I went back to the window, I saw the same people in the same places, and it dawned on me these were not real people. We bundled up and went out to the beach to see the most amazing sight

—one hundred identical iron sculptures scattered along the beach and into the sea, some semicovered by water, some buried in sand to their waists, and all staring out to sea. The image has never left me.

8. A more extensive discussion of Ong's analysis appears in my article "The Ethico-Political Agon of Other Criticisms: Toward a Nietzschean Counter-Ethic" in *Pre/Text* (11.3–4, Fall/Winter 1990: 289–309).

9. Information on Woods's exhibition can be found here: http://cryptome.org/woods-work.htm.

10. I wish to thank Victor Vitanza for pointing me to Agamben's work on refugees and the camps and Norman O. Brown's *Love's Body.* I also thank him enormously for careful readings of my work for the past thirty-two years.

11. That last sentence is, in the original: "Sie sagen das Verschwiegene" (*Wozu Dichter* 293). Unhappy with the Hofstadter translation ("the dots tell what is kept silent"), I prefer to translate it as follows: "The dots tell the secret."

12. Following the Afghan refugee crisis in Australia, the BBC reports that "legislation is being rushed through Australia's parliament to tighten up definitions of refugees, and put strict limits on their rights to challenge asylum decisions" (Knox).

13. Rebecca Gomperts, founder of Women on Waves, offers free abortions offshore in international waters, ignoring threats from antiabortion terrorists. "She is also arguably the first abortion rights activist aggressively to cross international borders" (Corbett).

14. As a graduate student at UTA from 1984 to 1994, I can personally attest to the rise and fall of the CACTIP program, the ramifications of which are still being acutely felt by all the faculty and students involved in the twenty-year history of that program and its integration with the graduate rhetoric program, which has also now been reduced to a mere shadow of its original conception.

15. Faigley first published the piece "Judging Writing, Judging Selves" in *CCC* journal (1989), and later included it in his award-winning book, *Fragments of Rationality* (1994).

16. If the CCCC Braddock award essays are salient barometers registering the pressures in our field, it is interesting to note that of the winning essays between 1975 (when the award was first announced) and 1998 (collected in Lisa Ede's edited volume *On Writing Research: The Braddock Essays 1975–1998*), only one deals explicitly with teaching argument. In "Moments of Argument: Agonistic Inquiry and Confrontational Cooperation" (published in 1997, winner of the Braddock in 1998), coauthors Dennis Lynch, Diana George, and Marilyn Cooper take issue with the practice of asking students to "establish their position before they interact with those with whom they disagree" (394). Arguing that this pushes "students to reproduce their disagreements rather than [move] towards negotiated and temporary resolutions of disagreements" (394), the authors recommend engaging students in negotiating "not 'conflicts of knowledge,' so much

as conflicts of positioning and power" (395). Understandably, they hope to teach students to sort through "the complexities of an issue" rather than to merely describe "stark controversies" (404); but their goals seem less motivated by a desire to teach students strategies for writing than a desire for them to change. When composing their assignments, the authors explained, "We reminded ourselves that the risk in argument is not that you may lose but rather that you may change" (407). Further: "We also knew full well the rhetorical force of the questions we asked; thoughtfully pursued, these questions could and did prompt change in our students" (407).

17. The logic of containment detains boat people on the high seas and on shore. Woomera is Australia's largest onshore internment camp. It is also the site of nuclear weapons testing, uranium mining, and an American CIA spy base pivotal to Bush's national missile defense system. Woomera2002 took place from March 27 to April 2, 2002, and Boat People Day was Good Friday (2002). Woomera2002 organizers declared:

> We refuse the death, pain, and confinements that are manufactured in the name of The Economy. We refuse the caging behind razor wire and the new world borders fashioned so that capital, by reserving for ITSELF the "right" to move around the world, can better enforce austerity, misery, the earth's destruction. (Woomera 2002)

18. Heeding Vitanza's moratorium on turning theory into praxis (160), yet mindful of the urgency of deregulating the argumentation industry that has our field so tightly in its grip, I offer the following assignment in the spirit of my title—writing offshore. Give your students (or yourselves) this *depth probe* assignment: Write something offshore (i.e., put a message in a bottle) in response to this statement: *WE ARE ALL BOAT PEOPLE*. Now take your paper and make a paper boat. Leave it in a prominent place such as a doorstep, a computer terminal, the university administration building, or wear it on your clothes, whatever. Then imagine its trajectory, where it will go, who will see it, what they will think (what you would *like* them to think). And then, put that in writing; trace the trajectories, and give it ballast—so that the main question you should ask yourself as you write is this: *will it float*?

5. Glitch Rhetoric (Gulzar e-Hijri, Pakistan)

1. The Pearl beheading was certainly not the first historically speaking, though it marked the debut of this horrific tactic by Islamist extremists. The power of this brand of tactical violence (now being used by ISIS) lies not only in its extreme brutality, but also in the "mediation" of the event—the filming and circulation of it on the Internet that broadcasts fear and terror. See Adam Taylor for a valuable perspective on the practice of Islamist beheadings.

6. Torture and Absolution (Gulfstream V N379P, Unknown Airspace)

1. This chapter is a slightly revised version of my article "Torture and Absolution: The Shadow Twin Towers of Atro/City" in *Fast Capitalism* 4.1 (2008). I am grateful to the editors for permission to reprint it here.

2. The significance of "thresholdy phenomena" is discussed at length in chapter 1; but this reference to Laurel indicates how long ago the threshold has appeared in my own thinking.

7. Postconflict Pedagogy (Ground Zero, New York)

1. This chapter is revised from an essay called "Postconflict Pedagogy: Writing in the Stream of Hearing," which was published in *Beyond Postprocess* (Utah State University Press, 2011). I am grateful to Sid Dobrin for inviting me to contribute to the book and to Utah State University Press for permission to reprint this revised version here.

8. Marine Media (1214 Middle St., Sullivan's Island, South Carolina)

1. Hauge's poem is translated by Robin Fulton and appears with permission from White Pine Press.

9. Accidental Metaphysics (Mendocino Ridge, Pacific Ocean)

1. The occasion for this chapter began with an invitation from Lynn Worsham, editor of *JAC* journal, to respond to Frank's essay "Heidegger, Captain Paul Watson, and the 'Look' of the Leviathan" (*JAC* 30.3–4, 2010). My response essay appeared in an issue soon thereafter as "Accidental Metaphysics: What Animals Don't Think About" (*JAC* 32.1–2, 2012, pp 347–53). I want to thank Lynn and *JAC* for permission to reprint the essay here (with minor changes). I am also immensely grateful to Luanne Frank for introducing me to Heidegger, for her generous attention to my writing, for challenging me every day to have at least three good ideas, and for her steadfast friendship.

2. I am indebted to Anthony Collamati for making a short film on rodeos, the editing of which spliced and cut (for me) the rope that had tied me up for forty years, making it now un/impossible to write about my daughter. Collamati's film inspired me to figure out some things, in writing, that otherwise continue to float in a sea of unthinking me's.

10. Armageddon Army (Umm Qasr, Iraq)

1. I would also like to, but can't, introduce you to this unnamed Iraqi guard, killed on March 21, 2003, by a direct hit of "perceptions management." In the US Army's *On Point: The United States Army in Operation Iraqi Freedom*, in chapter 3 on "decapitation" strikes, we learn that while engaged in an aerial leaflet drop, "a box of leaflets that fell out of a Combat Talon aircraft when a static line

broke. . . . impacted on the Iraqi guard's head, and 9th PSYOP Battalion may have achieved the first enemy KIA of Operation IRAQI FREEDOM" (Lieutenant Colonel Carl Ayers; qtd in Fontenot et al., 108). This chapter is a revision of my article published in the first issue of *Games and Culture* (2006), reprinted here with permission from Sage Publications.

2. For links to examples of these design attitudes of game modifications, see Engeli's shooter game art taxonomy here: http://maia.enge.li/gamezone/taxonomy.html.

3. See http://www.landoverbaptist.org/news0304/ut2k4mod.html (6 March 2015).

4. See http://www.darwinia.co.uk/ (6 March 2015).

5. See http://www.simtropolis.com/stex/index.cfm?mode=files&filetype=BAT&startrow=1&category=Modds&sortby=DatePosted&show=12&Str=Pegasus (6 March 2015).

6. See http://www.svatopluk.com/diablo/download/bobafett.stm (23 May 2005).

7. See http://www.gamefaqs.com/computer/doswin/code/556765.html (6 March 2015).

8. For information about the Jarhmann and Moswitzer antiwar shooter see http://www.climax.at/nybble-engine-toolz/shooter.html, where their "radical meta-art system shooter and practical model of mediapoiesis" is further explained.

9. "SITREP (Situation Report) is defined as 'an update to an existing report, issued as conditions change or events begin to unfold.' Put simply, it's a method of keeping everyone informed. Similarly, the computer game America's Army also issues SITREPs, providing updates to our community on a variety of topics, ranging from development progress, new features, upcoming events, and much more" (http://battletracker.com/forum/general/battletracker-news/46640-sitrep-strikes-back/) (2 March 2004; accessed 6 March 2015).

11. Endgame Rhetorics (Utøya Island, Norway)

1. An earlier version of this chapter is forthcoming as "Endgame Rhetorics: Theorycraft at the End of Play" in *Pre/Text* 21.1–4 (2016). I am grateful to Victor J. Vitanza, editor of *Pre/Text*, for permission to reprint this revised version of my essay here.

2. Herbrechter made this comment during an open discussion at the Game Studies and Literary Theory Workshop, University of Malta, March 2012. For a more specific examination of his views on posthumanism, see his review essay in *Culture Machine*.

3. A "rare spawn" is gamer parlance for a rare monster that is on a different timer from other mobs in the game.

4. Portions of this section are drawn from my essay "Muddy Waters, Serious Games" (*Ludic Society* 1, 2005).

Works Cited

Aarseth, Espen. *Cybertext: Perspectives on Ergodic Literature*. Baltimore: Johns Hopkins UP, 1997. Print.

———. "Doors and Perception: Fiction vs. Simulation in Games." *Proceedings of the Digital Arts & Culture Conference*. IT University of Copenhagen, 2005. 59–62. Print.

Aarseth, Espen, and Gordon Calleja. "The Word Game: The Ontology of an Undefinable Object." Lecture delivered at *Philosophy of Computer Games Conference 2009*, University of Oslo, Norway, 13 Aug. 2009. Web. 7 March 2015. <http://www.hf.uio.no/ifikk/english/research/projects/thirdplace/Conferences/video/02_aarseth_1200.mov>.

Agamben, Giorgio. *Means without End: Notes on Politics*. Trans. Vincenzo Binetti and Cesare Casarino. Minneapolis: U of Minnesota P, 2000. Print.

———. *State of Exception*. Trans. Kevin Attell. Chicago: U of Chicago P, 2005. Print.

America's Army. 2002. Web. 6 March 2015. <http://www.americasarmy.com/>.

Auckland, R. G. "The First Leaflet of the First World War." *Falling Leaf* 49 (June 1970). Web. 3 March 2015. <http://www.psywarsoc.org/FallingLeaf/firstwwi.php>.

———. "German 'Black' Propaganda to Denmark." *Falling Leaf* 75 (Winter 1976). Web. 3 March 2015. <http://www.psywarsoc.org/FallingLeaf/black.php>.

Bambach, Charles R. *Heidegger's Roots: Nietzsche, National Socialism, and the Greeks*. Ithaca: Cornell UP, 2003. Print.

Barthes, Roland. *Camera Lucida: Reflections on Photography*. Trans. Richard Howard. New York: Hill, 1981. Print.

Battletracker.com Forum. 19 Sept. 2005. Web. 3 April 2016. <http://battletracker.com/forum/general/battletracker-news/p1389757-sitrep-is-up/#post1389757>.

Baudelaire, Charles. "Crowds" in *Paris Spleen*. Trans. Louise Varese. New York: New Directions, 1988. 20–21. Print.

Benjamin, Walter. "A Berlin Chronicle" in *Reflections: Essays, Aphorisms, Autobiographical Writings*. Trans. Edmund Jephcott. Ed. Peter Demetz. New York: Harcourt, 1978. 3–60. Print.

———. "One-Way Street" in *Reflections: Essays, Aphorisms, Autobiographical Writings*. Trans. Edmund Jephcott. Ed. Peter Demetz. New York: Harvest, 1978. 61–94. Print.

———. *The Origin of German Tragic Drama*. New York: Verso, 1977. Print.

———. *Werke und Nachlaß. Kritische Gesamtausgabe 8: Einbahnstraße*. Ed. Detlev Schöttker. Berlin: Suhrkamp, 2009.

Bertha, Csilla. "Introduction: Desmond Egan's Poems." Hungarian Electronic Library. Web. 13 March 2015. <http://www.mek.iif.hu/porta/szint/human/szepirod/vilagir/egan_d/selected/html/intro.htm>.

Berthoff, Ann E. "Abstraction as a Speculative Instrument." *The Territory of Language: Linguistics, Stylistics, and the Teaching of Composition*. Ed. Donald A. McQuade. Carbondale: Southern Illinois UP, 1986. 227–37. Print.

———. *Forming/Thinking/Writing: The Composing Imagination*. Montclair: Boynton, 1982. Print.

Black, Edwin. "At Death's Door: Archivist Finds IBM Site near Auschwitz." 2002. Web. 20 Feb. 2009. <http://www.scrapbookpages.com/AuschwitzScrapbook/History/Articles/IBMpunchcards.html>.

———. *IBM and the Holocaust: The Strategic Alliance between Nazi Germany and America's Most Powerful Corporation*. New York: Crown, 2001. Print.

Blanchot, Maurice. *The Writing of the Disaster*. Trans. Ann Smock. Lincoln: U of Nebraska P, 1986. Print.

Boat People Organization. Web. 2 March 2015. <http://www.boat-people.org/>.

"Boat People's Plea to Australia." BBC News. 3 Sept. 2001. Web. 20 Feb. 2015. <http://news.bbc.co.uk/1/hi/world/asia-pacific/1522728.stm>.

Bock, Wolfgang. "Lost Orders of the Day: Benjamin's *Einbahnstraße*." *A Companion to the Works of Walter Benjamin*. Ed. Rolf J. Goebel. New York: Camden, 2009. 70–90. Print.

Breivik, Anders Behring. "2083—a European Declaration of Independence." Web. 3 April 2016. <https://fas.org/programs/tap/_docs/2083_-_A_European_Declaration_of_Independence.pdf >.

Brown, Norman O. *Love's Body*. New York: Vintage, 1966. Print.

Bunch, Ralph. "Some Reflections on Peace in Our Time." Nobel Peace Prize lecture. Oslo (11 Dec. 1950). Nobel *e*-Museum. Web. 3 March 2015. <http://www.nobelprize.org/nobel_prizes/peace/laureates/1950/bunche-lecture.html>.

Burke, Kenneth. *Attitudes toward History*. 3rd ed. Berkeley: U of California P, 1984. Print.

———. *Counter-Statement*. 2nd ed. Chicago: U of Chicago P, 1953. Print.

———. *A Grammar of Motives*. Berkeley: U of California P, 1969. Print.

———. *Language as Symbolic Action: Essays on Life, Literature, and Method*. Berkeley: U of California P, 1966. Print.

———. *Permanence and Change: An Anatomy of Purpose*. Indianapolis: Bobbs, 1965. Print.

———. *The Philosophy of Literary Form: Studies in Symbolic Action*. New York: Vintage, 1957. Print.

Burlas, Joe. "'On Point' Shares OIF Lessons Learned." Army News Service (26 May 2004). Web. 3 March 2015. <http://www.dau.mil/pubscats/pubscats/atl/2004_09_10/new-s004.pdf>.

Büsing, Kirsten, and Claus Seebacher. "Mykologen im Exlibris." *Mykologie Forum* (2006): 15–17. Web. 26 July 2015. http://www.dmykg.de/fileadmin/download/MykForum_15-17_Heft0206.pdf.

Callot, Sean. Personal interview. 24 March 2008.

Caputo, John D. *Against Ethics: Contributions to a Poetics of Obligation with Constant Reference to Deconstruction*. Bloomington: Indiana UP, 1993. Print.

———. *The Mystical Element in Heidegger's Thought*. New York: Fordham UP, 1986. Print.

Carter, Daniel. Personal email. 27 Sept. 2001.

Carter, Michael P., Carolyn R. Miller, and Ann M. Penrose. "Effective Composition Instruction: What Does the Research Show?" *Center for Communication in Science, Technology, and Management Publication Series*. No. 3 (April 1998). North Carolina State University. Web. 2 March 2015. <http://writing.uncc.edu/sites/writing.uncc.edu/files/media/docs/Effective_Writing_Instruction_What_Research_Shows.pdf>.

Chamberlain, Charles. "From 'Haunts' to 'Character': The Meaning of Ethos and its Relation to Ethics" *Helios* 11.2 (Winter 1984): 97–108. Print.

Christian Coders Network. 2005. Web. 4 April 2016. <http://ccnarchive.christiandevs.com/thread.php?f=GeneralDiscussions&t=000555&h=cheesestorm>.

Cixous, Hélène. "My Algeriance, in Other Words: To Depart Not to Arrive from Algeria." In *Stigmata: Escaping Texts*. New York: Routledge, 1998. 153–72. Print.

———. "The Oklahoma Nature Theatre Is Recruiting." *Autodafe* 3/4 (2003): 63–78. Print.

———. *Three Steps on the Ladder of Writing*. Trans. Sarah Cornell and Susan Sellers. New York: Columbia UP, 1993. Print.

———. "What Is It O'Clock? or The Door (We Never Enter)." *Stigmata: Escaping Texts*. New York: Routledge, 1998. 57–83. Print.

Clifford, John. "Toward Real Philosophic Laboratories: Ann Berthoff on Writing Theory and Practice." *The Territory of Language: Linguistics, Stylistics, and the Teaching of Composition*. Ed. Donald A. McQuade. Carbondale: Southern Illinois UP, 1986. 330–39. Print.

Commission on English. *Examining the Examination in English: A Report to the College Entrance Examination Board*. Cambridge: Harvard UP, 1931. Print.

Conansen, Joe. "See What Happens When You Don't Read?" *Observer.* 16 Feb. 2004. Web. 3 March 2015. <http://observer.com/2004/02/see-what-happens-when-you-dont-read/>.

Connors, Robert J. "Overwork/Underpay: Labor and Status of Composition Teachers since 1880." *Rhetoric Review* 9.1 (1990): 108–26. Print.

Corbett, Sara. "Rebecca Gomperts Is Trying to Save the World for Abortion." *New York Times Magazine.* 26 Aug. 2001. Web. 2 March 2015. <http://www.nytimes.com/2001/08/26/magazine/26ABORTION.html>.

Coupland, Douglas. *Generation X: Tales for an Accelerated Culture.* New York: St. Martin's, 1991. Print.

Critchley, Simon. *Infinitely Demanding: Ethics of Commitment, Politics of Resistance.* London: Verso, 2007. Print.

Crowley, Sharon. *Composition in the University: Historical and Polemical Essays.* Pittsburgh: U of Pittsburgh P, 1998. Print.

Davidson, Martin. *The Perfect Nazi: Uncovering My Grandfather's Secret Past.* New York: Berkley, 2010. Print.

Davies, Martin. "Gamers Don't Want Any More Grief." *Guardian.* 14 June 2006. Web.

Davis, D. Diane. *Breaking Up [at] Totality: A Rhetoric of Laughter.* Carbondale: Southern Illinois UP, 2000. Print.

Dean, Martin. *Robbing the Jews: The Confiscation of Jewish Property in the Holocaust, 1933–1945.* New York: Cambridge UP, 2008. Print.

De Landa, Manuel. "Extensive Borderlines and Intensive Borderlines." *Border-Line.* Ed. Lebbeus Woods and Ekkehard Rehfeld. Vienna: Springer, 1998. 18%–24%. Print.

De Man, Paul. *The Resistance to Theory.* Minneapolis: U of Minnesota P, 1986. Print.

Demetz, Peter, ed. Introduction. *Reflections: Essays, Aphorisms, Autobiographical Writings.* By Walter Benjamin. Trans. Edmund Jephcott. Ed. Peter Demetz. New York: Harvest, 1978. vii–xliii. Print.

Department of Justice. 2006. President George W. Bush pardons press release. Web. 3 March 2015. <http://www.usdoj.gov/opa/pr/2006/August/06_opa_544.html>.

Derrida, Jacques. "Canons and Metonymies: An Interview with Jacques Derrida." *Logomachia: The Conflict of the Faculties.* Ed. Richard Rand. Lincoln: U of Nebraska P, 1992. 195–218. Print.

———. *Cinders.* Trans. Ned Lukacher. Lincoln: U of Nebraska P, 1991. Print.

———. "Displaced Literatures." *Autodafe* 1 (2001): 63–66. Print.

———. *Dissemination.* Trans. Barbara Johnson. Chicago: U of Chicago P, 1981. Print.

———. "Intellectual Courage: An interview by Thomas Assheuer." *Culture Machine* 2 (2002). Web. 2 March 2015. <http://www.culturemachine.net/index.php/cm/article/viewarticle/303/288>.

———. *Of Hospitality*. Translated by Rachel Bowlby. Stanford: Stanford UP, 2000. Print.

———. *On Cosmopolitanism and Forgiveness*. Trans. Mark Dooley and Michael Hughes. London: Routledge, 2001. Print.

———. "Otobiographies: The Teaching of Nietzsche and the Politics of the Proper Name." Trans. Avital Ronell. *The Ear of the Other: Otobiography, Transference, Translation*. Trans. Peggy Kamuf. Ed. Christie V. McDonald. New York: Schocken, 1985. 1–38. Print.

———. *Paper Machine*. Trans. Rachel Bowlby. Stanford: Stanford UP, 2005. Print.

———. *Rogues: Two Essays on Reason*. Trans. Pascale-Anne Brault and Michael Naas. Stanford: Stanford UP, 2005. Print.

———. "Structure, Sign and Play in the Discourse of the Human Sciences." *Writing and Difference*. Trans. A. Bass. London: Routledge, 1978. 278–94. Print.

———. *Without Alibi*. Trans. Peggy Kamuf. Stanford: Stanford UP, 2002. Print.

Doerr, Andrew. *All the Light We Cannot See*. New York: Simon, 2014. Print.

Dorner, Adolf (Hrsg.). *Mathematik im Dienste der nationalpolitischen Erziehung mit Anwendungsbeispiel aus Volkswissenschaft, Geländekunde und Naturwissenschaft*. Frankfurt/Main, 1935. Print.

Drabble, Margaret. "Why Authors Need a Refuge." *Guardian*. 7 Dec. 2001. Web. 2 March 2015. <http://www.theguardian.com/books/2001/dec/08/politics>.

Dudenhefer, Paul. "A Guide to Writing in Economics." EcoTeach Center at Duke University. Dec. 2009. Web. 4 March 2015. <http://gsme.sharif.edu/~rms/files/manual.pdf>.

Egan, Desmond. "Needing the Sea." *Seeing Double*. Newbridge, Ireland: Goldsmith, 1983. Print.

Eisenstadt, Merry Madway. "Counted for Persecution; IBM's Role in the Holocaust." *Washington Jewish Week*. 17 Sept. 1998. Web. 26 February 2009. <http://www.stockmaven.com/ibmstory.htm>.

Elam, Diane. *Feminism and Deconstruction: Ms. en Abyme*. London: Routledge, 1994. Print.

Ellia, Linda. *Notre Combat*. Paris: Éditions du Seuil, 2007. Print.

Engeli, Maia. "Changing the Game—A Taxonomy of Artistic Alterations of First-Person Shooter Games." Featured presentation at "Shaping Consciousness: New Media, Spirituality, and Identity Symposium." 6 April 2005. Dallas, Texas. Web. 6 March 2015. <http://maia.enge.li/gamezone/taxonomy.html>.

Eskelinen, Markku. "The Gaming Situation." *Game Studies* 1.1 (July 2001) Web. 6 March 2015. <http://www.gamestudies.org/0101/eskelinen/>.

Faigley, Lester. *Fragments of Rationality: Postmodernity and the Subject of Composition*. Pittsburgh: U of Pittsburgh P, 1992. Print.

———. "Judging Writing, Judging Selves." *CCC* 40.4 (1989): 395–412. Print.

Flusser, Vilém. *The Shape of Things: A Philosophy of Design*. London: Reaktion, 1999. Print.

Fontenot, Gregory, E. J. Degen, and David Tohn. *OnPoint: The United States Army in Operation Iraqi Freedom*. Annapolis: US Naval Institute, 2005. Print. Web. 6 March 2015. <http://www.globalsecurity.org/military/library/report/2004/onpoint/ch-3.htm>.

Foucault, Michel. "The Discourse on Language." *The Archaeology of Knowledge and the Discourse on Language*. Trans. A. M. Sheridan Smith. New York: Pantheon, 1972. 215–37. Print.

Frank, Luanne T. "Criticism and the Meaning of Writing." *Pre/Text* 8.3–4 (Fall/Winter 1987): 185–94. Print.

———. "Heidegger, Captain Paul Watson, and the 'Look' of Leviathan." *JAC* 30.3–4 (2010): 583–617. Print.

———. "Heidegger and the Sign." Unpublished seminar lectures. University of Texas at Arlington. Spring 1990. Print.

Frasca, Gonzalo. "Ludology Meets Narratology: Similitudes and Differences between (Video) Games and Narrative." 1999. Web. 6 March 2015. <http://www.ludology.org/articles/ludology.htm>.

Fried, Gregory. *Heidegger's* Polemos*: From Being to Politics*. New Haven: Yale UP, 2000. Print.

Friedrich, Jörg. "'The Apartment Keys Are to Be Relinquished to the House Manager': The Cannibalization of Jewish Estates." *The German Public and the Persecution of the Jews, 1933–1945. "No One Participated, No One Knew."* Ed. Jörg Wollenberg. Trans. Rado Pribic. Atlantic Highlands, NJ: Humanities, 1996. 141–53. Print.

Gabriel, Peter. "Signal to Noise." *Up*. Virgin Records, 2002. CD.

Gaffney, Nik, and Maja Kuzmanovic. "topology of error: digital art and the glitch [b+m+n]." Digital Arts and Culture Conference. Bergen, Norway, July 2000. The Libarynth. Web. 3 March 2015. <http://lib.fo.am/digital_art_and_the_glitch>.

Galloway, Alexander R. *Protocol: How Control Exists after Decentralization*. Cambridge: MIT P, 2004. Print.

Galloway, Alexander R., and Eugene Thacker. *The Exploit: A Theory of Networks*. Minneapolis: U of Minnesota P, 2007. Print.

Garfinkel, Simson. "Welcome to Sealand, Now Bugger Off." *Wired* 8.7 (July 2000). Web. 2 March 2015. <http://www.wired.com/wired/archive/8.07/haven.html>.

Gayles, Gloria Jean Wade, ed. *Conversations with Gwendolyn Brooks*. Jackson: UP of Mississippi, 2003. Print.

Genosko, Gary. *Undisciplined Theory*. London: Sage, 1998. Print.

Gera, Vanessa. "Maurizio Cattelan's Statue of Praying Hitler in Ex-Warsaw Ghetto Sparks Emotions." *Yahoo News*. 28 Dec. 2012. Web. 4 April 2016. <https://www.yahoo.com/news/praying-hitler-ex-warsaw-ghetto-sparks-emotion-161124083.html>.

Gold, Jonathan, and Friedrich Nürnberger. "A Tribute to Abraham Buschke." *Journal of the American Academy of Dermatology* 26.6 (June 1992): 1019–22. Print.

Gormley, Antony. "Another Place." Installation at Stavanger, Norway, 1997. 100 cast iron figures 189 × 53 × 29 cm. Web. 2 March 2015. <http://www.antonygormley.com/projects/item-view/id/230#p6>.

———. "Extracts from interview with Udo Kittelmann on Total Strangers." Kolnischer Kunstverein, 1999. Web. 2 March 2015. <http://www.antonygormley.com/resources/interview-item/id/109>.

Graff, Gerald. "Hidden Intellectualism." *Pedagogy*. 1.1 (Winter 2001): 21–36. Print.

Guthrie, W. K. C. "Flux and Logos in Heraclitus." *The Pre-Socratics*. Ed. Alexander P. D. Mourelatos. New York: Anchor, 1974. 197–213. Print.

Gutman, Roy. *A Witness to Genocide*. New York: Macmillan, 1993. Print.

Haraway, Donna. *Simians, Cyborgs, and Women: The Reinvention of Nature*. New York: Routledge, 1991. Print.

Hauge, Olav. *Selected Poems*. Trans. Robin Fulton. Buffalo: White Pine, 1990. Print.

Haugo, Marita. "Breivik forklarte seg." *Drammens Tidende*. 17 Apr 2012. Web. 4 Apr 2016. < http://www.dt.no/nyheter/utoya/nyheter/breivik-forklarte-seg/s/2-2.1748-1.7185696 >.

Hawk, Byron. *A Counter-History of Composition: Toward Methodologies of Complexity*. Pittsburgh: U of Pittsburgh P, 2007. Print.

Haynes, Cynthia. "Absolution and the Rhetorical Sanction of Rogue Responsibility." Paper delivered at the Rhetoric Society of America (RSA) conference (Seattle 2008).

———. "Accidental Metaphysics: What Animals Don't Think About." *JAC* 32.1–2 (2012): 347–53. Print.

———. "Armageddon Army: Playing God, God Mode Mods, and the Rhetorical Task of Ludology." *Games and Culture: A Journal of Interactive Media* 1.1 (January 2006): 89–96. Print.

———. "Cities of Rendition: Interrogation on/of the Extrajudicial Edge." Paper delivered at the CCCC conference (New Orleans 2008).

———. "The Ethico-Political Agon of *Other* Criticisms: Toward a Nietzschean Counter-Ethic." *Pre/Text*. 11/3–4 (Fall/Winter 1990): 289–309. Print.

———. "Glitch Rhetoric: Shock Design and the Mediation of Global (T)error." Paper delivered at IT University of Copenhagen (Oct. 2005).

———. *In the Name of Writing: Rhetoric and the Politics of Ethos*. Dissertation. University of Texas at Arlington, 1994. Print.

———. "Marine Media: Composition and the Deep Play of Fluid Structures." Paper delivered at the Watson Conference on Rhetoric (Louisville, Oct. 2008).

———. "Muddy Waters/Serious Games." *Ludic Society* 1 (Nov. 2005): 15. Print.

———. "Playing Just, *Just Cause*: The Internet as Ace in the Language Game of Regime Change." Paper delivered at the 30th International Wittgenstein Symposium (Kirchberg, Austria 2007).

———. "Postconflict Pedagogy: Writing in the Stream of Hearing." *Beyond Post-process*. Ed. Sidney I. Dobrin, J. A. Rice, and Michael Vastola. Logan: Utah State UP, 2011. 145–62. Print.

———. "Torture and Absolution: The Shadow Twin Towers of Atro/City." *Fast Capitalism* 4.1 (2008). Web. 3 March 2015. <http://www.uta.edu/huma/agger/fastcapitalism/4_1/haynes.html>.

———. "When Peace Is in Style." Paper delivered at the CCCC conference (San Antonio, 2004).

———. "Writing Offshore: The Disappearing Coastline of Composition Theory." *JAC* 23.4 (2003): 667–724. Print.

Heidegger, Martin. "Building, Dwelling, Thinking." *Poetry, Language, Thought*. Trans. Albert Hofstadter. New York: Harper, 1971. 143–61. Print.

———. *An Introduction to Metaphysics*. Trans. Ralph Manheim. New Haven: Yale UP, 1959. Print.

———. "Letter on Humanism." *Martin Heidegger: Basic Writings*. Ed. David Farrell Krell. New York: Harper, 1977. 189–242. Print.

———. "Logos." *Early Greek Thinking: The Dawn of Western Philosophy*. Trans. David Farrell Krell and Frank A. Capuzzi. San Francisco: Harper, 1984. 59–78. Print.

———. *On the Way to Language*. Trans. Peter D. Hertz. New York: Harper, 1971. Print.

———. "The Origin of the Work of Art." *Poetry, Language, Thought*. Trans. Albert Hofstadter. New York: Harper, 1971. 17–87. Print.

———. *Parmenides*. Trans. André Schuwer and Richard Rojcewicz. Bloomington: Indiana UP, 1992. Print.

———. "Poetically Man Dwells." *Poetry, Language, Thought*. Trans. Albert Hofstadter. New York: Harper, 1971. 211–29. Print.

———. "The Self-Assertion of the German University: Address, Delivered on the Solemn Assumption of the Rectorate of the University Freiburg" and "The Rectorate 1933/34: Facts and Thoughts." Trans. Karsten Harries. *Review of Metaphysics* 38 (March 1985): 467–502. Print.

———. "What Are Poets For?" *Poetry, Language, Thought*. Trans. Albert Hofstadter. New York: Harper, 1971. 89–142. Print.

———. *What Is Philosophy?* Trans. William Kluback and Jean T. Wilde. New York: Twayne, 1958. Print.

———. "Wozu Dichter?" *Holzwege*. Frankfurt am Main: Klostermann, 1950. 248–95. Print.

Heller, Peter. *Whale Warriors: The Battle at the Bottom of the World to Save the Planet's Largest Mammals*. New York: Free, 2007. Print.

Herbrechter, Stefan. "Review: Rosi Braidotti's *The Posthuman*." *Culture Machine* (2013). Web. 7 March 2015. <http://www.culturemachine.net/index.php/cm/article/viewFile/495/516>.

Hitler, Adolf. *Mein Kampf*. Trans. Ralph Manheim. Boston: Houghton, 1971. Print.

———. *Mon Combat*. Trans. J. Gaudefroy-Demombynes and A. Calmettes. Paris: Nouvelles, 1934. Print.

Hölderlin, Friedrich. *Hymns and Fragments*. Trans. Richard Sieburth. Princeton: Princeton UP, 1984. Print.

Holmevik, Jan Rune. *Educating the Machine: A Study in the History of Computing and the Construction of the SIMULA Programming Language*. Trondheim: U of Trondheim Center for Technology and Society, 1994. Print.

———. *Inter/Vention: Free Play in the Age of Electracy*. Cambridge: MIT P, 2012. Print.

Holtzman, Elizabeth. "Bush Seeks Immunity for Violating War Crimes Act." *Nuclear Age Peace Foundation*. 23 Sept. 2006. Web. 3 March 2015. <http://www.wagingpeace.org/bush-seeks-immunity-for-violating-war-crimes-act/>.

Hopkins, Gerard Manley. "Pied Beauty." *Modern British Poetry*. Ed. Louis Untermeyer. New York: Harcourt, 1942. 47. Print.

"Huddled Masses, please stay away." *Economist*. 15 June 2002. Web. 4 April 2016. <http://www.economist.com/node/1177390>.

Hussein, Aqeel. "Google Earth, the survival tool of war-torn Iraq." Telegraph.co.uk. 15 Feb. 2007. Web. 4 March 2015. <http://www.telegraph.co.uk/news/worldnews/1542775/Google-Earth-the-survival-tool-of-war-torn-Iraq.html>.

Huyssen, Andreas. "Nostalgia for Ruins." *Grey Room* 23 (Spring 2006): 6–21. Print.

IBM. "History of IBM in Germany." Web. 3 August 2015. <https://www-05.ibm.com/de/ibm/unternehmen/geschichte/index.html>.

Ibsen, Henrik. "The Master Builder." *"Hedda Gabler" and Other Plays*. New York: Bantam, 1995. 281–387. Print.

Jahrmann, Margarete. "Ich Spiele Legen: The president@whitehouse.gov Shooter and Enlightenment as Mass Deception." *Economising Culture: On the (Digital) Culture Industry*. Ed. Geoff Cox, Joasia Krysa, and Anya Lewin. New York: Autonomedia, 2004. 205–11. Print.

Jahrmann, Margarete, and Max Moswitzer. "nybble-engine-toolz." 2003. Web. 6 March 2015. <http://www.climax.at/nybble-engine-toolz/shooter.html>.

Jarvis, Bob. "Mind/Body: Space/Time: Things/Events." *Urban Design Studies* Vol. 2 (1996): 101-14. Print.

Jenks, Chris. "Watching your Step: The History and Practice of the *Flâneur.*" *Visual Culture*. Ed. Chris Jenks. New York: Routledge, 1995. 142–60. Print.

Jonson, Ben. *Discoveries* Wks. 1846, 759. [1637] *Oxford English Dictionary*. Web. 3 March 2015.

Just Cause. Eidos Interactive and Avalanche Studios. 2006. Software. Web. 3 March 2015. <http://en.wikipedia.org/wiki/Just_Cause_(video_game)>.

Kaplan, Marion A. *Between Dignity and Despair: Jewish Life in Nazi Germany*. New York: Oxford UP, 1998. Print.

Katz, Steven J. "The Ethic of Expediency: Classical Rhetoric, Technology, and the Holocaust." *College English* 54.3 (March 1992): 255–75. Print.

Kennedy, George A. *Classical Rhetoric and Its Christian and Secular Tradition from Ancient to Modern Times*. Chapel Hill: U of North Carolina P, 1980. Print.

Kent, Thomas. *Post-Process Theory: Beyond the Writing-Process Paradigm*. Carbondale: Southern Illinois UP, 1999. Print.

King, John. "Bush Calls Saddam 'The Guy Who Tried to Kill My Dad.'" CNN.com. 27 Sept. 2002. Web. 3 March 2015. <http://edition.cnn.com/2002/ALLPOLITICS/09/27/bush.war.talk/>.

Kingston, Maxine Hong. *The Fifth Book of Peace*. New York: Knopf, 2003. Print.

Kleist, Heinrich von. "On the Marionette Theatre." *Essays on Dolls*. Trans. Idris Parry. London: Syrens, 1994. Web. 2 March 2015. <http://www.southerncrossreview.org/9/kleist.htm>.

Knox, Angie. "Howard's Refugee Gamble Paying Off." BBC News. 21 Sept. 2001. Web. 2 March 2015. <http://news.bbc.co.uk/1/hi/world/asia-pacific/1557082.stm>.

Kogon, Eugen, Hermann Langbein, and Adalbert Rückerl. *Nazi Mass Murder: A Documentary History of the Use of Poison Gas*. Trans. Mary Scott and Caroline Lloyd-Morris. New Haven: Yale UP, 1993. Print.

Koran. Trans. Rev. J. M. Rodwell. London: Dent, 1929. Print.

Kress, Gunther. "'English' at the Crossroads: Rethinking Curricula of Communication in the Context of the Turn to the Visual." *Passions, Pedagogies and 21st Century Technologies*. Ed. Gail E. Hawisher and Cynthia Self. Logan: Utah State UP, 1999. 66–88. Print.

Kwiet, Konrad. "The Ultimate Refuge: Suicide in the Jewish Community under the Nazis." *Leo Baeck Institute Yearbook* 29.1 (1984): 135–67. Print.

Kwinter, Sanford. *Architectures of Time: Toward a Theory of the Event in Modernist Culture*. Cambridge: MIT P, 2001. Print.

———. "The Fallacy of Misplaced Concreteness and the 'Avant-Garde' in America." *Autonomy and Ideology: Positioning an Avant-Garde in America*. Ed. R. E. Somol. New York: Monacelli, 1997. 262–75. Print.

Labash, Matt. "Psyching Out the Taliban—the Army Plans Mind Games at Fort Bragg" *Weekly Standard* 7.15 (24 Dec. 2001). Web. 6 March 2015. <http://www.weeklystandard.com/Content/Public/Articles/000/000/000/691yjwkt.asp>.

Ladd, Brian. *The Ghosts of Berlin: Confronting German History in the Urban Landscape*. Chicago: U of Chicago P, 1998. Print.

Landow, George. "Writing Poetry in Stretchtext: Literature and a New Form of Hypermedia" *Tekka* 3.2. Web. 4 March 2015. <http://www.tekka.net/login/>.

Lanham, Richard A. *Style: An Anti-Textbook*. New Haven: Yale UP, 1974. Print.

Laurel, Brenda. *Computers as Theatre*. Reading, MA: Addison, 1991. Print.

Lester, David. *Suicide and the Holocaust*. New York: Nova Science, 2005. Print.

Lévy, Bernard-Henri. *Who Killed Daniel Pearl?* Hoboken: Melville, 2003. Print.

Libeskind. Daniel. "Architecture Intermundium" *Threshold* 4 (Spring 1988): 114–21. Print.

———. *Countersigns*. London: Academy, 1991. Print.

———. *The Space of Encounter*. New York: Universe, 2000. Print.

Lupton, Ellen. "Fluid Mechanics: Typography Now." EllenLupton.com. 2000. Web. 4 March 2015. <http://elupton.com/2009/10/fluid-mechanics-typography-now/>.

Lutz, William. *Doublespeak*. New York: HarperPerennial, 1981. Print.

Lynch, Dennis A., Diana George, and Marilyn M. Cooper. "Moments of Argument: Agonistic Inquiry and Confrontational Cooperation." *CCC* 48.1 (February 1997): 61–86; reprinted in *On Writing Research: The Braddock Essays*. Ed. Lisa Ede. Boston: Bedford, 1999. 390–412. Print.

Lyotard, Jean-François. *The Differend: Phrases in Dispute*. Trans. Georges Van Den Abbeele. Minneapolis: U of Minnesota P, 1988. Print.

———. *Heidegger and "the jews."* Trans. Andreas Michel and Mark Roberts. Minneapolis: U of Minnesota P, 1990. Print.

Lyotard, Jean-François, and Jean-Loup Thébaud. *Just Gaming*. Trans. Wlad Godzich. Minneapolis: U of Minnesota P, 1985. Print.

Mackenzie, Suzie. "Rebuilding the Rubble." *Guardian Unlimited* (29 June 2002). Web. 3 March 2015. <http://www.theguardian.com/culture/2002/jun/29/artsfeatures.arts>.

Manovich, Lev. "Database as Symbolic Form." *Database Aesthetics: Art in the Age of Information Overflow*. Ed. Victoria Vesna. Minneapolis: U of Minnesota P, 2007. 39–60. Print.

Marshall, Margaret J. *Contesting Cultural Rhetorics: Public Discourse and Education, 1890–1900*. Ann Arbor: U of Michigan P, 1995. Print.

Merewether, Charles. "Traces of Loss." In *Irresistible Decay: Ruins Reclaimed*. Ed. Michael S. Roth, Claire Lyons, and Charles Merewether. Los Angeles: Getty Research Institute for the History of Art and the Humanities, 1997. 25–40. Print.

Metasploit Project. 2003. Web. 4 March 2009. <http://www.metasploit.com/>.

Meyer, Beate. *A Fatal Balancing Act: The Dilemma of the Reich Association of Jews in Germany, 1939–1945.* Trans. William Templer. New York: Berghahn, 2013. Print.

———. "The Fine Line between Responsible Action and Collaboration: The Reichsvereinigung der Juden in Deutschland and the Jewish Community in Berlin, 1938–45." *Jews in Nazi Berlin: From Kristallnacht to Liberation.* Ed. Beate Meyer, Hermann Simon, and Chana Schütz. Chicago: U of Chicago P, 2009. 310–62. Print.

"Most-Wanted Iraqi Playing Cards." *Wikipedia.* Web. 4 March 2015. <http://en.wikipedia.org/wiki/Most-wanted_Iraqi_playing_cards>.

Mukherjee, Bharati. *Jasmine.* New York: Grove, 1989. Print.

Mumford, Lewis. *The Pentagon of Power.* New York: Harcourt, 1970. Print.

Nagel, Thomas. "War and Massacre." *Mortal Questions.* Cambridge: Cambridge UP, 1979. 53–74. Print.

Natsios, Deborah, and John Young. "Jerusalem SKY." *The Next Jerusalem: Sharing the Divided City.* Ed. Michael Sorkin. New York: Monacelli, 2002. Web. 3 March 2015. <http://www.cartome.org/jerusalem-sky/introduction.htm>.

———. "Parallel Atlas: 38° N." Web. 3 March 2015. <http://www.cartome.org/parallel-atlas/dmz-intro.htm>.

Nietzsche, Friedrich. *Beyond Good and Evil: Prelude to a Philosophy of the Future.* Trans. R. J. Hollingdale. New York: Penguin, 1973. Print.

———. *The Birth of Tragedy and Other Writings.* Ed. Raymond Geuss and Ronald Speirs. Cambridge: Cambridge UP, 1999. Print.

———. *The Gay Science.* Trans. Walter Kaufmann. New York: Vintage, 1974. Print.

———. *On the Genealogy of Morals* and *Ecce Homo* [1887 and 1888]. Trans. Walter Kaufmann and R. J. Hollingdale. New York: Vintage, 1969. Print.

Novak, Marcus. "Liquid Architectures in Cyberspace." *Cyberspace: First Steps.* Ed. Michael Benedikt. Cambridge: MIT P, 1991. 225–54. Print.

Olsen, Lance. "Innovative Fiction as Liquid Architecture." *PIF Magazine.* 30 July, 2007. Web. 4 March 2015. <http://www.pifmagazine.com/2007/07/innovative-fiction-as-liquid-architecture/>.

Olson, Gary A. "Toward a Post-Process Composition: Abandoning the Rhetoric of Assertion." *Post-Process Theory: Beyond the Writing-Process Paradigm.* Ed. Thomas Kent. Carbondale: Southern Illinois UP, 1999. 7–15. Print.

Ominous Horizons. N'Lightning Software Development. Web. 14 May 2005.

Ong, Walter J. *Fighting for Life: Contest, Sexuality, and Consciousness.* Ithaca: Cornell UP, 1981. Print.

———. *Ramus, Method, and the Decay of Dialogue.* Cambridge: Harvard UP, 1983. Print.

"Pacific States Step into the Breach." BBC News. 3 Sept. 2001. Web. 3 March 2015. <http://news.bbc.co.uk/1/hi/world/asia-pacific/1520388.stm>.

Paley, W. Bradford. TextArc. 2002. Web. 3 March 2015. <http://textarc.org/>.

Pensky, Max. *Melancholy Dialectics: Walter Benjamin and the Play of Mourning.* Amherst: U of Massachusetts P, 2001. Print.

"Pentagon Releases Memo on Harsh Tactics." *Washington Post.* 1 April 2008. Web. 3 March 2015. <http://www.washingtonpost.com/wp-dyn/content/article/2008/04/01/AR2008040102392_2.html>.

Porter, Thomas E. "Composition, Analysis of Texts, Critical Thinking Integrated Program (CACTIP)." NEH proposal application. 1 April 1983. Print.

PsyWar.org. Web. 3 March 2015. <http://www.psywar.org>.

PsyWar Society. Web. 3 March 2015. <http://www.psywarsoc.org/history.php>.

RainbowSix 3 forum. Ubisoft Games forums. 2004. Web. 5 March 2015. <http://forums.ubi.com/eve/ubb.x/a/tpc/f/424105901/m/166100004/r/197003037#197003037>.

Rajchman, John. *Constructions.* Cambridge: MIT P, 1998. Print.

Rapaport, Herman. *Heidegger and Derrida: Reflections on Time and Language.* Lincoln: U of Nebraska P, 1989. Print.

Rasch, William. "In Search of Lyotard's Archipelago, or: How to Live with Paradox and Learn to Like It." *New German Critique* 61 (Winter 1994): 55–75. Print.

Ratti, Carlo, ed. "Digital Water Pavilion." MIT Sense*able* City Lab. 2008. Web. 4 March 2015. <http://senseable.mit.edu/papers/pdf/2008_Ratti_Nicolino_DWP.pdf>.

Readings, Bill. *Introducing Lyotard: Art and Politics.* London: Routledge, 1991. Print.

Regime Change. Turbulence.org. Web. 4 March 2015. <http://www.turbulence.org/Works/twotxt/>.

Rilke, Rainer Maria. *Duino Elegies.* Trans. C. F. MacIntyre. Berkeley: U of California P, 1961. Print.

———. *The Notebooks of Malte Laurids Brigge: A Novel.* Trans. Stephen Mitchell. New York: Vintage, 1990. Print.

Ronell, Avital. *The Telephone Book: Technology, Schizophrenia, Electric Speech.* Lincoln: U of Nebraska P, 1989. Print.

Roth, Michael S. "Irresistible Decay: Ruins Reclaimed." *Irresistible Decay.* Ed. Michael S. Roth, Claire Lyons, and Charles Merewether. Los Angeles: Getty Research Institute for the History of Art and the Humanities, 1997. 1–23. Print.

Schellenberg, Walter. *The Labyrinth: Memoirs of Walter Schellenberg, Hitler's Chief of Counterintelligence.* Boston: Da Capo, 2000. Print.

Schiesel, Seth. "On Maneuvers with the Army's Game Squad." *New York Times.* 17 Feb. 2005. Web. 6 March 2015. <http://www.nytimes.com/2005/02/17/technology/circuits/17army.html?_r=0>.

Scholem, Gershom, Ed. *The Correspondence of Walter Benjamin and Gershom Scholem, 1932–1940*. Trans. Gary Smith and Andre LeFevre. Cambridge: Harvard UP, 1992. Print.

Scholz, Albrecht, and Werner Aberer. "History of Sexually Transmitted Diseases in the 19th and 20th Centuries." *Geschichte der deutschsprachigen Dermatologie—History of German Language Dermatology*. Ed. Albrecht Scholz, Karl Holubar, and Günter Burg. Bilingual edition. Weinheim: Wiley, 2009. 489–518. Print.

Scott, Charles. *The Question of Ethics: Nietzsche, Foucault, Heidegger*. Bloomington: Indiana UP, 1990. Print.

Shachtman, Noah. 2008. "Hayden Admits: Contractors Lead 'Enhanced Interrogations' at CIA Black Sites." *WIRED Blog Network*. 28 June 2008. Web. 3 March 2015. <http://blog.wired.com/defense/2008/02/in-testimony-be.html>.

Shields, Rob. "Fancy Footwork: Walter Benjamin's Notes on Flânerie." *The Flâneur*. Ed. Keith Tester. London: Routledge, 1994. 61–80. Print.

Sirc, Geoffrey. *English Composition as a Happening*. Logan: Utah State UP, 2002. Print.

Speer, Albert. *Inside the Third Reich*. Trans. Richard and Clara Winston. New York: Macmillan, 1970. Print.

Spivak, Gayatri Chakravorty. *A Critique of Postcolonial Reason: Toward a History of the Vanishing Present*. Cambridge: Harvard UP, 1999. Print.

———. "Decolonizing Feminisms: Between Narcissus and Echo." Keynote lecture delivered at "Issues in Cultural Theory Symposium: Gender, Pedagogy, and Psychoanalysis." University of Texas at Arlington, February 1992.

———. *Outside in the Teaching Machine*. New York: Routledge, 1993. Print.

Stein, George. "Information Warfare: Words Matter." *Infowar: Ars Electronica 98*. New York: Springer, 1998. 51–59. Print.

"Street Smarts." Warner Brothers TV Show. 2000–2005. Web. 3 March 2015. <http://www.warnerbros.com/studio/news/%E2%80%9Cstreet-smarts%E2%80%9D-reflects-top-entertainment-trends-may-reality-tv-nostalgia-and-musical >.

Taylor, Adam. "From Daniel Pearl to James Foley: The Modern Tactic of Islamist Beheadings." *Washington Post*. 20 Aug. 2014. Web. 3 March 2015. < http://www.washingtonpost.com/blogs/worldviews/wp/2014/08/20/from-daniel-pearl-to-james-foley-the-modern-tactic-of-islamist-beheadings/>.

Taylor, Mark C. *Nots*. Chicago: U of Chicago P, 1993. Print.

TGS Gamers. Two Guys Software. 2005. Web.

"Theorycraft." WoWWikki. Web. 7 March 2015. <http://www.wowwiki.com/Theorycraft>.

Tjønneland, Eivind. *Ibsen og moderniten*. Oslo: Spartacus, 1993. Print.

Toge, Sankichi. "Give Back the People." Hiroshima Peace Site. Web. 3 March 2015. <http://www.pcf.city.hiroshima.jp/virtual/VirtualMuseum_e/tour_e/ireihi/tour_23_e.html>.

Tostrup, Elisabeth. *Architecture and Rhetoric: Text and Design in Architectural Competitions, Oslo 1939–1997.* London: Papadakis, 1999. Print.

"Transport I/75 from Berlin, Germany, to Theresienstadt, Czechoslovakia on 4/11/1942." Yad Vashem. Web. 25 Feb. 2015. <http://db.yadvashem.org/deportation/transportDetails.html?language=en&itemId=5093058>.

Tresniowski, Alex, and Steve Helling. "Watching Him Die." *People.* 70.23 (8 Dec. 2008): 106. Print.

Trimbur, John. "Delivering the Message: Typography and the Materiality of Writing." *Rhetoric and Composition as Intellectual Work.* Ed. Gary Olson. Carbondale: Southern Illinois UP, 2002. 188–202. Print.

Tuman, Joseph S. *Communicating Terror: The Rhetorical Dimensions of Terrorism.* Thousand Oaks: Sage, 2003. Print.

Turquand d'Auzay, Béatrice. 21 Feb. 2015. Web. <http://www.turquand-dauzay.com/?page_id=1887>.

Ulmer, Gregory L. *Heuretics: The Logic of Invention.* Baltimore: Johns Hopkins P, 1994. Print.

———. *Internet Invention: From Literacy to Electracy.* New York: Longman, 2002. Print.

United States Memorial Holocaust Museum. Web. 12 Feb 2009.

"US Army Officer Puts 'Solution to Iraq War' on eBay." Australian Broadcasting Corporation (ABC). 16 July 2007. Web. 4 March 2015. <http://www.abc.net.au/news/2007-07-17/us-army-officer-puts-solution-to-iraq-war-on-ebay/2504618>.

"US Issues Deck of Cards on Iraq's Archaeology." Telegraph.co.uk. 21 June 2007. Web. 4 March 2015. <http://www.telegraph.co.uk/news/worldnews/1555148/US-issues-deck-of-cards-on-Iraqs-archaeology.html>.

"U.S. Opposition to the International Criminal Court." *Global Policy Forum.* 2008. Web. 3 March 2015. <http://www.globalpolicy.org/intljustice/icc/usindex.htm>. <http://www.ushmm.org/>.

Virilio, Paul. *Open Sky.* Trans. Julie Rose. London: Verso, 1997. Print.

Vitanza, Victor J. *Negation, Subjectivity, and the History of Rhetoric.* Albany: SUNY P, 1997. Print.

———. "Three Countertheses: A Critical In(ter)vention into Composition Theories and Pedagogies." *Contending with Words: Composition and Rhetoric in a Postmodern Age.* Ed. Patricia Harkin and John Schilb. New York: MLA, 1991. 139–72. Print.

Vranic, Seada. "Interview: Breaking the Wall of Silence." *Bosnia Report* 17 (Nov. 1996–Jan. 1997). Web. 3 March 2015. <http://www.bosnia.org.uk/bosrep/n096ja97/rape.cfm>.

Wagner, Aleksandra, and Alexander Stein. "The Trouble with Borders." *BorderLine.* Ed. Lebbeus Woods and Ekkehard Rehfeld. Vienna: Springer, 1998. 89%–96%. Print.

Ward, Mark, Sr. *Deadly Documents: Technical Communication, Organizational Discourse, and the Holocaust*. Amityville: Baywood, 2014. Print.

Wark, McKenzie. *Gamer Theory*. Cambridge: Harvard UP, 2007. Print.

Weizman, Eyal. "Military Options as Human Planning." Interviewed by Philipp Misselwitz. *Cities without Citizens*. Edited by Eduardo Cadava and Aaron Levy. Philadelphia: Slought, 2003. 167–99. Print.

Wellerstein, Alex. "A Day Too Late." *Restricted Data*. 26 April 2013. Web. 3 March 2015. <http://blog.nuclearsecrecy.com/2013/04/26/a-day-too-late/>.

"West Germany Faces 15 Year Housing Task." *Chicago Tribune*. 27 Sept. 1951. Web. 25 Feb 2015. <http://archives.chicagotribune.com/1951/09/27/page/39/article/west-germany-faces-15-year-housing-task>.

Wiedergutsmachtungsämter (Restitution) Project. Landesarchiv Berlin. Web. 25 Feb 2015. <http://wga-datenbank.de/en/background.html>.

Williams, Josette H. "The Information War in the Pacific: Paths to Peace." *CIA Studies in Intelligence* 46.3 (14 April 2007). Web. 30 July 2015. <https://www.cia.gov/library/center-for-the-study-of-intelligence/csi-publications/csi-studies/studies/v0146n03/article07.html>.

"Wipe." WoWWikki. Web. 7 March 2015. <http://www.wowwiki.com/Wipe>.

Wiscombe, Tom. "The Haptic Morphology of Tentacles." *BorderLine*. Ed. Lebbeus Woods and Ekkehard Rehfeld. Vienna: Springer, 1998. 25%–31%. Print.

Wittgenstein, Ludwig. *On Certainty*. Ed. G. E. M. Anscombe and G. H. von Wright. Trans. Denis Paul and G. E. M. Anscombe. New York: Harper, 1969. Print.

Woods, Lebbeus. "Libeskind's Machines." Web. 24 Nov. 2009. 6 March 2015. <https://lebbeuswoods.wordpress.com/2009/11/24/libeskinds-machines/>.

Woods, Lebbeus, and Ekkehard Rehfeld, eds. *BorderLine*. Vienna: Springer, 1998. Print.

Woomera2002. NoBorder.org. Web. 3 March 2015. <http://www.noborder.org/camps/02/aus/display.php%3Fid=73.html>.

Worsham, Lynn. "Reading Wild, Seriously: Confessions of an Epistemophiliac." *Rhetoric Society Quarterly* 22.1 (Winter 1992): 39–62. Print.

———. "Writing against Writing: The Predicament of *Écriture Féminine* in Composition Studies." *Contending with Words: Composition and Rhetoric in a Postmodern Age*. Ed. Patricia Harkin and John Schilb. New York: MLA, 1991. 82–104. Print.

Young, Julian. "What Is Dwelling? The Homelessness of Modernity and the Worlding of the World." *Heidegger, Authenticity, and Modernity: Essays in Honor of Hubert L. Dreyfus*. Vol. 1. Ed. Mark A. Wrathall and Jeff Malpas. Cambridge: MIT P, 2000. 187–203. Print.

Index

Page locators in italics indicate figures.

Cynthia Haynes is a professor of English at Clemson University, where she serves as the director of first-year composition. Her previous publications include *High Wired* and *MOOniversity* (both with Jan Rune Holmevik). Her essays have appeared in *Enculturation*, *Games and Culture*, *JAC*, *Pre/Text*, *CyberText Yearbook*, *Fast Capitalism*, *Kairos*, the *Writing Center Journal*, and numerous edited collections. She received the 2003 James L. Kinneavy Award for her article "Writing Offshore."